995

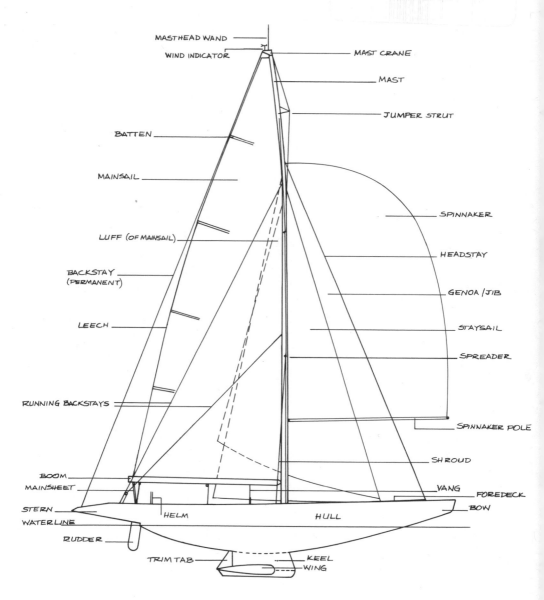

MASTHEAD WAND

WIND INDICATOR

MAST CRANE

MAST

JUMPER STRUT

BATTEN

MAINSAIL

SPINNAKER

LUFF (OF MAINSAIL)

HEADSTAY

BACKSTAY
(PERMANENT)

GENOA / JIB

LEECH

STAYSAIL

SPREADER

RUNNING BACKSTAYS

SPINNAKER POLE

SHROUD

BOOM

MAINSHEET

VANG

FOREDECK

STERN

HELM

HULL

BOW

WATERLINE

RUDDER

TRIM TAB

KEEL

WING

COMEBACK

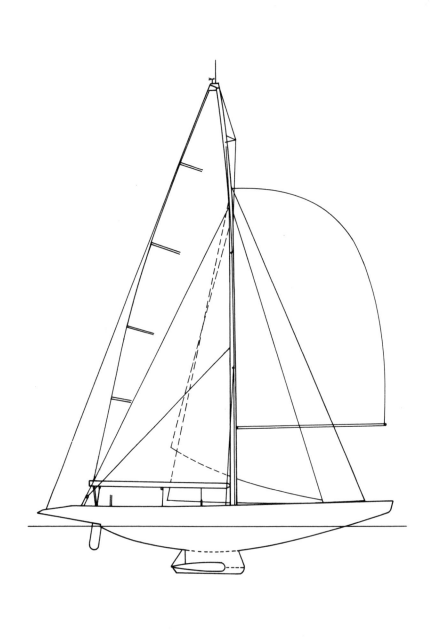

COMEBACK

MY RACE FOR
THE AMERICA'S CUP

BY

DENNIS CONNER

WITH

Bruce Stannard

FOREWORD BY

Walter Cronkite

Paul C. Larsen,
Consulting Editor

ST. MARTIN'S PRESS
New York

Grateful acknowledgment is made for permission to reprint the following photographs:

© Carlo Borlenghi: 2, 12, 15, 16, 19, 22, 23, 26, 27, 35, 43, 47, 51, 55.

© Margherita Bottini: 6, 24, 33, 37.

© Enrico Ferorelli/DOT: 40, 45.

© Daniel Forster/Duomo 1983: 17; © 1986: 4, 8, 9, 10, 11, 13, 20, 21, 25, 28, 29, 31, 32, 36, 39, 41, 42, 44, 46, 48, 52, 53, 56; © 1987: 49, 61, 63, 64.

© Roger Garwood: 1, 30.

© Dan Nerney/DOT: 3, 7, 14, 54, 57, 58, 59, 60.

© Tom Martin/Aspen Photography: 5, 62.

© Adam J. Stoltman/Duomo 1983: 18.

© Bruce Stannard: 38, 50.

Design by Claire Counihan

Library of Congress Cataloging-in-Publication Data

Conner, Dennis.
    Comeback: my race for the America's Cup.

    1. America's Cup races. I. Stannard, Bruce.
II. Title.
GV829.C68   1987   797.1'4   87-4729
ISBN 0-312-00900-3

First Edition
10 9 8 7 6 5 4 3 2 1

This book is dedicated to all the men and women of **Stars & Stripes** *whose commitment to the commitment helped us bring home America's Cup.*

AMERICA'S CUP BUOY

CONTENTS

CONTENTS

ACKNOWLEDGMENTS

ANY have contributed to winning the America's Cup. Obviously I would not be writing this book without the support and dedication of my family, Judy, Julie, and Shanna, as well as my many friends and supporters. Several individuals have been especially important to me, providing special friendship and assistance. They are Malin Burnham, Ed du Moulin, Fritz and Lucy Jewett, and Michael Dingman.

I have worked and sailed with Malin Burnham since long before we created the idea of an organization to promote international understanding through competitive sailing. He is a brilliant executive and sailor as well as a friend. In fact, he was a childhood hero of mine and one of my role models.

Ed du Moulin is one of the most influential America's Cup participants in its history and his influence continues with me. His attention to detail is legendary and will have a lifetime impact on me.

Fritz and Lucy Jewett are close friends and were the key supporters of my involvement with the Cup. I can't say how much I appreciated their help and support over the years.

Michael Dingman's steadfast support of the *Stars & Stripes* campaign makes him one of the most important individuals involved in bringing the Cup home to America. He is the type of person who helped make America the great nation it is today.

A big thank-you to the *Stars & Stripes* design team, John Marshall, Britt Chance, Bruce Nelson, and Dave Pedrick, as well as the involvement of SAIC's Dr. Robert Beyster, Nils Salvesen, and Clay Oliver. The design team was a critical factor in my success, especially in the creation of *Stars & Stripes '87.*

Special thanks also to my longtime friends and fellow 12-meter sailors Tom Whidden, Jack Sutphen, and Jon Wright.

The many young men and women of *Stars & Stripes,* both at sea and ashore, deserve a great deal of credit. They are responsible for much of the work that has made my success possible. My special gratitude goes to bowman Scott Vogel and tailer Bill Trenkle for leading the way in building and maintaining the boat. Also deserving are the sailmakers, the boat and keel builders, and riggers.

Thanks also to the corporate sponsors that supported this effort when we needed their help the most: Allied-Signal, Anheuser Busch, Atlas Hotels, Ford Motor Company, The Henley Group, Merrill Lynch, and Science Applications International Corporation.

Bruce Stannard is to be singled out for the personal sacrifices he made in putting up with me night and day for six months at the expense of everything else. I deeply appreciate his friendship.

FOREWORD

●●●●●●●●●●●●●● ★ ●●●●●●●●●●●●●●

ENNIS CONNER rewrote the book on America's Cup competition. Since he became involved it has not been the same, and it never will be again.

In the years B.C. (Before Conner), challenging for and defending that one hundred guineas worth of Victorian silver was a sometime sport, almost an after-office-hours sort of game.

Gentlemen yachtsmen, usually from the comfort of their leather chairs, talked idly of racing for the Cup and on occasion decided to pool some of their idle money and do something about it.

They talked to a naval architect or two and commissioned the building of a boat that sometime early in the year of the race was launched with due ceremony. Then a captain was selected, not infrequently one of the gentlemen himself, and he selected a crew of ten other stalwarts with a couple of substitutes, also not infrequently relatives of the other gentlemen. These were young men who could afford to spend a good part of the summer in Newport, Rhode Island, racing their boat.

They practiced in the late afternoons of spring in Long Island Sound and then moved to Newport when summer vacations began to permit. They raced other boats, usually entered and manned by friends, for the right to defend the Cup, and then in September the winner met the boat that came over from abroad to challenge. In later years, that boat was the survivor of an elimination series between three or four boats from other nations.

The United States, that is, the New York Yacht Club entry, won, the crews went back to school or the stock brokerage that had let them off for the summer, the owners went back to their leather chairs, and nearly all thought of the America's Cup went into another two- or three-year hibernation.

Then along came Dennis Conner—hyper Dennis Conner. Probably the world's best racing boat skipper and hyper-ambitious, hyper-dedicated. The lackadaisical approach to defending the Cup was not for him. He wanted to begin practice the minute the challenge was decided upon, and he wanted the latest state-of-the-art boat to practice with. And he wanted a second boat to practice against, and a skilled crew in that one as well. And then he expected to build more boats as possible improvements became apparent.

A three-year training program with two full crews that would be full time at the job and a fleet of boats—all of that took money, a lot more money than the few old boys could raise no matter how deeply they dug into their tweed pockets. And it would take a permanent organization of managers, fund raisers, and all the paraphernalia of a going business.

Dennis Conner made it all work, and the sport was forever changed.

At Perth, Western Australia (or more properly Fremantle, for that is the port city for Perth) in the antipodes' summer of '86–'87, those of us who were lucky enough to be there exulted in the changes he had wrought.

There may have been some moaning at the bars by those who mourn the passing of the gentler age of big boat racing, but the cries of despair were unheard in the excitement along the Fremantle waterfront.

Here was a real international competition, a really world-class event. Whatever exclusivity had still surrounded 12-meter racing at Newport had disappeared at Fremantle.

From the docks of the seventeen competing clubs lining the wharves —"pens," the Aussies called them—flew the flags of seven nations. Back behind the security walls, twenty-six sleek 12-meter boats crouched to spring out into Gage Roads to challenge for the America's Cup.

Never had there been assembled such a 12-meter fleet.

Three hundred or more of the world's best sailors, in the rare moments when they weren't practicing or fine-tuning their boats, mixed with a throng of thousands that paraded along the waterfront's new roads, savored the fast foods, and favored the dozen kiosks peddling T-shirts and a wild assortment of other souvenirs.

The carnival lasted almost six months. It took about 360 races for each of the boats to meet all the others in a series of elimination contests that eventually selected the one Challenger to meet the one Defender.

Dennis's drive for perfection, his three-year, multiboat training program, had forced everyone to compete on equal grounds. The success in 1983 of the radical Australian innovation, the winged keel, had forced all others to move into the high-tech world of computers and exotic underwater designs.

All of this brought America's Cup racing into the realm of high finance. The clubs that by the rules sponsored the entries really only were fronts for syndicates that raised and supervised the expenditure of huge amounts of money.

Those that built a single boat and sent a single crew to Australia never were seriously in the running, although they gave the big boys a scare now and again. Their expenditure of only seven, eight, or nine million dollars wasn't nearly enough.

The "serious" syndicates with the multiboat programs spent fifteen or twenty million, maybe more, to make their bid. That kind of money can't be raised by popular subscription or the largesse of a few dedicated yachtsmen. As of now, commercial sponsorship is the only way, and that is as big a change as any in this 12-meter sport.

Dennis made another contribution to all this—but one that even his single-mindedness never intended. By losing in '83 he opened up the race. He inspired a lot of the '86–'87 Challengers to enter by proving that someone other than the New York Yacht Club really did have a chance.

No, the pursuit of the America's Cup never will be the same as it was B.C. No man has had a greater impact on this venerable competition.

—Walter Cronkite
New York, February 1987

PROLOGUE

Y name is Dennis Conner. I was born in San Diego, California, forty-four years ago and I've lived there ever since. I have a beautiful wife named Judy and two lovely daughters, Julie and Shanna. By trade I'm a draper but for the better part of my life I've been a sailor. It's my hobby, my passion, the way I've chosen to live my life. It's what I've spent more time at than anything else, and it's certainly the one thing I do best.

Most of the values and philosophies I live by are the result of lessons I've learned while racing sailboats. My closest friends are those who have sailed with me or who have been associated with my sailing. I love my life onshore but when I'm on the water, I'm at peace and almost always happy, especially when I'm winning.

The story you're about to read is of a quest, a journey long in distance and time, a treasure hunt. I won't call it a personal quest because there were so many dedicated people involved. I played a part, but the story could never have had the same ending without the participation of all those who helped me find the way.

It's hard to know just where to begin. Maybe the right moment is when as a kid I decided to learn how to sail. A more suitable time might be when I first heard the words "America's Cup." A fitting start might also be how I decided to commit myself to winning an Olympic medal.

It's a story of lessons learned, dreams dreamed, and sacrifices made in complete dedication. And it's also the story of something that began in stuffing an empty shoe box and ended in carrying home the oldest trophy in sports.

1

★

"What Do You Mean, Wings?"

HEN the telephone rang, Johan Valentijn answered it. It was June 16, 1983, and Johan was in the middle of an America's Cup summer in Newport, Rhode Island. With our boat *Liberty*, we were one of three teams fighting to be chosen by the New York Yacht Club as the American Defender later in the summer. As the designer of our boat *Liberty*, he had little time to take calls, but this particular one would change his life, every idea he'd ever had about 12-meter yacht design, and, eventually, the entire future of the America's Cup.

"Johan, I've just seen something incredible." The voice was excited, even desperate. Johan recognized it as that of Paul Doppke from Cove Haven Marina in Barrington, Rhode Island. Earlier that day, Paul had been responsible for blocking *Australia II* when she was hauled out of the water for her final measurement. He was most probably the first American to see the unusual configuration on the bottom of this yacht's hull.

"*Australia II* has wings on her keel and they're made of lead. It's the damnedest thing I've ever seen. Do you know anything about this?"

Doppke's anxious question would haunt us all for a long time. Johan's answer was anything but satisfactory.

"What do you mean, 'wings'?" asked Johan. "What do you mean, 'lead'?"

1

COMEBACK

Actually, I had heard something about a peculiar keel back in January 1983. A journalist (I think it was Jay Broze) had told me that *Australia II* had an unusual keel. In those days, we didn't have the resources to go to Australia and investigate. But then I didn't hear anything more and before long I forgot all about it.

Looking back, I'd say that neglecting espionage was probably the biggest mistake we made in preparing for the 1983 races. But the America's Cup is supposed to be a sporting competition, not a battle between intelligence agencies, and back then I really didn't think it was necessary to set up a network of spies. I couldn't have been more wrong!

Johan got terribly tense about Doppke's revelation. When he relayed the news to me, I asked a few questions.

"Who was at the measurement, Johan? Any of our guys?"

"No, Dennis. Just Savage, Watts, and Vinbury." These three comprised the International Yacht Racing Union measures committee. (IYRU). "Doppke said the Aussies insisted on a private shed and on having two armed guards there. Everything was done in secrecy. No one from the New York Yacht Club was anywhere around."

I didn't like the sound of that. I told Johan to have Doppke make a sketch of what he saw. In the meantime, I checked with the Yacht Club guys and found out that they should have shown up, but didn't. They were certainly entitled to, under the rules that they themselves had established, but they seemed to have been unaware of them. It was just one of a long list of screw-ups—a perfect example of how the Australians outmaneuvered us on land all summer long.

The next morning Doppke appeared with his sketch and told us about this incredible keel. Johan and our navigator Halsey Herreshoff turned green, then red, then very pale. Johan had had a lot of experience in this game, dating back to 1977, when he worked with Bob Miller (who later changed his name to Ben Lexcen) on creating *Australia*. Lexcen had come to town with wings on and Johan was in turmoil.

Halsey is a descendant of the great yacht-design family that included Nathanael and L. Francis. His ancestors had known everything worth knowing about shaping a boat, so when he said he couldn't figure out what the wings did, we all looked at each other with foreboding. While I shared their concerns, I was still chiefly involved with getting *Liberty* and her crew up to speed. I believed my main job was steering the boat. But as reports began to drift into our camp about *Australia II* being fast in her tune-up against the English, that she was very fast in a breeze and that she was pulverizing the competition in the foreign trials, alarm bells started.

I guess what finally moved me to action was when our tactician, Tom Whidden, relayed his conversation with his counterpart on *Australia II*, Hugh Treharne. The affable Aussie, known around the circuit as "Hughie," told Tom that they were able not only to beat their opponents, but to blow them right out of the water.

By now, I had heard enough!

Johan supplied me with some more drawings and I went alone to meet with Bob McCullough. A former America's Cup sailor, McCullough was both past Commodore of the New York Yacht Club and chairman of the America's Cup Committee. Clearly, he was the man to make our case, if indeed we had a case.

"Commodore, we have a problem here and you had better do something about it," I said. "*Australia II* has a peculiarity on the bottom of her keel and we don't think it's legal."

The Commodore was unmoved, but willing to hear me out. I showed him Johan's sketches, which weren't precise, but as it turned out, the concept was correct. I felt that our attack should be on the legality of the keel because I believed the rule stated a 12-meter "shall draw no more than nine feet." We knew that *Australia II*'s keel, when the boat was heeled over in a breeze, would extend below the nine-foot draft.

"The way we see it," I said to McCullough as we both looked at the drawings, "is that *Australia II* simply can't sail in nine feet of water, which is the intent of the 12-meter rule. Heeled over with those wings, she would run aground. We think the keel is illegal and we ought to ensure that the Australians take steps to adhere to the rule or else they don't sail."

McCullough looked at the drawings, but he didn't have a clue as to their implications. He just stood there and scratched his head—as I had done the first day I saw them. I couldn't make him feel the urgency of the situation. He didn't see the practicality of pressing the issue immediately, so he didn't do a damn thing. Instead, he told me to go back to Johan to find out more about this.

Disappointed, I did what he asked. We continued our research and learned more about what we were up against. We also studied the rules and I asked Britton Chance, an experienced and very capable designer, to help us. He dug up interpretations from the 5.5-meter-class rules that clearly showed the concept to be illegal.

When we had our case together, we took it to the IYRU measurers.

Tony Watts, the British chief of the crew, told us that our contention that the boat drew more than nine feet when heeled didn't mean a damn thing. The boat had to be measured vertically, he maintained.

We didn't get anywhere with the other measurers either. The Australian on the team was Jack Savage, whose son was at the helm of *Challenge 12*, the other Ben Lexcen-designed boat. Enough said. Mark Vinbury, who with Watts and Savage made up the "holy trinity," is from the United States, but the most he could bring himself to do was to recommend to Watts that they refer the question to the IYRU Technical Keel Boat Committee.

But chairman Watts had already made up his mind on the issue. He was standing up for his IYRU team, which had judged the keel previously in Australia and found it to be legal. His position was: If Watts's team has ruled, they shall not be overruled.

The more *Australia II* won in the foreign trials, the more the New York Yacht Club's attention to our keel complaints grew. But it really wasn't until the next incident occurred that Bob McCullough and the rest of the Cup Committee finally began seriously to plan an attack on the keel.

Word had drifted into our camp that the Dutch had helped in the design of the Australian yacht. If this were true, if the yacht was designed outside of Australia, it would be a definite infringement of the rules. Johan's uncle in Holland heard about this and went to see the guys at the Netherlands Ship Model Basin in Wageningen, where Ben Lexcen was testing different designs in the test tank. It was reported to Johan that these guys had admitted helping with ideas for the keel. Now we really had something to go on, but again, the Australians had already anticipated our moves and had prepared a defense.

Johan, Halsey, and Bob formed a "keel unit" with Johan in charge. They made a concentrated effort to get the NYYC to mount a protest, and it wasn't that the Club was deaf to all they were being told; they were just inept. The Club never formulated a clear-cut plan. They didn't know what to do. The Australians had their syndicate's Executive Director Warren Jones as their public spokesman and he had become the ultimate tactician in the land-battle part of the Cup fray. The biggest problem was that the Club hadn't listened to Johan, Halsey, and me in the beginning, and when they finally agreed to take some action, it was too late.

The Club brought in someone from Chicago who was to advise on the rules. In retrospect, I guess we should have sent someone from our team, but I didn't feel that was our responsibility. We were supposed to be sailing the boat and that's just what we were doing, every day, every hour we could. We were out on the water fighting for our lives to be the Defender. It was up to the New York Yacht Club to follow through on the land-based issues.

Things went from bad to worse. As a result of reports from Holland, McCullough helped dream up the idea of asking the Dutch to design a new boat for our use. Johan then wrote a telegram that our syndicate manager, Ed du Moulin, agreed to send. Unfortunately, I never saw the cable, and I don't think Ed had much of a look at it either, although he did sign it. Johan was in such a big rush, and since Johan was in charge of all the undercover work, Ed let the cable go. Eventually he regretted sending it because it backfired on us.

On July 16 the cable was sent. It read: "I understand you and your team are responsible for development and design of special keel for *Australia II*. We are finally convinced of her potential and would therefore like to build same design under one of our boats. We will keep this confidential as not to jeopardize your agreement with Alan Bond. However, due to complexity of problems, need your maximum input. We can start next week and be ready by August 25."

The whole idea was ridiculous. Here we were trying to prove the keel was illegal, but asking them to build us the same thing. Later it would be said that the cable was not a genuine attempt to get the design but merely a ploy to trap the Dutch into acknowledging they had helped design the Australian boat—a clear breach of rules by Bond—but in the hands of the clever Warren Jones it was used to make the Club look like a cheat and a fool simultaneously.

I wasn't really involved in all the intrigue. I was sailing the boat. But Johan began to see the handwriting on the wall and he realized that his old buddy Ben Lexcen was going to emerge from the races as the hero. Johan, on the other hand, stood to be the goat if all the speed rumors we were hearing proved true.

At this point we still had a lot of confidence in Johan, but I must say, it was beginning to fade. First, he had designed *Magic* too short to even be entered in Cup competition. Then he built *Liberty* with the keel so far back we had to load 1,800 pounds of lead three feet from the bow so she would sit on her lines at the launching. Eventually, we had to take the keel off and move the whole thing a foot forward. No one ever found out about that, but it was the first indication to me that *Liberty*'s design was a bit flawed.

The other big problem for us was the modifications made on *Freedom*. We had successfully defended the Cup in 1980 in the fine blue yacht (beating *Australia* 4–1), and she was to be a big part of our 1983 campaign.

Unfortunately, we blew it big when we lost our "grandfather clause." One of *Freedom*'s best assets was her low freeboard. This lowered her center of gravity, made her more stable, and allowed her less weight. But following the 1980 races, there was a change in the international 12-meter-class rule that affected freeboard. *Freedom* would have been greatly penalized under this rule, but her grandfather clause allowed her to be sailed, as she was already built.

Although Johan and I discussed the changes to be made on *Freedom*, I was unaware that they would mean we would be unable to sail her in competition. He moved the rudder and made some minor structural changes, and in doing so, we lost the grandfather clause because the yacht was considered altered. Looking back, I should have been more on top of this, even though it was the designer's responsibility.

Perhaps I should have become more involved in both the design and in the growing keel controversy. But as far as 1983 was concerned, it's important to understand that the New York Yacht Club pulled all the strings. The sailors were the puppets. The Club had total control of the Defense, and our syndicate had not yet even won the right to race. The *Defender/Courageous* syndicate was attempting the same thing.

So there was a question of just how far our syndicate could push the keel issue. We followed the proper course by working through the Club, and they had a strict protocol on who did what. McCullough was the chairman of the America's Cup Committee—which was itself an arm of the Club, a blurry arrangement that had raised eyebrows for a century. His right-hand man was Vic Romagna, who had been his tactician when the two sailed aboard *Valiant* in 1970. Romagna is a smart, scrappy little guy who might have had a real impact on all this if he'd become involved a little earlier in the game.

"Listen, Dennis, you guys go sail," he used to say. "Don't worry. We'll beat 'em."

"Fine, Vic," I'd shoot back. "But we know how to sail. Sailing's the least of our problems. It's what you guys are doing ashore that really bothers us."

"We'll take care of it," was the answer we'd always get, and those words still echo in my head on cold, dark nights.

Vic took the hard line. He soon became as convinced as I that the keel was illegal and he felt Bond and his boys should be disqualified. The Club had given Bond an affidavit in which he was to swear he hadn't violated a number of rules. Bond refused to sign it. That pushed Vic over the edge and he did everything he could to get the Club out of the contest. He was the leader of the dissent when the now famous, or should I say infamous, committee vote aboard Bus Mosbacher's boat *Summertime* was taken on whether or not the Yacht Club should allow the Cup races to start. They were convinced that Bond's group had violated the rules on several scores, but, preoccupied—as our member cited—"with thousands of people having come from all over, with all the money that had been spent," they could not bring themselves to say, "We won't race." As Fritz Jewett, the *Freedom* syndicate chairman, expressed it: "They put expediency ahead of principle. We were counting on the New York Yacht Club to represent us in these issues . . . [and the] Club let us down."

In retrospect, I can see exactly where the Club went wrong. They were functioning more as a selection committee than as a Defense committee. Their major concern was which boat to put on the starting line, but they neglected the other critical areas of the Defense. I now realize they should have had their own people around the world watching the foreign challengers, gathering information, and reporting back. They should have had somebody responsible for reading the rules, understanding them thoroughly, and making sure they were adhered to. And they should have had someone responsible for public relations.

Of course, I'm speaking from hindsight. It's not my intention here to rehash all the melodrama that went on on land during 1983. A separate book could be written about all that; in fact, several have been.

My intent is simply to give my perspective, not as an excuse but as a lesson well learned. You can never excuse losing, *but* if you're going to grow, to learn, to achieve, you have to understand *why* you lost, what *your* mistakes were, and then take steps to correct them.

My major mistake in 1983 was not having enough control. After we lost and I had a chance to gain some perspective, I knew what I had to do to win the Cup back. If I was going to be tagged as the guy who lost the Cup, then the least I could do was be the guy who had a say in trying to win it back. I wanted control of my own destiny; I wanted to call the shots.

The year 1983 showed me just how big a deal the America's Cup is, not just to the New York Yacht Club, but to all Americans. To me, the Cup stood for excellence at sea—a great American tradition—but unfortunately, for many it had evolved into a social occasion: red trousers, straw hats, blue blazers, club ties, cocktails and canapés. It was all very elegant, but no way to win a boat race.

I know people have complained that my approach to sailboat racing in general and the America's Cup in particular is too "professional," that I'm too serious, too dedicated, too keen a sailor, too obsessed with winning. I make no apologies for any of those things. I believe that's what it takes to win, and unless I've missed something, that's the object of the game. It seems to me there's no point in competing unless you're determined to win, unless you're going to give it all you've got. I hate to lose. That's why I take every precaution I can to guard against it. It's true; I really won't accept from myself any excuse to lose.

As I write this, the legality of the wing keel is a moot point. We all know *Australia II* was allowed to sail. My attitude at the time was that the Club lost a battle on land, but since I'm a sailor, I'd have to win the one on the water. In the end, that's all that mattered to me—doing our best on the water. By race time I knew we were up against a faster boat, but I believed in my heart of hearts that we could somehow pull it off. By the time we were towed out to the course for the first race against the Aussies, I had put all the bullshit behind me and I told my guys to do the same.

"Forget everything that's happened, except what we've achieved on the water," I remember saying. "We're here to race sailboats and each one of you knows your job. We're here because we're the best in America. Now let's prove we're the best in the world."

I suspected as we left the dock in Newport that September morning that we were in for the battle of our lives. But because you never know for sure just what your competition has until you actually meet them on the race course, my suspicions weren't confirmed until we actually came up against *Australia II* for the first time. No, this wasn't going to be just a battle, it was going to be all-out war. And what a glorious war it was!

The first race of the 1983 America's Cup was scheduled for September 13. As we were being towed out to the course, I reflected back on the summer that had just passed and everything that had happened. As a sporting event, this America's Cup had been a great political clash.

We had won the right to defend the Cup by beating two good people in Tommy Blackaller and John Kolius. They were the skippers for the *Defender/Courageous* syndicate. In addition, Gary Jobson was sailing with Tommy as the tactician. Despite their talent, we won two out of every three races we sailed.

Even though we were winning, it was not the most pleasant of summers. On top of the wing-keel controversy, I was getting clobbered in the press by Tom and Gary. Nothing I did seemed to be right in their eyes. At first, they jumped me for not helping them, not trialing against them. They said this was hurting the American effort. But we were competitors and we were both entered in a contest in which there would only be one winner. What really got them howling was when they discovered *Liberty* had been granted multiple-rating certificates. These allowed us to remove or add lead ballast and change sail area depending on weather conditions.

It was a perfectly legal concept, as long as we complied with the 12-meter formula, and I had taken the idea to the America's Cup Committee in May, before the trials began. I told them what we had in mind and they said okay. We were granted three separate rating certificates.

The *Defender/Courageous* boys didn't figure this out until the end of July, and by then they were so frustrated with their new boat *Defender* because she was such a woofer that they took it out on me. Tom and Gary proclaimed to the press that we had an unfair advantage, that I was unethical, that the rules had been compromised. They were particularly vehement about the Committee's not sharing our ideas with them for "the good of the Defense." It was the old "let's get together for the American effort" argument. If you took that to its logical conclusion, we would have had to turn over our sail shapes, crewmen, computers, everything. But in the end, nothing would have helped *Defender*.

Several books about the '83 races say Gary and I ended up bitter enemies. That's not true. We have been competitors for a long time and there may have been times when we had some heated battles on and off the course, but I don't think either one of us has ever held a grudge. The fact is I have great respect for Gary's abilities as a sailor and admiration for the job he did as a television commentator. He's done as much as anyone in the sport to help popularize 12-meter racing in the United States.

2

★

The White Shark

WHEN *Australia II* and *Liberty* met on the race course for the first time, they were escorted by the largest spectator fleet I'd ever seen. If there was any question about the growing popularity of this event, this immense turnout seemed to answer even the most jaded observer.

The first thing I remember about that race was that we had a terrible time getting it started. When the ten-minute gun sounded at noon, the wind was out of the northeast at about eight knots. But there was an enormous windshift of something like 40 or 50 degrees to the east, which meant that instead of the first leg being a beat (heading into the wind), it would have turned into a reach (wind coming across our beam).

I sailed up alongside the committee boat, the *Black Knight*, and began signaling frantically to Dyer Jones, the race committee chairman: "This is a negatory, for God's sake get rid of this. Abort the race, abort the race." We all laugh about it now, but at the time, with *Australia II* down to leeward, we anticipated an immediate massacre because of a fluky wind.

Tom Whidden was lying out over the hull making hand signals to the *Black Knight*. Sure enough, at about two minutes before the starting gun was set to go off, the postponement flag went up. We saw Dyer later and he said, "Don't get the impression I'm going to do what you

10

guys ask, but in this situation, we certainly couldn't have had a fair start." They set a new course and a new starting time, but finally the day's race was abandoned.

I remember very clearly how astonished we all were during that first encounter with *Australia II*. After the ten-minute gun had gone off, we met the Aussies in the starting arena and began prestart maneuvers. During the very first circle, we tacked and John Bertrand, the Australian helmsmen, tacked and then bore off right inside us. We all looked at each other in silent amazement, but no one dared utter a word even though we were all thinking the same thing.

We were going to jibe onto starboard, which was the prescribed match-racing tactic in that situation, but Bertrand just slid down inside and threw a block at us that numbed me. That's when we knew that everything we had heard about *Australia II*'s ability to turn was no exaggeration. She turned faster than any boat we had ever seen.

During that first encounter I decided to abandon the usual prestart tactics of circling and maneuvering in order to get the best position. Since that little white marauder was able to cut us off at the pass whenever she wanted, there was no point in playing their game. I decided to go for time-on-distance starts, keeping away from them, giving them whichever side of the starting line they wanted while I tried to have *Liberty* right on the line going full speed when the gun sounded. Time-on-distance is my long suit anyway, and it sure worked in 1983. *Liberty* won every start except in the first race.

In that first race, Bertrand got the start by three seconds, but we were to windward and I liked our position. After about nine minutes the two boats converged and *Australia II* crossed in front of us, then immediately executed a "slam-dunk," meaning they tacked right on top of us, took our wind, and forced us to tack away to find clear air.

Bertrand rounded the first mark eight seconds ahead, the first time in modern America's Cup history that a foreign challenger had rounded the first mark in the lead. In front of us were the two reaching legs, where the wind blows roughly perpendicular to the boat. We felt at the time that we were faster than *Australia II* on this point of sail, but we didn't think Bertrand knew that yet. We were setting our trap, and my crew was ready to spring it.

Australia II had us by ten seconds at the wing mark, but now we were prepared to attack. We jibed around the mark and immediately set our staysail. They neither matched our staysail nor did Bertrand bother to cover us. He ignored one of the principal rules of match-racing, which is to keep your boat between your opponent and the next mark. Our trap worked; we had lulled them into thinking their boat was as fast or faster on the reach. Bertrand was much too overconfident, so he just kept going down the course with reckless disregard for us.

We simply powered right over the top of them. We couldn't have done that if they had covered. Although it was one of the most exciting moments of the entire summer, our boat was very quiet. No emotion, no rebel yells. We're like a well-oiled machine in situations like that. Once we got ahead, we kept our lead and rounded the third mark sixteen seconds in front. That was pretty much the race right there.

However, probably the most dramatic part of the day was the fifth leg, a downwind run. We were still ahead by about a half-minute, but *Australia II* started gaining fast. I think I recognized this first, and the rest of the guys probably thought I was just being negative. But when you've raced as much as I have, you acquire a sixth sense about that type of thing.

I called for a spinnaker change, but Bertrand kept gaining. It was simply amazing. The day before we had seen how that boat could turn and today we were seeing how fast she could charge downwind. In less than one leg she ate away our twenty-nine-second lead and had drawn even. We had mast-abeam, which according to the rules gave us controlling position, but then the unbelievable happened. Bertrand bore off, taking his yacht lower. When he opened up the necessary three boat-lengths between us, he reconverged and now he had controlling position. I was dumbfounded; it was like he'd turned on an engine.

That particular lesson was all-important. We had no idea that *Australia II* was that fast on that point of sail. *Liberty* was terribly slow downwind, particularly in about 7 or 8 knots of true wind and lumpy seas. There wasn't a lot we could do, and that situation would come back to haunt us in the final race.

Now that Bertrand was back in control, I had to do something and do it fast. We were heading for the fifth mark and I was pretty sure he would round first unless we pulled a rabbit out of the hat. The next move has received a great deal of attention in the press, and many people have said it was one of the most secretive and daring moves of the entire summer. In truth, it was completely unplanned and totally spontaneous.

Without any notice to my crew, I said, "We're jibing." Scotty Vogel, our bowman, was below deck working on packing and unpacking sails, and he had about ten seconds to jump up and get set. This is where my men really help me. They're always ready to do whatever I ask.

THE WHITE SHARK

Australia II was only about two boat-lengths to leeward and I decided to jibe right at them. By doing so, we went on starboard tack and gained the right of way. That meant Bertrand had to react instantly because the burden was now on him to keep clear. His options were either to jibe with us, which would have given us inside position going around the mark, or cross our stern in an attempt to get inside us.

Bertrand chose the latter, and as he went into his emergency left-hand turn he threw the wheel hard to port. The tremendous stress placed on the steering gear caused the rudder quadrant to break and *Australia II* went into a wild, out-of-control broach. This enabled us to round the mark ahead with a nice lead; then all we had to do was cover them and the first race of the 1983 America's Cup was ours by 1:10.

By the time we reached the dock after the race we all felt damn relieved to have won. The secret was out—these guys were fast, not only upwind, but downwind as well. I kept thinking about one of my favorite movies, *Butch Cassidy and the Sundance Kid,* when Butch and Sundance are being relentlessly pursued by a posse of the best hotshots in the West. Our heroes keep riding like hell, but every time they turn around, there's the damn posse. Butch and Sundance keep asking "Who *are* those guys?" That's just the way we felt with that little white shark on our fanny.

If the first race had me mumbling those words, Race Two made me shout them. Who are those guys who can suffer another gear break (their headboard, which takes the mainsail to the top of the mast, broke), lose the start, then round the first mark by forty-five seconds in the lead? Forty-five seconds! With a sagging main and a jib crew way up in the air so they could trim the main. *Who* are *those guys?*

But there was no give-up on our boat, now or at any time during the entire series. Now we were on the reaching legs, where we felt we could outperform *Australia II*. Bertrand sent his mainsail trimmer, Colin Beashel, up the mast to try to secure the sagging mainsail. We kept attacking.

While we were sailing the two reaching legs, our afterguard got together and formulated a plan for the next beat. It was a gutsy call, but dictated by our position and by the weather conditions. People say we outsailed the Aussies here, but actually we just employed a little American ingenuity and out-thought them. I keep hearing they won the Cup because they psyched me out. Well, we pulled off a little psych-job ourselves.

Tactician Tom Whidden, navigator Halsey Herreshoff, sail trimmer John Marshall, and I figured that after Bertrand's blunder of not covering us on the third leg of the first race, he'd play strictly by the book from now on. We knew the wind was dying and was shifty. When they rounded the third mark twenty-one seconds ahead of us, we put our plan into motion.

The idea was that because we were behind, we could force the action; we could make them tack when we wanted because they would feel obligated to cover us. We'd divided up responsibilities so that Tom was concentrating on how wind shifts were affecting our boat, Halsey kept feeding us information about where we were in relation to the next mark, and John was our scout, watching for signs of wind hundreds of yards away and trying to identify their strength and direction.

My job was to absorb all the information, keep my eye on the White Shark in relation to us, and tack when I thought they'd be out of phase with the wind. When a boat is out of phase, it is heading in a direction other than the optimum direction given the current direction of the wind. We were trying to find spots where we'd have the wind and they wouldn't. This is called "sailing them into a hole."

The strategy worked perfectly. Bertrand never figured out what we were doing and we managed to sail him into a hole in which he had no wind but we did. We caught up to them and then passed them. As we tacked in front of them, we threw a slam-dunk at them. This can be a very effective maneuver to trap your opponent on your leeward side where the wind has been weakened by its passage around your own sails and is accomplished best in winds of 10 knots or more. Just as the bow of the boat you are crossing in front of passes beneath your stern, you immediately start to tack. If your boat makes it onto the new tack and accelerates fast enough before the bow of the now leeward boat lines up with the bow of your boat, you have "slam-dunked" your competitor by taking his wind and slowing him down.

Our maneuver against *Australia II* was very close, only just legal. They protested, but the jury dismissed them just as we had done on the course. *Liberty* by 1:33 for a 2–0 score. We felt pretty good.

The first Race Three was on Saturday, September 17. Once again, the spectator fleet was enormous. The main impression I have of that race is that the White Shark just blew us out of the water. I remember thinking we were doing okay and then we got on the first run and hoisted our number-one spinnaker. That was our smallest chute and it had always been good to us. But *Australia II* just put her head down and raced through the water.

By the end of the run the Aussies were ahead by an unbelievable five minutes and fifty-seven seconds. That was the largest lead a foreign Challenger had ever had over an American Defender. The only thing that saved us was that the wind died and time ran out. *Australia II* was still about a mile and a half from the finish line when the Committee boat raised the "Race Abandoned" flag. The score remained 2–0, but we knew the Aussies had gained a lot of confidence.

The real Race Three, held the following day, wasn't much better. The White Shark had tasted blood and now began to move in for the kill. We won the start again, but we were just no match for their lighter, smaller boat in the zephyrs. At the first mark *Australia II* showed us her stern by one minute, fourteen seconds. Again, we made up some time on the reaches, but *Australia II* piled it on over the last three legs and won by 3:14.

Everyone thinks we must have been devastated, but my guys have lost boat races before and they wouldn't have been where they were if they became too upset over a loss. We didn't like it, but we just don't get too down over it. But I might say we were a little bit shocked at how fast the Aussies were, so we decided to call for a lay-day to regroup.

At the press conference that night, I remember trying to fend off a lot of silly questions about what the loss *really* meant. But one question I remember thinking was pretty funny was from an Aussie reporter. The night before someone asked me how I felt about having the race abandoned with *Australia II* so far in front. My reply was, "God must be an American." Tonight, the question was, "Yesterday you claimed God was an American. Does your loss today mean He has Sunday off?" Now there's a journo with a little wit! I laughed and said, "Not even He could have coped with *Australia II* today."

The fourth race was perhaps the finest race we had ever sailed up to that point. Bertrand tried to get us in a circle game during the prerace maneuvers, but with about three and a half minutes to go before the gun, I just peeled *Liberty* off and sailed way off to the left. I had a feeling Bertrand thought we'd gone too far and he let his guard down. We'd never been too impressed with his starting ability—he was always hunched over the wheel looking so white and nervous and sick—and I had an idea we could stick one to him today.

When I turned to make the dash for the line, I was pretty confident I was spot on. I was on port tack and *Australia II* was on starboard tack, which under sailing's rules of the road meant Bertrand had right of way. I had to stay clear *if* we were on a collision course. We both headed for the line, going right at each other. Fifty tons of aluminum and lead were bearing down on each other and something had to give. Bertrand was trying to make me take his stern, but I thought I sensed some daylight in front of his bow.

I asked Tom Whidden, "Can we cross their bow?" He said, "Probably not," but I took a hard look and said, "Hell, we can make it." I flicked up on the wheel and took him by maybe ten or fifteen feet. We were over the starting line first by six seconds, but by port-tacking him I think he got pretty demoralized. You're just not supposed to let something like that happen if you're an America's Cup helmsman with the starboard tack advantage. It was a real faux pas. He completely miscalculated time and distance. I had to laugh at that. There are five moves in match-racing that you should never let happen, and that was one of them. It was the ultimate insult, and I believe it hurt the Australians psychologically because they were never really in the race after that. Bertrand said after we won the race by forty-three seconds, "I'll never endure a humiliation like that again."

Some people have described that race as the "most perfect America's Cup race ever sailed." I'm not sure I go along with that, but I will admit it was memorable. What made it so satisfying wasn't just that we made the right moves at the right time, but that we were able to neutralize a faster boat.

Now we only had to win one race before the Aussies could win three. We felt good to have gotten there by sheer sailing ability, because without question the White Shark was the faster boat. All we needed now was to keep sailing hard and a little racing luck.

Racing luck. I'm not a very superstitious person. I don't go in for rabbit's feet or garlic cloves or lucky pennies or any of that. To me, luck is work, preparation, ability, attitude, confidence, skill. When something breaks or the wind shifts, I don't see it as a result of the stars being aligned in a certain pattern or because our bowman walked under a ladder. But if there is such a thing as racing luck, ours ran out about an hour before the fifth race in 1983.

For me, the most dramatic, traumatic, and suspenseful part of the '83 series was before the start of that race. I joke with John Marshall about what happened, but back then he felt dismal about it. While tuning up we were on a starboard tack, and John was pumping out the hydraulic pistons in the jumper struts that control the top third of the mast. What he didn't realize was that he had left both valves open so all the fluid drained out and the pistons froze. There was some pressure in the windward piston, so it wasn't too badly damaged, but the leeward rod went out 20 percent farther than it had ever been before.

When we tacked, it broke off and the jumper strut bent over like the skin of a peeled banana. This occurred just one hour before the start.

That was just the beginning of a comedy of errors. Our first big mistake was that we didn't have a spare part on the water. I immediately radioed to Ed du Moulin, our syndicate chairman, who in turn requested help from the Coast Guard. They denied the request. That left us with only a couple of options, one of which was to hacksaw the piston off and then reattach it.

To accomplish this, we sent Scotty Vogel and Tom Rich up the mast. It was blowing twenty knots true and those two guys performed a Herculean job in adverse conditions. In the meantime, our chase boat raced to our dock, picked up a spare, and got it to us just a few minutes before the ten-minute gun. However, our problems were far from over. The new piston was about two inches too long. It was absolute agony waiting for the gun, with the minutes ticking away, and realizing that we were in deep trouble.

Scotty and Tom came down after fifty minutes aloft, tired and beat to hell. They immediately went back into action to hoist the jib we had chosen especially for the wind condition. No sooner was it up than it ripped. Down it came to be replaced by another. All this was happening about eight minutes before the start, while we were supposed to be concentrating on prestart maneuvers.

The White Shark smelled blood again and came at us. But Bertrand was still having problems with the start, and despite being wounded, we came back at him aggressively. We were to leeward of the starting line and I got the better position and just forced him over the line by about one second. _Australia II_ had to reround and by the time she got squared away, we had a thirty-seven-second lead on him.

You had to like our situation at that moment. We were ahead on the board 3–1, we were ahead on the course by more than a half-minute, the wind conditions suited us perfectly, and right then, we had _Liberty_ moving well.

But about four minutes into the race, the jumper strut broke again. Without proper tension, the mast sagged and we were just unable to point up into the wind. With blood on the water, the white shark started charging and soon she was just a few boat-lengths behind us. We were both on port tack and then Bertrand tacked to clear his air. As he took off to the left side of the course, I kept driving on our same heading.

In his book, Bertrand criticizes us for not covering. What he does not mention is that in our crippled state we couldn't have possibly engaged in a tacking duel. There was no way we could have won the race on boat speed in close proximity. Actually, he gave us the only chance we had by splitting away. The only way for us to win was to be a mile apart and have the windshifts come in our direction. Unfortunately, it just didn't happen that way.

Australia II won by 1:47. I still feel we should have won that race. It was the kind of breeze in which the boat didn't heel over too much but she could still use her waterline. She had enough sail area so that she could go full speed, but not so much that she would heel over and have to reduce power. She was a longer boat than *Australia II* so she had a little more potential when she was able to use her full power. That's one of the reasons we were faster reaching.

Race Five was a lesson we took into the 1986/87 Cup. We now have an even more comprehensive list of spare parts on our tender *Betsy* (named of course after Betsy Ross, maker of the first American flag). One of the reasons *Betsy* is such a satisfactory tender is that she is big enough to stow all sorts of gear on board. We had booms, spinnaker poles, winches, mainsheets, halyards, guys, blocks, pump handles, and yes—pistons for the jumper struts.

The sixth race was a real ballbreaker. It started off with Bertrand misjudging his start yet again. He was too close with too much time so he had to jibe, circle, and cross behind us. We were over seven seconds in front of him.

The story of that race was that *Australia II* caught a spectacular windshift on the first leg and just kept powering out ahead of us. Bertrand had taken the boat to the left and we got the first lift, but then God must have come back from His day off and decided to help the Aussies. We had a good breeze, about 16 knots true, but then *Australia II* got her own private blast several knots more than we had and almost 20 degrees closer to the mark. I remember watching that damn boat go faster and faster and get farther and farther away. Who *are* those guys? They're the ones who got to the first mark two minutes, twenty-nine seconds before we did. Yes, 2:29. Kiss that one good-bye. In the end, they won by 3:25, the largest margin ever recorded by a challenging yacht.

So we went into the seventh race, the first time in history the America's Cup had gone the distance. At the press conference after the sixth race, Bertrand said something about how not even Hollywood scriptwriters could have cooked up a better scenario. Where he saw this as some big drama, I saw it as just another boat race.

A lot of people who don't know me imagine that the final race was the cause of all sorts of anxiety and that the result must have been heartbreaking. It's difficult to convince them that none of the eleven people on board felt that the end of the world was near. The fact is that we just shook hands and told each other we'd raced well.

What I remember most about that last race was that the Aussies called a lay-day, which enabled us to change the mode of our boat. Lee Davis, our meteorologist, gave us a firm prediction for light wind the next day, so we decided to take *Liberty* to Cove Haven Marina (the same place the Aussies' wing keel was first discovered) and make her as light as possible. *Australia II*, because of her shorter size, came out of the box a good deal lighter than we so she had always been a good light-air boat.

If the casual fan only understood what nerve it took for us to take the risk we did, there might be a greater appreciation of just how gutsy we were. Making the boat lighter would make her fast in 10 knots or less wind, but hopelessly slow in fresh air. We took out 1,000 pounds of ballast and we stripped the boat clean, trying to get every bit of weight we could off her. Normally we sailed with six jibs, six spinnakers, and several staysails. When we hit the starting line for Race Seven, we had just two jibs and two spinnakers. We had also taken off the spare winch drum, the spare afterguys, the spare halyards— every bit of weight that wasn't absolutely essential. The guys even left their sweaters and boots on the dock. They wore nothing but shorts and T-shirts.

But then on the way out to the course, the wind was blowing 15 true. We had been counting on 10 or less. We began to think Lee had made a colossal mistake, but just before the start the breeze died down as he had predicted. In the seventh race, *Liberty* was faster than she had ever been in such light air.

There were no pep talks, no "come on guys, let's go get 'em" talk. There never has been on any of my boats. Anyone who sails with me is at the top of his sailing career. He is the best, otherwise he wouldn't be there. And at that level there's no need for hype. The most that is ever said is, "Let's have a good one."

The early difference between the two boats in that final race was not so much that we sailed spectacularly well but that the Australians really screwed up by not covering us. We were almost to the starboard lay line, and they let us get back to the inside of the course. That was better for us because the wind went to the left, making the first reach so lopsided, and ultimately that's what won them the race. It meant that we couldn't make any gains to add to our 31-second lead. We got

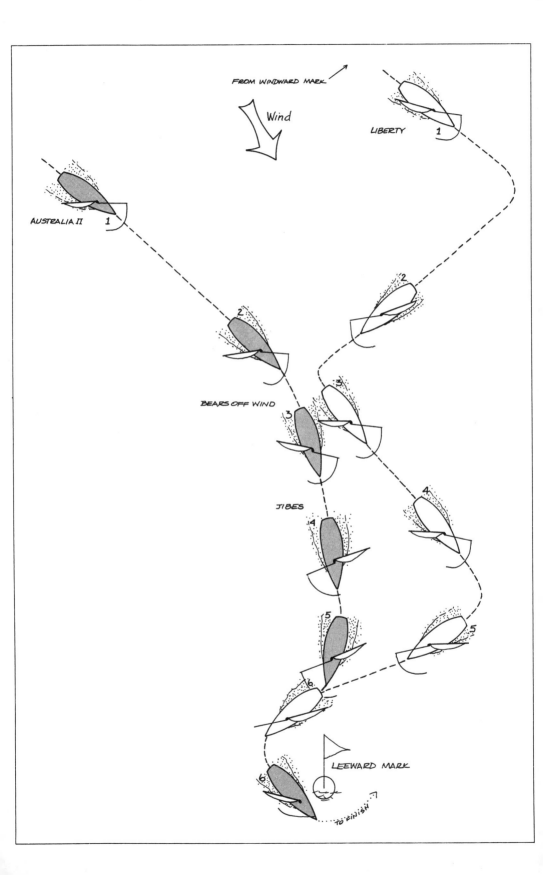

FROM WINDWARD MARK

Wind

LIBERTY

1

AUSTRALIA II   1

2

2

BEARS OFF WIND

3

3

JIBES

4

4

5

5

6

6

LEEWARD MARK

TO FINISH

THE WHITE SHARK

15 seconds on the first reach and then gave it all back when change in the direction of the wind turned the second reach into a run downwind. The rest of the race was fairly uneventful except that on the second windward leg we got quite a long way ahead, and right at the end we got in a little lighter wind up by the spectator fleet and got a little out of phase with the wind. It was my fault, not Tom's, that they closed up on us. The same left-hand shift that let us pass them on the first beat allowed them to pass and saved their ass. We knew that the Australians had been gaining an average of a minute on every spinnaker run and since we were only 49 seconds ahead at the last windward mark we knew we were in deep ca-ca. We were not at all confident that we were going to win.

We started the run by heading out to the right, but then we found there was more pressure on port than starboard so we jibed to port to get to the inside of the course. People who say we didn't cover just don't know what they're talking about. The truth is that we did exactly the right thing to cover. We got to the inside of the course so that we could have clear air on the jibe and when we got to the inside we jibed back to starboard. The Aussies came down on us with a real bone in their teeth. I could see them out of the corner of my eye gaining bearing, gaining bearing, gaining bearing. Tommy was calling out the number of diminishing boat-lengths that once was our lead, but no one was getting excited. That's when I said, "Anyone got any ideas?"

I don't think I had any emotions one way or another. I certainly didn't say to myself, oh boy, here goes the Cup. As far as we were concerned it was still a boat race that we were going to win. When we converged on opposite jibes they were very close to being able to pass before us so we jibed onto a course parallel to theirs and they still just sailed up right through us. The fact that the lead had changed didn't make a scrap of difference. After we both rounded the leeward mark and bore upwind toward the finish line we said right, we'll tack them down and we did. There were 47 tacks on that last leg and a lot of times I went head to wind and got Bertrand all screwed up. At the end I took

Opposite: **1983, America's Cup.** *Australia II* **grabs lead that wins her the Cup during the last leeward leg.** *Liberty* **leads** *Australia II* **after rounding the windward mark and they each set a spinnaker. The two boats choose to take separate routes to the leeward mark. As they converge near the leeward mark,** *Australia II* **bears off and jibes (2–3–4) and** *Liberty* **jibes to port (2–3) to stay inside of** *Australia II* **(3).** *Liberty* **then jibes back to starboard (4–5).** *Australia II* **leads** *Liberty* **around the leeward mark (6).**

him over into the spectator fleet. I thought I might get lucky and someone might run him down! In Bertrand's book he claims there was a fist fight on board *Liberty*. If you will pardon the expression that's just plain bullshit. It's an absolute fabrication. It never happened and what's worse when the author called to check the story, he was told it definitely did not happen. It wasn't true, they knew it wasn't true, but they included it anyway. That's the way history gets distorted.

Going across the line 41 seconds astern was no big deal either. When it happened the guys shook hands and said, "Nice going. Good race. We gave it our best shot." There were no tears shed by anyone except Kyle Smith, the biggest, toughest, meanest guy on the boat. Of course there was a lot of emotion later, especially when I went aboard *Australia II*'s tender, *Black Swan*. That's when I said hi to Sir James Hardy, one of the world's great yachtsmen, who sailed for Australia in several America's Cups. I said, "Jim, I can't sail any better than that." He replied, "You sailed a great race, Dennis. You were beaten by a faster boat." I tried to put a brave face on, but the truth is I was ready to go home.

Perhaps my greatest disappointment was the reaction of the members of the Cup Committee from the New York Yacht Club. They simply abandoned me and all the guys. No one ever showed up even to say "nice try." We'd done the best we could in a situation that their inaction and ineptness helped to create, but not one of them had the guts to face any of us.

The night of the last race I went to the press conference by myself. It wasn't easy walking alone onto a stage full of exuberant Aussies, but I felt it was important for someone representing the Yacht Club's team to be there. It seemed to me the sportsmanlike thing to do—to offer our congratulations. I said well done, the better boat won, we have no excuses.

We've received criticism from some quarters for not showing up at the Marble House when the Cup was officially presented to the Royal Perth Yacht Club. The truth is that the New York Yacht Club changed their plans at the last minute and decided to present the Cup in Newport the day after our loss, instead of later in the week at the Club in New York. They neglected to tell us such a ceremony was planned. The first we heard about it was when some of the crew was having lunch at the Pier restaurant (others had gone home) and someone came up to us and said, "Hey, why aren't you guys at the trophy presentation?" Halsey Herreshoff was the only guy who got wind of it, and he mentioned it to Ed du Moulin and they both decided to go. When

Halsey showed up they didn't even have the courtesy to let him on the dais. They made him walk out back with the crowd. I understood later that Ed du Moulin, the syndicate manager, did present our syndicate flag to John Bertrand prior to the presentation of the Cup to Alan Bond.

The day after the last race my wife Judy, my close friend and fellow-sailor from San Diego, Malin Burnham, and his wife Roberta and I got on an airplane headed back to San Diego. Later that day, the White House called Ed du Moulin to invite the crew to Washington to take part in a ceremony in the Rose Garden. I would have been thrilled to meet President Reagan, but the timing just didn't work out, as we were already on our way home. However, Ed managed to round up nine crew members, including those who had already returned to their homes. Together with Chairman Fritz Jewett they all flew to Washington to meet the President the next morning.

When we arrived in San Diego there were hundreds of people at the airport to meet us and their warmth and affection were gratifying. We all went to the Yacht Club and had a big party and the next day I went to work. That was that. Life goes on.

3

★

Aloha
Winds

OW that I've had the opportunity to reflect on the 1983 America's Cup, I'd have to say there were three major factors accounting for the victory of *Australia II*. They are Warren Jones, Ben Lexcen, and Alan Bond.

Jones handled the political end of the keel controversy brilliantly and he did a superb job managing the crew. From my perspective, Jones was the real leader in that camp. He ran the day-to-day operation and did a super job.

Ben Lexcen came up with the greatest innovation in 12-meter yacht design in decades. He deserves all the credit he has received and more.

John Bertrand has been very critical of the wing keel, but I feel he ought to thank his lucky stars because without it, with just a conventional boat, he would never have won the Cup.

Bondy was the money man, but perhaps even more important, he had the courage to go along with Lexcen's idea. Imagine if you were doling out millions of dollars and your designer says he has an idea to turn the keel upside down and put wings on it. Most businessmen have a hard time dealing with the artistic temperament, but Bond had the guts to invest in Lexcen's vision.

For a while after the Cup was lost, no one really seemed to know how the next event would shape up. The initial word was that because Perth was so far from everything, no one was going to show. It took a little while for interest to build, but then we began hearing that a number of yacht clubs were considering campaigns. I knew the New York Yacht Club would certainly want the Cup back, but I never thought that by the time entries closed, twenty-four different Challengers would put their money on the table. I was flabbergasted.

So while other sailors around the world were thinking about Perth, I really hadn't got too excited. People assume that somehow I was mesmerized by the aura of the Cup. Certainly the third time around was not as exciting as the first time. Sailboat racing is the thing I like to do most in life and I get a great deal of personal pleasure out of it. Certainly the America's Cup is the pinnacle of yachting and the Holy Grail of our sport. However, looking back, my greatest thrill in yachting was winning the Star Boat Worlds for the first time in 1971. My second-biggest thrill was going to the Olympics in 1976 and standing on the dais with the bronze Medal around my neck listening to the National Anthem. My third-greatest thrill was in 1977 when I won the Star Boat World Championship with five consecutive firsts.

There were a few tears when we got back to the dock the night we lost the Cup and that seemed natural enough. But at that point my mind was a long way from focusing on bringing the Cup home.

It wasn't until Christmas 1983 that I seriously began thinking about trying again. At that time I was in Hawaii visiting Fritz and Lucy Jewett and we began talking about the Cup. I realized that the amount of time I had spent on the water in 12-meter yachts almost demanded another attempt. In 1974, with the *Mariner* campaign, the boat was in the shed so much I spent more time sanding than sailing, but we still managed about five hundred hours at sea. The 1980 *Freedom* campaign began in Newport; in the winter we went to San Diego, then back to Newport in the spring. Total time: three thousand hours. 1982–83 aboard *Liberty* was pretty much the same, so add another three thousand hours.

The Jewetts had first become interested in the America's Cup in 1958 when Briggs Cunningham anchored *Columbia* in front of their house in Woods Hole, Massachusetts. Fritz and Lucy rowed out to see the Cup Defender and Briggs gave them a guided tour. That's all it took to get them hooked and they've been in this game ever since.

During the 1960s Fritz was involved in various campaigns, mostly from afar, but by 1973 Gerry Driscoll, the San Diego designer and yachtsman who skippered *Intrepid* in 1974, had persuaded the Jewetts to become directly involved. They campaigned *Intrepid,* which became known as the first "people's boat" because of their fund-raising appeal to grass-roots America instead of to just the rich. They started the "people-to-people" campaign in conjunction with the Seattle Sailing Foundation and away they went.

To Fritz in those days, Dennis Conner was the enemy. Ted Hood and I were the ones who beat them and went on to race in the Cup. By 1978 the time had come for the Jewetts and me to team up, so they invited me to their house in Woods Hole. It is a magnificent home situated right on the water and it intimidated this carpet and drapery salesman. I was doing my best to stay cool and act socially adept, but I committed a piercing faux pas. Lucy served iced tea and I mistook the salt cellar for a sugar bowl and starting spooning salt into the tea. Lucy immediately realized my predicament and put me at ease by making it seem like her mistake. She is a Lady with a capital L.

Since then they have become more than just friends. I consider them family. Lucy became the den mother of the 1980 and 1983 efforts, and Fritz has always been someone whose counsel I take to heart. They believe in Dennis Conner and his dream and they've been among the best and most loyal friends I have.

So when we met during Christmas in 1983, the conversation turned to the Cup. By now we had forsaken iced tea for rum and tonic, and after a couple I started thinking another campaign might not be so bad. The Jewetts were disappointed in the way the New York Yacht Club conducted itself in 1983 and in the way it treated me. We knew the Club had revealed that the first announced candidate for the next Cup would have John Kolius as the helmsman. They had already begun to approach individual and corporate sponsors, so they had a step up on any other groups contemplating making a run.

The Jewetts offered financial backing if I wanted to go out on my own—to try to put together my own syndicate. It was a tremendous offer and one that took me a little by surprise. The Jewetts were certainly no newcomers to the game, but they had always invested their America's Cup dollars in a bona-fide organization. Now they were saying, "Dennis, you form your own group and go get that Cup."

I began to give that idea a lot of thought and by the time I met with Malin Burnham several weeks later, I was adamant about having nothing to do with the New York Yacht Club. Malin is a legend in San Diego sailing circles and has been ever since he won the Star Boat World Championships at the age of seventeen. He helped teach me to sail on the waters around San Diego when I was a kid and he's been like an older brother to me for many years. I've always had a great respect for his opinion and when he insisted that our first loyalties, as far as the Cup was concerned, lay with the New York Yacht Club, I eventually agreed.

Malin pointed out that we were both long-time members in good standing and that I had successfully defended the Cup for the Club in 1980 and then unsuccessfully in 1983. He convinced me that we owed it to New York to first offer our services there.

I came to think then—and in many ways I still believe—that the Cup was such a part of that club for so long, it almost belonged there. And since I had a part in losing it for them, I wanted to have a part in winning it back.

There is a lot to be said for tradition. No other sporting trophy in the world has ever had just one custodian for a hundred thirty-two years. There are many things about the trophy that make it very special, and for me, very American. It's as much a symbol of our country as the Statue of Liberty.

So I flew to New York and spoke with Ed du Moulin. A meeting was arranged at the Club on January 6, 1984. It was held in the Commodore's Room on the third floor. We were informed that the Club also planned to interview two other groups. One of the groups was proposing Chuck Kirsch as an administrator with John Kolius as the helmsman, and the other had Leonard Greene as manager and Dave Vietor skipper. Actually, these two groups had sort of split apart from the once-united 1983 *Defender/Courageous* campaign.

When I had the opportunity to address the group, I laid out my plan. I said I wanted a multiboat program, with the maritime college at Fort Schuyler Foundation as the tax-free vehicle, that we would use *Liberty* as our basic yardstick, that Fritz Jewett would be our chairman and that Ed du Moulin would help me manage. I was confident our key guys would return and that we could harness the best American technology.

I also spoke about improving the image of the Club. It wasn't necessary to spell this out, because everyone in the room knew that the rancor of 1983 had taken its toll. Irritation with the Club was so great that many Americans had actually rooted for the Australians, and even within the Club some members were quite annoyed with the actions of the hierarchy. Obviously, it was time to make some changes. I said we had to get the entire country behind us and that included all yacht clubs, not just the one on West 44th Street.

I felt the presentation went well and that a number of the men in the room had a positive reaction. I ended my pitch by saying that while deciding which group to go with, the Committee should consider that time was of the essence. The Kirsch/Kolius group was already out there calling my former backers. My attitude was that if they wanted me, fine, but if not, I had to know sooner than later so I could go in other directions.

The feedback from the inner circle was very good. I was told the Committee liked the idea of having me return. We thought we'd get the order any day. But then no decision was made and it began to look like none would be forthcoming. Bus Mosbacher had gone to Florida on vacation right after the original meeting and several weeks later there still was no word.

At the time, I was Commodore of the San Diego Yacht Club helping to organize the Manzanillo Race, which is a biennial event. So on January 20 I called Mosbacher's office in New York and was informed he was out of town. I explained that I needed to know what decision had been reached about my participation in the next Cup effort. The next day I received a call from the Secretary of the New York Yacht Club. It went like this:

"Good morning, Mr. Conner. I'm calling on behalf of Commodore Mosbacher. He requests your presence here at the Club on January 29 at four P.M. We look forward to seeing you then."

"Thank you very much, but I'm afraid I have a real scheduling conflict on that day. As Commodore of the San Diego Yacht Club, I will be hosting an affair in conjunction with our Manzanillo Race. Two hundred people are expected at my house. Could you ask Commodore Mosbacher to call me back and we can make other arrangements."

Several hours later I got another call from Ann Carroll of the Secretary's office of the New York Yacht Club.

"The Commodore says that in order to accommodate your schedule he has changed the meeting from four P.M. to eleven A.M."

"Thank you," I said, not really believing what I was hearing. "On what day?"

"The same day, Mr. Conner."

"Please inform the Commodore I will not be able to attend. As I've said, I have an obligation here."

"Yes, the Commodore is aware of that. That's why he changed the time."

"I'm afraid it will be impossible for me to be there. Please ask the Commodore to call me."

I guess that was the straw that broke the camel's back. I blew my top and called Fritz and Malin. "If they can't even schedule a meeting, how the hell are we ever going to put together an entire syndicate? I've been thinking about this twenty-four hours a day and Mosbacher doesn't even have the courtesy to call me back. This just isn't going to work out."

Fritz repeated his suggestion to go out on my own. Malin now agreed. That day I decided I'd do it. It may have been the most important decision made during the entire run for the Cup.

I organized a board meeting at the San Diego Yacht Club and put forth my plan. Malin Burnham heroically stated that he would be personally liable for any debts the syndicate incurred. It was an unbelievably gutsy thing to do and it showed me just how much faith he had in my abilities. Without Fritz and Malin, there would never have been a campaign.

We also assured the Club that we would not spend any of its funds. The board gave its approval. Before announcing it to the press, at Ed du Moulin's suggestion Fritz Jewett and I called Bus Mosbacher and Bob Stone of the NYYC to advise them of my decision.

When things settled down a bit and I had a chance for some quiet reflection, I began to wonder exactly what I'd done. I realized that it was going to take millions of dollars to be competitive and at that time, aside from Fritz, Malin, and Dennis Conner, I didn't have any sponsors nor did I really have any idea where I would get them. I had just launched myself off a cliff with Fritz Jewett supplying my parachute.

On the race to Mexico, I thought quite a bit about the organization of the campaign, and when we arrived in Manzanillo, Joanne Fishman arrived to help me get started. Joanne had been the *New York Times* correspondent during the 1983 America's Cup and she had a lot of excellent contacts in the world of yachting. She became the first employee of our as-yet-unnamed syndicate, and much of our early success was due to her loyalty, drive, and enthusiasm.

The early months of our unorganized organization were literally run out of a shoe box kept in the back of Vera's Drapes in San Diego. I used to put all our unpaid bills in it, and since we were spending a lot more than we were bringing in, the box filled up in a hurry.

Most of those phone calls went to my old backers, people who had been with me since 1974. Since most of them were either members or supporters of the New York Yacht Club, I was in effect declaring war on the Club. Of course, the Kirsch/Kolius group was already well organized and they had been out there scooping up backers before we got going. The Club became my enemy. To me, they were just as big a threat as the Australians, and I knew if I were going to win the Cup back, I'd have to go through them to do it.

So, having made the big announcement, I wasn't exactly deluged with offers of support. The number of bills in the shoe box grew at an astonishing rate, but the cash register rarely opened. Then a couple of guys from the Club, David Kennedy and Bob Aron, came up with solid cash gifts and said let's see how you go. I have a great deal of respect for them because I know what it took to break old ties and back a brand-new endeavor.

Joanne's forte was fund raising and in the beginning our campaign was really the Dennis and Joanne show. During the first few months we went hat-in-hand to a lot of people and corporations asking for money, and we had a lot of smoke blown in our faces. For more than a century the America's Cup had been very much an exclusive game played by the East Coast yachting establishment, and here we were bucking up against the New York Yacht Club. A lot of the boys in blazers and straw hats didn't like it and the word got out fast to secure wallets when Dennis and Joanne came to town.

The smoke in our faces began to clear when Terry Brown of the Atlas Hotels in San Diego came in with a $500,000 donation. That was the first substantial contribution and it got us going. Terry deserves a lot of credit for taking the plunge because at the time he was the only San Diego businessman who had faith in us.

The next significant sponsor was the Ford Motor Company. Joanne had set up a meeting with Edsel Ford and right from the beginning the reaction was positive. Edsel understood immediately what our program could do for his company and he had the courage to back our dream with a very large check. He later doubled the amount, and we also received a number of cars for our use in Hawaii and Australia. Throughout the entire campaign, Edsel was one of our staunchest supporters.

Chasing dollars has never been my favorite aspect of the America's Cup. However, I'm the first to realize the importance of a well-financed effort. In this new era of very high-ticket campaigns, financing is as crucial to winning the Cup as design or sails or seamanship.

In the very beginning, Malin and I isolated two key ingredients essential for success. They were excellence in design and lots of money. We might come up with the best design in the world, but without the money to refine and exploit it, it wouldn't be a winner. Conversely, we could have all the money in the world, but without the right design, dollars wouldn't make it faster. Two perfect examples of this thinking were San Francisco's *USA* and New York's *America II*. *USA* was a revolutionary boat that showed a lot of speed in certain conditions but was insufficiently developed because of lack of adequate funding. *America II* just wasn't designed well, and no matter how much money was thrown at it—and an awful lot was—she didn't get any faster.

While we were putting together our campaign, I realized how important a role the Challenger of Record would play. This was to be the official body, chosen by the Royal Perth Yacht Club, that would administer all aspects of the Challenger side of the races. The Royal Perth was in charge of everything on the Defender side and, ultimately, the actual America's Cup best-of-seven series.

Politics play an enormous role in the America's Cup. Trade-offs and compromises in smoke-filled rooms affect what happens on the water in a thousand different ways. An example is a move the Royal Perth tried to pull early in the organizational process. They wanted all Challengers to be restricted to one boat per entry and there could be no substitutions. On the other hand, the Royal Perth was quite happy to allow two boat campaigns in the Defender trials, which gave an enormous advantage to all Defenders. One boat could be built for light air, the other for heavy air, and depending on the conditions, whichever boat was appropriate could head out to the starting line. This demand was later modified somewhat, but there was no question Royal Perth gave itself an advantage whenever possible.

Actually, Royal Perth could have been a lot worse. I thought the moment the Aussies got their hands on that trophy they'd say, "Okay, here's our big chance to spit in the eyes of the New York Yacht Club just like they've done to Challengers for a hundred thirty-two years." But except for a few incidents, they were fair.

I lobbied hard for the role of Challenger of Record. We commissioned a $20,000 videotape presentation illustrating the strengths and accomplishments of the San Diego Yacht Club. The club's history was given, from 1883 to the modern 12-meter era. The SDYC involvement in this class has been particularly illustrious, perhaps second only to the New York Yacht Club in the United States. Gerry Driscoll sailed aboard *Columbia* in the Defender trials in which *Constellation* emerged as the victorious defender. Driscoll also sailed *Intrepid* against *Courageous* and *Mariner* in 1974.

In 1977, Fritz Jewett commissioned the design of *Enterprise* and organized a syndicate with himself as chairman and Ed du Moulin as manager. Lowell North and Malin Burnham, perhaps the two most famous sailors in the San Diego Yacht Club, were recruited to campaign *Enterprise*. Obviously, San Diego Yacht Club sailors have been deeply involved in the America's Cup.

The videotape we produced to sell the Royal Perth Yacht Club on the SDYC becoming the Challenger of Record was indeed impressive. I felt we had the credentials to be taken seriously: a solid history, two decades of 12-meter experience, a number of Olympic medalists, and expertise and experience in all types of sailboat races. We had the whole proposal packaged in a beautiful red velvet teak box.

I flew to Perth and made the presentation on April 21, 1984. The officers of the Royal Perth in attendance were clearly impressed—I remember mouths falling open during the more spectacular scenes. But open mouths do not a positive decision ensure, for the offer went to the Yacht Club Costa Smeralda on the island of Sardinia in Italy. Royal Perth never justified their decision; they just announced this was the way it would be. My guess is they figured they could steamroll the guys from Costa Smeralda while he'd have difficulties dealing with a hardass like Dennis Conner.

But the trip to Perth didn't go for naught. I spent some time acquainting myself with Fremantle and started some real-estate deals going for our syndicate. Fremantle was still a mess at the time with so much construction going on in preparation for the races, but I'm involved in real estate in the San Diego area and I think I have a pretty good feel for how things might develop. With the help of Steve and Lynn Soares, we tied up crew quarters and waterfront facilities. Now Fremantle was ready for us when we were ready for Fremantle.

On the trip home, I stopped in Hawaii. This beautiful paradise had been central to my plans from the very beginning. It was where Fritz and I originally talked about putting together our own run for the Cup, and from previous race experience, the waters and conditions were known to me. The more I considered Hawaii as a training area, the more perfect it seemed.

My primary consideration was that the wind and water were very similar on a year-round basis to those conditions in which the Cup would be held. For the design of the boat and the making of sails, nothing was more important. Also, Hawaii is in the United States and while it is a long plane trip from the mainland, it isn't halfway around the world. By that time we were already planning to build extra boats. The shipping time to Fremantle alone would have meant that we couldn't have completed our program and applied our results to building the final boat. We knew we had to have that boat in Hawaii on July 1, 1985, so therefore we had to start work four months earlier. The plans had to be drawn and in the hands of the builder by March 1, so the results had to be in by the first week of February. We could not have built '86 and shipped it to Fremantle in time to be tested. As it

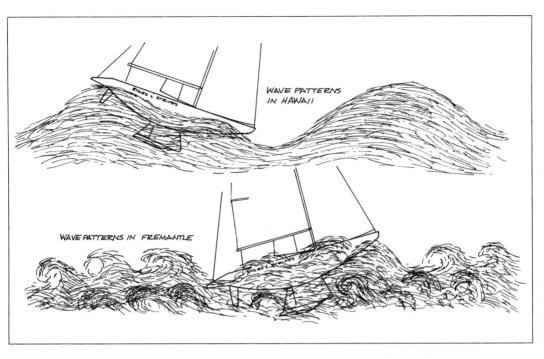

WAVE PATTERNS IN HAWAII

WAVE PATTERNS IN FREMANTLE

We chose to train in Hawaii because the winds there are similar to those we expected in Perth during the Cup races. In 20 knots of wind the waves in Hawaii build to six-to-eight-foot rolling swells. In the same wind conditions in Gage Roads off Fremantle, where the seas are relatively shallow, three-to-four-foot swells with a choppy surface were more common.

was, John Grant had to go through considerable heroics to organize the effort of getting it to Hawaii on time. He had to persuade the governors of three states to issue special waivers to allow the long load to travel on the weekend. We knew it took a month to get a boat to Fremantle, so instead of five days we would have lost another twenty-four. At one stage we looked at the cost of flying the boats out but it was just staggering: approximately $140,000 more than by ship.

Training in Hawaii also meant that our key crewmen, guys like Tom Whidden and Jon Wright who had full-time jobs, could get to our camp and train for ten days instead of traveling for two days to Western Australia, recuperating, practicing a little, then flying home for two days.

Another critical factor in the decision to train in Hawaii was security. As warm and wonderful as our welcome in Fremantle was, we were still the enemy, and if we had trained there, we would have had a thousand eyes watching our every move. Americans root for Americans just like Aussies root for Aussies. When we set up shop in Hawaii, we became a part of the local scene and we felt comfortable. The island people always watched out for us. Whenever spies came to see what we were doing, we'd know before they were even out of customs. Whenever they chartered boats or helicopters, we had advance warning. A perfect example was when Chris Bouzaid, in charge of sail design for the *America II* syndicate, came to Hawaii to try and pick up a little intelligence on our sails. We never put up any of our good sails when Chris was around.

I've never really understood why we were the only American syndicate to figure out the benefits of Hawaii. Every day we were out slugging through 22–28 knots of wind and three-to-five–foot seas, we were developing our seamanship. Our guys were used to those conditions when we finally did get to Fremantle. The record proves that most of the other crews were not.

Those conditions also gave us a tremendous amount of data that fed into our computers aboard the tender *Betsy*, which were used to design our heavy-weather boats and refine our heavy-air sails. It would have been impossible to come as far as we did in sail design in Fremantle. The really boisterous conditions that prevailed for the majority of the Cup races are prevalent off Fremantle only two, maybe three months of the year. Those months happened to be when the Cup would be held. Otherwise, the wind usually comes from the east in the morning and then shifts to the west. But in Hawaii, we got the same wind direction and pretty much the same wind velocity every day. There is absolutely no question that in terms of testing, we got the most bang for our buck by being in Hawaii.

Local friends helped us secure the facilities at Snug Harbor, just outside Honolulu. Fred Smailes was a good friend of ours who once lived in California. He knew the governor and was very well respected by the local business and yachting community. Cy Gillette and Fred Smailes showed me around Hawaii in April of '84.

Cy Gillette is Mr. Hawaii. Because he was so well known there, he played a fundamental role in helping to bring us to Honolulu. He and Fred Smailes, Ken Morrison, and Dick Gooch all made sure Sail America had the facilities we needed in Hawaii. I liked Cy right away because he stood up to me. I couldn't intimidate him. He had maturity, self-respect, and confidence in his expertise. I came to respect his knowledge of the racing rules. He is a very wise man. That's why I asked Cy to go down to Fremantle and help with the rules. I also asked

Mort Bloom to help us on the rules and act as our liaison with the Race Committee. Together, they worked as an excellent team. Both are senior IYRU judges.

We looked at three or four options that were going to be free, but I picked Snug Harbor right away because it had a nice wharf, a crane, and good security. The waterfront facilities were great, but the crew accommodations certainly left something to be desired. There weren't that many choices and they were all expensive. We wanted all the guys to be together. That's why we ended up in a high-rise out at Pearl City. It was in bankruptcy so the owners had not been able to sell it. It was only 20 percent occupied so we were able to get everyone on the same floor and organize a gym down in the garage. We got three units and put them together to create a dining hall. It worked fine.

A typical day in Hawaii saw us all get up at five-fifteen for aerobics from six o'clock to seven. Breakfast at seven-fifteen and leave for the boat at eight A.M. We used to work on the boat until ten and then sail until five-thirty, clean the boats up, go home, have dinner at eight o'clock, then hit the hay until the next morning. That is more or less the same routine we've had since 1979. In Fremantle I was a little more lenient. I used to allow the guys an hour off to shower and have breakfast instead of the usual ten minutes.

By the time I got back to San Diego from the Perth/Fremantle/Hawaii journey, I could sense we were beginning to roll. Joanne Fishman had made great strides on the organizational and fund-raising fronts. I had a lot of messages from my key guys that they were ready to come back and make the boat go. Plans for a design team were beginning to crystallize, and there was now no doubt we were going to make a strong run.

Now what we needed was a name for the syndicate, a name for the boats, some kind of logo, and so on. Putting together an America's Cup campaign has often been described as setting up a small company or a political organization. I can testify to the truth of that.

I called Sandy Purdon and asked if he would help. Sandy is an old friend of mine. In fact, I was in his wedding and he is a very good sailor in his own right. I asked him to come on board and help administer the tax-free foundation that would oversee the finances. Sandy, Malin Burnham, the president of our foundation, Doug Alford, our foundation attorney, and I talked about what the name of the foundation should be. Sandy asked me what I wanted to call it and I told him I felt strongly that our team should represent all of America, not just a region or a particular yacht club.

Doug Alford came up with the name "Sail America Foundation for International Understanding." Everyone called us just "Sail America," but we were officially established to foster and promote international understanding through yachting. In addition to liking kids I was also active in helping to promote junior sailing in Fremantle to help fulfill the foundation's obligations. I took kids sailing with us sometimes and we had several open-house parties and receptions to discuss sailing with youngsters.

Without a tax-free status, we couldn't offer potential donors the ability to write down their contribution on their tax forms. Doug Alford did a great job in getting the show together and we were granted a seven-year tax-exempt status by the IRS. Formation of Sail America was an important development in our at-that-time very short history.

Now that we had a name for the syndicate, we had to find one for our boats. I received a lot of suggestions and was urged to adopt names like *Revenge* or *Vengeance.* While they may have had a certain appeal, I felt we had to come up with a name with more marketing appeal.

One day several of us were throwing names around and I said, "How about *Stars and Stripes*?" The room got quiet and everyone nodded and smiled. It was perfect, exactly what we wanted to project. We wanted a name people throughout the United States could identify with, one symbolizing our intent to campaign on behalf of the entire nation. It was like Mom and apple pie. No one could argue with *Stars & Stripes.*

Then we began discussing different colors for the boat. We immediately discarded "liberty red," and I was amused to see no other syndicate showed up in Fremantle with a red boat. We wanted something striking, and one night Bill Trenkle and I sat around mixing up colors. Besides serving as part-tailer, Bill had a lot of influence over many aspects of the campaign, from crew selection to dinner menus. I place a lot of trust in him. As Bill poured, I watched; as I poured, Bill watched. Our conversation went something like this:

"Well," said Bill, "with a name like *Stars and Stripes,* we oughta be red, white, and blue. We don't want a red hull, so we go with either white or blue. What do you think?"

"Sounds about right," I agreed. "What kind of paint you got there?"

"Several colors, but I'm strong in the blues."

"Go for it. Make up four or five different shades and we'll take 'em over to Roberta Burnham's and see what she thinks. She has good taste and a good eye for color. In fact, let's see if we can match the trim on the Burnhams' house. I've always liked that color. Sort of a gunsmoke blue."

"Gunsmoke blue, coming up," said Bill. "A dab of this, a snitch of that, and abracadabra. This what you had in mind?"

"Will it make the boat go faster?" I asked.

Bill laughed. "Like a bat out of hell."

4

★

A Bunch of
Picassos

ROM September 1983 until early in 1984, I received hundreds of messages each week urging me to go after the Cup once again. Among the telephone calls, letters, and telegrams were a lot of far-out ideas concerning keel shapes. It was apparent that *Australia II*'s design had caught the imagination of a lot of people, and there were some ideas that were pretty weird, to say the least.

One of the calls Malin answered was from Barry Shillito, a retired senior naval officer and a member of the San Diego Yacht Club. He explained that he worked with Science Applications International Corporation, which did a great deal of work for the Department of Defense. He told Malin that SAIC had something very interesting for us to see.

Now that the campaign was fully underway, I didn't want to take much time to do anything that was merely "interesting." I needed every minute to look after the thousand details that go into preparing for a winning effort.

"Barry's a neighbor and I think we ought to hear him out. He says he might have some ideas about design," Malin argued. He knows how to deal with me when I don't want to do something he thinks I should. He's one of the few guys who always seems to know which buttons to push. Since he and I had already had numerous discussions about the design of the boat and we had determined to leave no stone unturned, he had me in the car within minutes.

On the drive to SAIC's headquarters in La Jolla, Malin explained a little about the company. Following *Australia II*'s victory, the U.S. Navy had become so intrigued with the possible defense and commercial applications of the wing keel that it commissioned SAIC to study the design. Malin said he suspected the afternoon would be "eye opening."

I told him that I was open to everything, but I really couldn't spend more than a half-hour at SAIC. He said "fair enough" with a wry little grin that I knew meant trouble.

From the time we entered the front gate until we walked into the conference room, it felt as though we were escorted by armed guards, sniffed over by German shepherds, led through forty-two locked doors, and passed through a dozen lead-lined, soundproofed corridors. Clearly, this was the land of high tech and high security.

In the conference room were about fifteen guys who, after introductions all around, sat down at a large mahogany table. The room got dark and up on the screen appeared a very professional show I've always thought of as "the wing keel as brought to you by the Department of Defense." Malin and I sat transfixed, amazed by what we saw.

The night that *Australia II* won the Cup, Alan Bond and Ben Lexcen allowed the keel to be exposed. Instantly, thousands of photographs and miles of videotape recorded the size and shape of the until-then "secret" keel. In one impromptu move that I imagine Bond and Lexcen have come to deeply regret, three years of proprietary design became public domain with the flip of a lens shutter.

Some of the photos and film footage were acquired by SAIC, which in turn fed shapes and images into computers. The analysis revealed that, compared to a conventional keel, the wing keel provided the boat with added stability and maneuverability, as well as increased lifting qualities. While the scientists had everything neatly defined in terms of formulas and percentages and quotients, sailor Dennis translated it all to mean that the little white boat from Australia turned on a dime, headed higher into the wind, and footed lower off the wind. Although I knew all of this from my experience on the race course, it was indeed "eye opening" to see it on paper. I suppose it was somewhat comforting to have all these scientists spend several million dollars to tell me I was doomed from the start.

It had been a fascinating afternoon for both Malin and me. The half-hour I had insisted on had turned into almost three hours, but it may have been the most productive time we spent in the early stages of the campaign. What we had seen was the dissection of a design revolution. SAIC wanted to help us. Their sense of the 1983 races was that the Australians had taken a chapter out of the book on American ingenuity. Where Australia saw potential for a quantum advance in technology, we remained convinced of only marginal refinements. The Aussies were aggressive and we were complacent. They beat us to the punch and that punch seemed to leave the greatest sting on the collective nose of the scientific community. SAIC said they were embarrassed because it was proof that America was not the leader in technology we always thought we were.

What SAIC had concluded was that by using the old design methods we would be greatly limited in experimentation. Having one man sit all day at a drafting table drawing lines and curves would allow us to test only four or five basic designs in the time we had. They felt they could develop certain computer codes that would enable our designers to compare and contrast hundreds of alternatives that hopefully would lead to the single best design. They wanted to put naval architecture into the computer, to convert design from an art to a science.

SAIC, through their chairman Dr. Bob Beyster, offered its help as well as a cash donation. When we left, Malin and I shared a sense that all our Christmases had come at once.

On the way back we discussed the concept of merging design and computers. It was one thing to copy the wing keel—as we suspected everyone would do—but it was something else to truly understand what every change, every alteration meant to the overall performance of the boat. The days of designers flying by the seat of their pants were over.

Malin made a very apt comparison. He said, "Remember when President Kennedy set the challenge to land a man on the moon in our lifetime? NASA didn't go out and hire just one contractor or one engineer. They harnessed the best and the brightest from all across America. If we're going to catch up to, and then surpass the Australians—and surpass them in this technology game—we're going to have to land our own man on the moon. We'll have to create our own mini-NASA."

I started out as head of design because traditionally the skipper has a lot to say about the shape of his boat. But as we worked more and more with SAIC, it became clear I was in over my head. In previous America's Cup campaigns I think I tried to manage too much of the effort, and if I had delegated more responsibility, some areas might

have been improved. What I'd finally learned was the difference between controlling and managing. This time, while I insisted on control,
I realized it would be foolhardy to demand I be involved in every
detail. "Control" didn't mean never delegating; it meant having the
power to delegate only to people I respected and trusted, people I
chose myself.

In past campaigns I had achieved some success by using two, sometimes three, different sailmakers to create the same sails. While they
worked independently, they knew they were in competition with their
business rivals and I always felt this spurred them on to be more
creative. I tried the same approach in 1983 with a design competition
between Sparkman & Stephens (the grand old firm of America's Cup
design) and Johan Valentijn. It didn't work out well in this case for a
variety of reasons, but I still believed in the concept.

For this campaign, I decided to use a design team. Not just one guy
or two guys, but a whole team to which each individual could bring
his special qualities and viewpoints. SAIC had convinced me of the
potential of the computer, and I knew most boat designers didn't have
access to anything like SAIC was prepared to use.

With the team-selection process started, SAIC going full bore, and
my time being eaten up by fund-raising pressures I knew I needed
someone to manage the whole project. I was happy with SAIC's involvement, but I was nervous that they might spend more time in the
think tank than in the testing tank and that we'd all end up either in
left field or left behind. We needed someone to pull together the
scientists, the sailors, and the designers.

The first person to come to mind was John Marshall. Although he
is not an engineer (he studied biochemistry at Harvard), he has one of
the highest IQs of anyone I know. He also has had vast experience
aboard 12-meter yachts, having sailed in 1974 (*Intrepid*), 1977 (*Enterprise*), 1980 (*Freedom*), and 1983 (*Liberty*). He is the guy who talks the
same language as the eggheads and the jocks.

Due to a corporate buy-out, John had recently been relieved of
duties as president of North Sails, so he was slowly coming down to
earth on a golden parachute. I told him my plans for a team approach
and offered him chairmanship of the design committee. Malin, Fritz
Jewett, Bob Beyster, and I (the trustees of Sail America), asked him to
join our board. I wanted him in a leadership role because I knew he
would not only help find the right guys and get them to work together,
but he would push the process along. He's not one to let things hang.
While he's a deep thinker, he's also a man who commands respect and

demands action. John inherited a team of three naval architects whom I had previously selected.

It was a very complicated decision as to who should be on the team. Since Johan had been involved with us for so long, he was our first consideration. We knew he had a great deal of knowledge about 12-meters, but he was pretty insistent about being a one-man band. It seemed to me that Johan's skills could be nicely balanced by someone with more formal training and by someone else who'd never worked on 12-meters but might bring fresh ideas to the party. It didn't work out with Johan because he had such a good reputation that he'd received several offers from other syndicates and he felt he could operate better with more control. He soon left to join the Eagle syndicate in Newport Beach, California.

I'm sure our final selection of the three main designers raised a few eyebrows among America's Cup aficionados. Dave Pedrick's 1983 experience with *Defender* was less than inspiring. Britton Chance's name was a concern to many as a result of his disaster known as *Mariner* (1974). Bruce Nelson had never worked on a 12-meter in his life. On paper our choices may have looked ill-considered, but I was interested in each man's potential, not in past failures or inexperience.

Dave Pedrick is a graduate of the Webb Institute and we felt that formal training was important. He was conservative in his approach. We knew that he'd check every detail, and that he knew the 12-meter Rule very well. After all, he was a protégé of Olin Stephens, and had worked on both *Courageous* and *Enterprise*. We were sure he would fit into the program perfectly. We had previously selected Gary Mull, but, like Johan, he was too much of an individualist for Marshall's team approach and soon left to join his hometown team in San Francisco. To me, Pedrick offered the same qualities Mull did—it was like trading one quarterback for another.

Bruce Nelson's name kept coming up whenever we discussed fresh new talent. He had recently graduated from the University of Michigan's School of Naval Architecture and he had designed a number of hot new IOR boats (a class of racing boats designed under the International Offshore Rule). He is a devotee of velocity prediction programs (VPPs), which are computerized models giving data on a boat's speed as a result of many different factors, so he was used to the new technologies. Instead of viewing his inexperience on 12-meters as a disadvantage, we believed it to be a great advantage. We wanted someone who didn't have any preconceived ideas. We selected Bruce because he had a proven record of being smart and he wasn't afraid of computers.

A BUNCH OF PICASSOS

To me, Brit Chance is a creative genius. He's the kind of guy who has nine ideas for a boat, eight of which are brilliant, but he can't figure out which one isn't. He's very smart and has produced a long list of trophy winners.

So there was our team. As I said, we were subject to a lot of second-guessing, but I felt from the beginning that if we could get these great minds working together, they'd come up with something special.

Since John Marshall was so directly involved with the entire design program, I asked him to elaborate on just how the project was developed. Here's what he had to say:

The major error of 1983 was the pervasive American thinking that 12-meter design had essentially peaked and there wasn't a lot more that could be achieved. Ben Lexcen certainly proved us wrong on that score.

When Dennis first approached me about the design-team idea, I became excited for two major reasons. First, while Dennis is not a scientifically trained person, he was smart enough to recognize the void American yacht design had fallen into and the need to seek answers outside the design community. He sought new ideas, new approaches, new viewpoints. He also changed his management style a great deal by deciding to delegate an enormous amount of responsibility.

The second reason for my excitement was that I could sense we were on the brink of a new era in naval design and architecture. I felt there would be a great opportunity to be involved in a very creative project that would probably affect how boats were shaped and built for years to come.

In order to make technology work you have to have both proper methodology and creativity. We lacked both in 1983. Our lack of conviction in certain parts of methodology, such as tank testing, doomed us to failure. The Australians relied on the test tank implicitly, but we felt it was of very little value. Therefore, any concept of a really radical boat was dealt with strictly in the abstract. If someone dreamed up a light boat that would be fast in rough water or a boat with minimum wetted surface and lots of sail area, there was no method of testing these concepts. We were unable at the time to quantify these abstractions and single out the effects of each trade-off.

Brit Chance's experiments with the test tank that led to *Mariner* did place tanks in doubt. A great deal of negative thought resulted from that, but no one bothered to pay attention to the very profound lessons that were there for the learning. Tank experimentation is a relatively crude approximation of nature. It's not exact and it's very subject to human error. The wrong resistor may be replaced in the electrical circuit when the tank is changed over from towing oil-barge models to 12-meter models. Something like that might indicate that your yacht model has an extra 2 percent of drag, so you discard that particular configuration. It may have been a rocket, but human error colored the results. Things like that happened over and over again.

In the States, models being used in tanks used to be made to one-seventh scale of the proposed design. Later, one-third scale became the accepted length. That length was used in the development of *Enterprise* and, to some extent, *Freedom*. Yet, while the data coming out were improved, it was still very inexact. That frustrated most designers, so there was a big lull in tank use, or at least the belief in tank results.

What we all had to get over was the fact that tank testing does not simulate sailboat racing. It is just one factor, a tool that, if used correctly, can help distinguish the advantages and disadvantages of two widely different concepts. But if you're trying to identify minute differences between two things that are very much alike, the tank shouldn't be used. Where Ben Lexcen had so much success was in using the tank to see if this new concept of a wing keel was any improvement over something like a *Courageous*-type boat. In that example Lexcen got out of the tank a whole raft of broadly valid numbers. He might not have known immediately how to interpret what he had, but I'm sure he recognized the intrinsic differences in design because they would have been big enough to be able to quantify them.

From there, Lexcen and the team in Holland worked up a methodology for predicting the boat's performance. A lot of data go into the program: model towing, meteorological records, information on lift and drag, input from ship hydrodynamics, resistance in different conditions, the integration of the hull and the keel, various building materials, a whole array of factors. This is where computer modeling is particularly helpful.

So I explained to Dennis that the key to getting a winning design was developing this methodology. I said if we couldn't duplicate the methodology that the Australians were using, and then surpass it, the design program would be a waste of time and money. I told him I thought it would take a year before we could come up with anything I'd feel right about. I'm sure when he heard that it nearly killed him. He wanted to have a new boat yesterday, he wanted to be out on the water testing her. And I'm sure that when America II built a boat almost overnight and took it to Australia, Dennis must have thought we were dragging our heels. But I was convinced the America II approach was too hit-or-miss and wasn't right for the long run. Dennis never said anything about hurrying up; he gave us our freedom and somehow the syndicate found the money to support the program.

Britton Chance was certainly one of my first choices to work with us because of his creativity, his brilliant flights of fantasy. His failure with *Mariner* didn't matter in the least. That was inevitable. Look at the works of Beethoven and you will see some catastrophies. You just can't have an entire life opus that's good, good, good, and at the same time be creative. I'd rather see someone take a creative leap and fail than not try for the breakthrough.

As a manager, I can take that problem and then set up a system in which the failure can't occur again. In other words, I try to establish criteria that identify the failure before it goes too far. But the idea is to give the person the chance to explore an idea and to express it until it's proven not to be right. Building a lousy 12-meter can be a bad thing but having a wrong idea can be a good thing. As it turned out, Brit had lots of ideas that greatly contributed to the program. Some of his ideas were dead wrong, but a lot were worth following quite a long way.

Dave Pedrick came to us with a very strong balance in 12-meter design, especially so far as the checks and balances are concerned. He has a very sure sense of what is right. Working at Sparkman & Stephens was probably responsible for this because they have had a very analytical approach over the years. Olin Stephens is a real scientist and as much of an intellectual as anyone in yacht design. So anyone with a strong academic background who had been through the S & S program has picked up a lot of the science of yacht design.

Dave had a good sense of what had been tested over the years and didn't have to be tested again. This saved a lot of time and helped channel ideas in certain directions. We would discuss something and someone would say, "What if we did this?" Dave would think a bit and reply, "That was tried in 1970 and proved ineffectual because of this, this, and this."

Bruce Nelson is one of America's leading young designers in the very competitive arena of IOR design. IOR is the one place today where a designer gets a quick answer on whether his ideas are right or wrong. It's a different game from 12-meters, but it uses the same test: Did you win or lose? You have to know where you stand and that's how you keep score in yacht design. Bruce Nelson has a track record that qualifies him as the lead guy in America right now.

Asking Bruce to join the team was a good idea in light of the development of *French Kiss* and *New Zealand*. Both those boats were designed by guys who have a lot of IOR background. Both boats were very, very strong contenders and both were developed from a design history outside of the 12-meter tradition.

It turned out that Dave, Brit, and Bruce had complementary personalities and styles to begin with, so they gravitated to their own areas of strength. Brit worked very closely with Grumman Aerospace on keel design. He and Dave worked on structural engineering, and Bruce worked extensively with the towing tank in Escondido, California. All three interfaced with a battery of computer programmers, physicists, aerodynamicists, and engineers from all over the country. This was truly a national effort. Dave and Brit are from the East Coast. Bruce is from the West. I live in Maine, as does our senior scientist John Letcher. The training site was in Hawaii. The towing tank was in California. Same with SAIC, based in La Jolla, but with key guys in Annapolis, Maryland. Our major computer resource, Cray, is in Minneapolis. Our boat builder, Derecktor's, is in Mamaroneck, New York. The aerospace resources were in Long Island (Grumman) and Seattle (Boeing).

Dave was also very keen on developing computer-assisted lofting that greatly helped facilitate building our boats quickly. His computer model allowed us to go directly from the computer to the floor of Derecktor's with only a modest amount of refairing of lines. Normally the lines are drawn at table scale and then they are expanded onto the lofting floor, faired there, and then parts are cut. We saved two time-consuming steps. Consequently, I suspect *Stars & Stripes '87* was built quicker than probably any of the other twelves that came to Fremantle.

The construction process was also quite different from other twelves built previously. Basically she is longitudinally framed rather than transversely framed. The result is that she is quite a lot stronger proportionally. She was built stiffer, more rugged than most twelves because of the conditions we expected off Fremantle. Longitudinal framing incurs practically no weight penalty, so you don't have to suffer the trade-off between strength and extra weight. The decision to build her that way was all part of the mounds of data that were fed into our Velocity Prediction Programs. That was the major tool created for this project.

While John Marshall deserves a great deal of the credit for his superb leadership and ability to keep the Picassos painting the same picture, certainly Pedrick, Chance, and Nelson must be held in high esteem for their creativity. As John says, "Yachts are designed by yacht designers." Before any work was started, everyone in the program signed a confidentiality agreement stating that no one could divulge who actually did the drawings or whose ideas were used in what manner. It was our version of the famous "Ranger Agreement," which Olin Stephens and Starling Burgess had in 1937 when they collaborated on the design of the great J-boat *Ranger*.

Another key player in our program was Robert Hopkins. He was hired by Marshall because of his intelligence and his skills as a sailor. As the former coach of the U.S. Olympic yachting team, he had had a lot of experience working with world-class athletes and he immediately earned the respect of everyone in the syndicate. He also served as another bridge between the scientists and the sailors. He worked closely with Marshall to make sure the needs of both were met.

During the tank testing and computer modeling, I was concentrating on assembling a crew, raising money, securing facilities in Hawaii, and trying to get our guys out on the boats we had. Those included *Liberty* and *Spirit*. We decided to modify *Spirit* and leave *Liberty* untouched to use her as a benchmark because, after all, she was the second-fastest 12-meter in the world in 1983.

Spirit was designed by Sparkman & Stephens so we contacted their offices on Madison Avenue in New York City and requested to purchase her plans. They refused to sell them, probably because they were then involved with the America II syndicate, so we tried to obtain the proper lines by using photogrammetry. This is a process used by the military to decipher the design characteristics of foreign aircraft. It gave us a set of digitized lines but they turned out to be inaccurate. I guess that was because we were looking at a big white boat and this device must have been set up for military gray.

During the summer of 1985 Bill Trenkle begin to work on *Spirit*. He turned her upside down and braced her with cross-struts to prevent her from springing, and then he cut off the conventional bottom of the boat a few feet below the sheer line. He then tacked on the new lines from the design team and set up the structure to support a wing keel. *Spirit* would become *Stars & Stripes '83*, about the same length and sail area as *Liberty*. The design team hoped she would be a step ahead of *Australia II* in design. In the meantime, *Stars & Stripes '85* was being completed, a longer and more powerful version of *Stars & Stripes '83*.

After *Stars & Stripes '85* was built at Derecktor's yard in New York, we began to sail her against the other two. Almost immediately I knew our design guys had done their job well. *Stars & Stripes '83* easily beat *Liberty*. In fact, she was a lot faster than *Australia II*. In heavy air, where we knew we would ultimately need to win, '85 was fast from the beginning.

There is an old saying in sailing that you can't turn a turkey into an eagle. But at the same time, no matter what you do to a good boat, she almost always stays a good boat. These theories were proven in our experience with *Stars & Stripes '85*. She was fast no matter what we did to her. We changed keels, moved the rig forward then backward, replaced rudders; she took it all in stride and just kept going. I knew then our design concept would pay off big dividends.

People often ask me whether I see a certain personality in a boat. The answer is no. To me, they are not living creatures. I don't go down to the dock and pet the boat before I take it out. When I do go out, I thrash the boat around the course. I punish it. I'm likely to crash it into other boats. To me, boats are simply a means to an end, although a boat's performance has a lot to do with my happiness.

Our original plan was to build two new boats at this stage. *Spirit* had been designed too small and with too much useless sail area for heavy air, so she wasn't much use to us once we knew the basic wing keel design was right.

When we trialed against '85 in heavy air, *Spirit* would get slaughtered. It was a combination of one boat being fast and one being slow, but we were still able to acquire a good deal of information to aid the progress of the design program. Most importantly, we learned exactly how much advantage '85's greater length gave her over '83.

The purpose of altering *Spirit* and building the two new boats was to zero in on different parameters of the ultimate boat: the size and shape of the hull, the sail area, the type of keel, the best position for the rigging, and so on.

Stars & Stripes '86 came next. She was built with what is best described as a double bow. There was a flat section and a rather ugly bump or breast right at the forward waterline. The idea was to have the volume forward and attempt to trick the water into behaving as if the boat were longer than she actually was. This seemed to work when it was windy. She really hauled the mail, especially reaching.

During the design of '86 we worked closely with Nils Salvesen at SAIC-Annapolis, who is recognized as one of the world's leading authorities on ship hydrodynamics, and with Carl Scragg, a scientist at SAIC-La Jolla. As a boat moves through the water, there are a number of forces that slow her down, such as the water itself. When it is windy, and the boat is going fast, it kicks up a large wave which it drags along behind. Since we knew Fremantle would be by and large windy, we were seeking the perfect design that reduced wave-making drag but still accommodated all the other needs we had identified.

SAIC pioneered a computer code that accurately predicted the wave-drag. I think this was a first in naval architecture. Nils and Carl worked with the designers to compute the drag of each hull and to suggest new ideas. On the keel design front, Marshall used two somewhat competitive approaches. On the one hand, he had John Letcher apply a purely theoretical analysis to wing keel configurations, in which he analyzed the energy lost in the vortex wake of the keel. The other attack on the problem was done by Charles Boppe of Grumman Aerospace and two of his colleagues using the VSAERO computer code running on Cray's super computer. Feeding results of the hull drag code and the keel analysis through Clay Oliver's VPP represented a breakthrough in analysis by SAIC. Marshall and his team, in conjunction with several dozen scientists, had established the methodology he previously described and we all believed they had caught up with, and perhaps even surpassed, the Australians and the Dutch.

Hawaii became not only the training camp for the crew, but the actual testing area for the different designs. As John wrote, tank towing, computer modeling, and all the other types of simulations used in an attempt to quantify abstract thoughts are inexact. We're never sure just how good a boat is until we get her in the water.

The basic idea behind modifying *Spirit* and building '85 was to have the same-shape boat, only in different sizes. In theory, real-life testing would provide the answer on the optimum length we sought. *Stars & Stripes '86* represented a radical step to the new type hull forms suggested by SAIC's work. Tank testing of the "stepped bow" concept proved so promising it became the essential new feature in this boat. When '86 was delivered and we sailed her, she proved fast, but the design team insisted they could still find more speed.

In the very beginning, I expressed to the team my overriding consideration in a boat: I wanted one with straight-line speed. I believed that because of the success of *Australia II*, most designers would go for quick, highly maneuverable little boats. I reasoned that match racing tactics and the new America's Cup course (two legs were added and the course became more compact) would seemingly put a premium on boats that could turn fast and accelerate out of a tack quickly. It was certainly logical because in match racing, the boat that gets the lead first usually controls the tactics. However, I was opting for straight boatspeed because I felt sheer power rather than maneuverability would win races in the strong winds off Fremantle, and I was confident I could always get off the starting line with at least an equal start.

We were all pretty satisfied with *Stars & Stripes '85 and '86*. The decision to build one more boat—to incorporate the best features of all the boats into *Stars & Stripes '87*—was very difficult. I was anxious to settle on a boat we would use to challenge for the Cup. Continuing the design program was costly and I was concerned about time.

In addition designers since the beginning of time have always said the next boat would be a lot faster than the last. In my experience, 90 percent of the time designers are wrong to be so optimistic. But in the end Marshall was persuasive. He felt that with everything we knew now about hull shape, waterline length, deck layout, cockpit shape, height of steering wheel, keel configuration, and even color, we were just one step away from that elusive "perfect" boat.

When 12-meter designers and sailors talk about "the Rule," they are talking about the formula, established in 1906, that governs such variables as length, girth, amount of freeboard, and sail area. It is a complex equation that has been fine-tuned over the past eighty years in an attempt to make all 12-meters uniform.

Although our designers had a good feel for the Rule, there were still a few screw-ups. For example, the shape of *Australia II*'s rudder was copied for use on *'85*. When the rudder was actually built and put on the boat, it had no balance, which meant that it imposed tremendous pressure on the wheel itself. However, when the boat was launched, it sat precisely on its lines. That's probably the first real test to see if a boat is correctly transferred from blueprints to blue water. Each of the three new boats we built hit their lines perfectly. In fact, *Stars & Stripes '87* was within 36 pounds of what she was designed to weigh. I considered that a magnificent achievement. Another great plus from this team was that we didn't have to move the keels in any of the new boats. The designs were spot on.

Following the problems we had with *Liberty* (when we were forced to add 1,800 pounds of ballast and then move the keel), I thought it something of a miracle that the designers figured out everything so well and so consistently on our three new boats. When *'87* was launched, my first thought was "Well, beauty is in the eye of the beholder." She wasn't going to win the Most Beautiful Twelve award, but then fast boats have their own way of looking good. To me, the straight sheer of *'85* was much more attractive. She had the look of a German Frers boat—clean, compact, and strong. When I saw *'87*, I was a bit taken aback by the pug nose, the gondola look. But the more she won, the more beautiful she became. Right now, I'd have to say I've never seen a prettier boat in my life!

5

━━━━━━━━━━ ★ ━━━━━━━━━━

Merger
Mania

━━━━━━━━━━━━━━━━━━

ITHIN a year of the 1983 loss, America's Cup fever was beginning to rage across the United States once again. News of international challenges being formed made the proposition seem real in the minds of many people, and before long there was talk of more than a dozen U.S. groups clamoring to get a piece of the action.

Although a number of legitimate groups were formed, there were also several with rather dubious credentials—a total of 24 in all. What astounded me was that some of them actually came up with the initial entry fee of $20,000 to attend the first meeting for all Challengers organized by the Yacht Club Costa Smeralda (the Challenger of Record). That meeting was held in Bermuda on February 20, 1985, and eighteen groups were present.

While some challenging groups were enough to make the more serious representatives pause to consider what the "new era" of the America's Cup had wrought, indications were that out of an initial twenty-four Challengers, maybe seven or eight groups from abroad would make it and perhaps an equal number of American groups. As it turned out, six U.S. Challengers and seven from abroad showed up in Fremantle for the first race.

For me, the America's Cup is a serious endeavor and not something to be taken lightly. The trophy itself is a symbol of excellence, and the long and glorious past is full of heroic deeds done by uncommon men. I'm all for humor—that's certainly an important ingredient in any Cup campaign—but I'm not a fan of whimsical attempts to profit by association or to attempt to share the glory of the Cup without paying dues. Those dues are hours and hours, even years and years, of personal sacrifice, pain, and suffering. A lot of people never see past the cocktails and canapés.

At any rate, from the beginning we considered our strongest American competition would be the *America II* syndicate from the New York Yacht Club and the *Golden Gate Challenge* from the St. Francis Yacht Club in San Francisco. We felt *America II* would raise a lot of money and *Golden Gate* had the always-dangerous Tommy Blackaller with a "revolutionary" boat concept.

Frankly, we didn't spend a lot of time thinking about what the other guy was doing. We had our hands full with our own program. But it soon became apparent the biggest hurdle for all American syndicates was money. We all had the same idea—hit the corporations—and at times it was like "Take a number and have a seat. Mr. Big will be with you after the other five syndicates." We tended to bump into each other a lot.

Personally, it was the Club that kept getting in my way. I've described our problems during and immediately after 1983, but they didn't end with the formation of Sail America. *America II* was vying for the role of Challenger of Record right alongside me. They continued to tie up my former backers, they had a massive effort to raise corporate dollars, and they were the first guys with a new boat on the water in Australia. While they appeared on the surface to be strong—and the press certainly bought their act—I sensed some chinks in the armor.

In June of 1985, some of their highly touted syndicate organization began to unravel. The first indication of discontent in the palace guard was when Chuck Kirsch was replaced as syndicate chairman by Arthur Santry. Kirsch had had a lot of experience as an administrator in previous campaigns and he had done all the spade work for 1987. Santry, chairman and CEO at Combustion Engineering Corporation, was in line to become the next Commodore of the Club.

While a little bit of executive shuffle is common in this game, the next major announcement from *America II* was a real bombshell. In September 1985, John Kolius resigned as skipper and helmsman of the boat. The sailing world was shocked! Kolius was the heir apparent to the sailing throne at the New York Yacht Club. Mosbacher called their boy wonder "the best and the brightest."

From what I was able to put together from certain "inside sources," the major reason Kolius resigned was that his hands were tied in several areas. One concerned sailmaking. The Club had a contract with Sobstad and North to build sails for their boats. The company wanted Kolius to sign an agreement stating he wouldn't build his own sails for use in the Cup campaign. Kolius refused. Santry, as syndicate chairman, said he did not feel it was in the syndicate's best interests to have Kolius make sails. Kolius was extremely upset. A year earlier, Butch Ulmer, who had run his own sailmaking business for years, had given John half of the business in order to acquire his name and talent. Butch obviously saw Kolius as an entree into the lucrative 12-meter business, so there was a lot of pressure on John to get the syndicate to buy Ulmer/Kolius sails.

Kolius also had problems on a head-to-head basis with Santry. Kolius wanted more control of the entire program, but the boys at the Club wanted him simply to sail the boat. Shades of 1983 all over again.

Santry had also floated the idea of bringing in another designer. There was speculation that the Club was attempting to procure a Green Card for German Frers, which would allow the Argentinian the opportunity to work on a U.S. boat.

Even before the problems within *America II* came to light, we were holding secret meetings with some of the powers-that-be at the Club. We felt our technical program was really snapping into focus and we believed we would produce a very fast and competitive boat. But the money was drying up and we were almost broke. We had heard that some of the guys in the *America II* program weren't very happy with what was going on, so we thought we should at least feel them out to see if there might be any possibility of a joint venture.

In July of 1985 Tom Whidden met with Charlie Robertson and John Marshall met with Bob Stone. Robertson and Stone are shrewd, articulate, smart men who were able to put past animosities aside in order to meet future goals. Their aim was the same as ours: bring the Cup back to the United States. They were willing to explore the possibilities of what might be the best way to do that.

While nothing was resolved, the door was left open a crack and there were promises of continued talks. The two camps kept in touch until Kolius resigned, and then all hell broke loose. A number of calls went back and forth between New York, San Diego, and Hawaii until a top-secret meeting was called at La Guardia Airport in New York. A number of people flew in, and it was on that day that I first recognized the demise of power of the New York Yacht Club. Until then, I believed the Club was in charge of their challenge.

The meeting produced what I call "the La Guardia Ultimatum."

What happened is that O.L. Pitts and Lee Smith, two very wealthy Texans, flew in and walked into the meeting room. Present was Arthur Santry, soon-to-be Commodore of the Club. The Texans told Santry to leave the room, that he would be called when he was needed. No one should talk to the Commodore like that, but they did and they got away with it. They got away with it because they had loaned $3 million to the Club to get the syndicate started. The Club didn't put up any money. The Texans said either give us our money back and you run the show, or stand aside and we'll call the shots. That was the moment the Club realized they no longer had control of their own syndicate.

A new executive committee was formed with only two Club flag officers on the eleven-member board. Syndicate chairman Santry stepped down and was replaced by Richard DeVos, founder and president of Amway Corporation. John Kolius, originally from Houston and very close to the Texans, was brought back.

I guess these actions just go to show how wide of the mark we were. There we were holding secret discussions with the Club hierarchy, when in reality they didn't have two cents worth of power over their own challenge. Their blue blazers were beginning to look no better than striped T-shirts. We had witnessed the end of an era, and they just sat there and took it as easily as flicking a flea off a dog.

The power was lost as it is in many similar situations. Money talks, nobody walks. The flag officers wouldn't ante up the money themselves, so they didn't have the chips, and you can't even bluff if you don't have chips in front of you.

While the "La Guardia Ultimatum" cooled things off between Sail America and America II for a while, it did not automatically bring an end to discussions. As we sank deeper and deeper into financial quicksand, we grasped at any straws that came our way.

One day John Marshall sat down with Malin and me and made an eloquent case for joining forces with *America II*. His view was that we had the better skipper and the superior technical program, while New York had the money and the facility in Fremantle up and functioning. Their organization and logistics were also strong. Marshall then pointed out that what the two groups would gain most from a merger was a coherent marketing strategy to sell to corporate America. With Dennis Conner and the New York Yacht Club joining forces, our marketing people could pitch a truly national, all-American campaign by the guys who won the Cup, lost the Cup, and now, with your help Mr. Executive, we'll bring it back. Conner is the guy who was knocked down in '83, but true to the American character, he's getting off the canvas and coming back with the knockout punch. The New York Yacht Club had a grand and glorious association with the America's Cup—they *were* the America's Cup for a hundred thirty-two years—and now they were just about guaranteeing the Cup would come home.

It was a good story and I knew John was right, but I was very guarded in my enthusiasm because I never really believed it would happen. I felt the guys from the Club were just too proud to concede any significant ground and without compromise from both sides, there could be no deal. Tom Whidden joined the conversation and agreed the idea was worth pursuing. He and John decided to try their two-prong attack again; Whidden would talk with Bus Mosbacher and Marshall would return to Bob Stone. Even though we knew the Texans held the power, Mosbacher and Stone still had influence.

When the talking began in earnest, the big issues revolved around who was going to be the skipper, who would design, and under what flag would the challenge be made. Our compromise was that if I were the skipper we would challenge under the New York Yacht burgee. This point was not agreed to by Malin, who felt the San Diego Yacht Club should be equal with the New York Yacht Club. We insisted on no tryouts between me and Kolius. Marshall made it clear he was not prepared to budge on that because he felt my record was far superior.

The New Yorkers were apparently very concerned about my personal style. They felt that in the past I had been a one-man show, that I was an autocratic manager unwilling to accept outside help. They said Cup campaigns had now grown too big to be a one-man show. Marshall listened to all they had to say and then he asked them to judge me on how I was operating today, not three years ago. He said I had changed, that I managed differently, that I was more prone to delegating responsibilities. As an example, he cited his increased role in the present campaign as compared to what he had done in 1980 and 1983 under Dennis Conner. He explained he had come in as the design coordinator, that he had joined the board of directors, and that Dennis was allowing him free reign.

Then the New Yorkers changed tacks a little by expressing doubts about my ability to come back. They wondered if the loss hadn't got to me, if I was the same guy who had won in 1980. Marshall said he'd never known Dennis to be as mentally and physically tough, and that *Stars & Stripes* had achieved more team unity than any campaign with which Marshall had been associated. Marshall said point-blank that what he was bringing to the negotiating table was the opportunity for New York to get on board the fastest boat steered by the most experienced 12-meter helmsman in the world.

Despite Marshall's persuasiveness and common-sense approach, the New Yorkers were so focused on their own program that they felt they were in the lead and that they didn't have much need for any of our help. Bob Stone was the only one who saw the wisdom of the proposition.

Arthur Santry then returned to the issue of the flag and stated unequivocally that under no circumstances would the NYYC have anything to do with any program that was to win the Cup for anyone other than the NYYC. Marshall proposed that in the event the Cup was won by *Stars & Stripes* it would be won under the NYYC burgee, but it would then be held by a new national institution—a club established for the specific purpose of helping American yachtsmen in international competitions. This should have had wide appeal at the Club since they had suffered for years by attempting to be both Cup trustee and to run fair and impartial races. The foreign Challengers were constantly accusing the Club of changing the rules to suit themselves.

We thought Marshall's idea was brilliant. Most of the NYYC members were aware of the untenable position holding the Cup and hosting the races posed. Most wanted out of the whole business. Here was an opportunity for New York to complete its cycle in history—of winning the Cup, losing it, and winning it back—and then it could pass the Cup over to the American people through a trustee organization representing the whole country. Again, Bob Stone was the only one who could make sense of the idea. Public relations has never been something the Club either understood or practiced very well.

When Marshall sat down with the flag officers in New York, I think they recognized deep down that America II had a number of problems —otherwise they wouldn't have given him the time of day. I think they also were aware that if I was successful, the NYYC would essentially be out of the America's Cup for many years to come. For if I won, the next defense would be managed by the San Diego Yacht Club. No matter which syndicate won any future defense, New York would have to wait until we lost it again, then they'd have to win it back. No one had to remind them how long the Americans had held it before.

Marshall further proposed that America II and Sail America bring their two programs together in Hawaii after the 12-meter World Championships were held in February 1986. America II was planning to enter the races in Fremantle, the same site where the Cup was to be held, but we had decided not to disrupt our program. We felt the risks of entering the Worlds far exceeded the possible gains. Marshall said Hawaii would be the perfect place to sort out which boats were faster.

If a joint venture were agreed upon, John proposed he take over the integration of the two design teams so costly and redundant test programs could be eliminated. He also proposed an outside auditor enter the design program to ensure final choices were made fairly. We were prepared to race the America II boats and if they proved faster, we would have used their boats in the Cup challenge. I rationalized that it was better to discover that our design team had not made the progress we thought they had and end up sailing an America II boat with a strong all-around team than to arrive in Fremantle with an unproven slow boat and be sent home early.

I give credit to the New Yorkers for listening to what John had to say. The meeting was concluded when the flag officers reminded him that the final decision was not totally up to them. *America II* was run by a large board of directors that included virtually all their major contributors. We were told that while several individuals in the meeting might see the merits of our proposal, there were a number of board members who had very strong allegiances to John Kolius and a strong antipathy toward Dennis Conner.

Two weeks later Bob Stone told Marshall that he had sounded out the board and they were pretty much split down the middle. Stone thought the pivotal person was Richard DeVos, and he suggested our man travel to see their man. John flew his own four-seat airplane from Maine to Ada, Michigan, headquarters for the Amway Corporation. When he touched down he requested space in the Amway hangar and was directed where to go. He expected a corporate jet or two in a small hangar, but he found a massive building housing enormous 727s, Lear jets, and a dozen or so smaller craft.

Marshall met DeVos in the entrepreneur's office and once again laid out all the tenets of his proposal. DeVos gave John a fair hearing, but then he said he believed the gulf between the two syndicates was too wide to be bridged by this proposal. DeVos felt that the competition between the two syndicates for funding and for public recognition had been so intense that they had established two completely different personalities in their own eyes and those of the media. DeVos couldn't imagine how the syndicates could ever be melded into a single effective unit. He felt we faced an insoluble management problem and he predicted that my insistence on remaining as skipper would lead to the mass resignation of the NYYC team.

That was that. His thumbs-down effectively ended all further thoughts of a merger and both syndicates went their separate ways.

All the talk didn't solve our money problems. By then we had put together a pretty effective fund-raising and marketing plan, but no matter how many dollars came in, many more went out. If the old saying about ocean racing being like sitting under a cold shower tearing up hundred-dollar bills is true, raising money for an America's Cup effort is like a blind man begging with his tin cup on Fifth Avenue.

By now we were truly on the brink of disaster. The debts were mounting and we feared the creditors would call them in any day. We had stretched our credit to the limit with sailmakers, spar manufacturers, designers, our paid (using the term loosely) employees, the tank-test facilities—everyone and every organization involved with us.

At this point Mike Dingman, chairman of the Henley Group, stepped forward to become our savior. Malin and I had met Mike about a year previously when we called on Malin's former school chum, Forrest Shumway, the Chairman and CEO of the Allied Signal Company. When we walked into Forrest's office, Malin commented on a photograph of Shumway and his wife Patsy on a sailboat. Malin knew Forrest was a powerboat man so he asked about the photo and was told it had been taken aboard Mike Dingman's yacht. Dingman, as chairman of Henley, a subsidiary of Allied, worked closely with Forrest. Shumway said, "As a matter of fact, you should meet Mike. He'll be able to talk your language."

Shumway called Mike immediately and within minutes the four of us began talking about the run for the Cup. That was the beginning of what may have been the single most valuable relationship ever developed by Sail America in the hunt for corporate dollars. Mike is on a first-name basis with almost every major CEO in the country and is personally a very generous and loyal man.

Mike immediately went to work for us setting up appointments across the country with leading money men and power brokers. His personal dynamism and his belief in us opened up dozens of doors that had previously been shut. In one way or another, Mike Dingman was personally responsible for securing more than half of all the corporate dollars that came our way. His pitch would go something like this: "Joe, how's the wife and kids? Great. Listen, you're an American and you must've felt terrible when we lost the America's Cup. You've got to help these guys win it back."

Dingman is a man of action and a tremendous salesman. But even with Mike's muscle, we met with a lot of uncertainty in corporate boardrooms. America loves a winner and since we were dealing with something as chancy as a boat race, it wasn't easy to convince the money men to come aboard. At that time yachting, particularly America's Cup (which was supposed to be the pinnacle of the sport), had never received much exposure on television. It seems if you're not seen on the tube, you're not a viable marketing bet.

The corporate chiefs quite rightly wanted to be sure they would get some return for their investment. Budweiser is a good case in point. When we visited the beer-maker, we met with about eight of their marketing people. They all had what looked to be a scorecard, and it soon became obvious we were not the first syndicate to approach them. Throughout our presentation, I had the feeling they were checking off what we had to offer in comparison to what *America II*, *Heart of America*, *Eagle*, and the others had already said. I guess we convinced them we had the best shot at winning because they soon informed us they were coming on as a major sponsor. They were a great supporter throughout the long grind, and I felt we paid them back in a small way the day our keel was revealed and on it was the Budweiser logo with the words "King of Beers."

We asked for a minimum of $500,000 in cash for a major corporate sponsorship. In return, we offered exposure to the media, especially print and television, by flying spinnakers with the company's name out front. Also offered were the exclusive marketing rights to advertise the company's association with us: If we won, they could tell the world they backed the victor. There were many other points to our program such as VIP treatment at the races, personal appearances at corporate functions, and so on.

As far as marketing of sporting events are concerned, the model for our times is the 1984 Olympics held in Los Angeles. Under Peter Ueberroth, the organizing committee raised not only enough money to run the event, but they actually ended up with a surplus. For the first time in Olympic history, all the money was raised from private and corporate sources. The organizing committee raised the bulk of the money by selling marketing rights to corporations for between $4 million and $12 million.

I thought that the same type of thing might work on a minilevel for us. I visited Ueberroth, who later became the Commissioner of Baseball, to discuss the details of their marketing program. He told me that he thought the same type of approach, albeit on a smaller scale, would work for us. He was helpful in his advice and even agreed to send some of his key people to San Diego to help us establish a game plan to determine what we might offer corporations in return for their financial support.

Eventually, seven companies joined us as major sponsors, more than any other American syndicate. By the time we were ready to move to Fremantle, we had signed on Allied-Signal, Inc., Anheuser-Busch, Atlas Hotels, Ford Motor Company, The Henley Group, Merrill Lynch, and Science Applications International Corporation.

But as I said, despite the help of these sponsors, after our merger talks with New York, we were on the brink of disaster. What saved us was the amazing personal courage of Malin Burnham and Mike Dingman. Once again, Malin secured loans at several San Diego banks by putting up his own resources. Mike Dingman also backed lines of credit. Both these men took enormous gambles because if we didn't prove fast on the race course, there would be no way we could raise the money to pay them back. Literally millions of dollars were at risk.

6

The
Committed

HILE our design team was hard at work testing lines and curves and attempting to pull all the technical aspects together, we were also putting in a concerted effort on our sails. As the engine of the boat, this aspect of the program was crucial, and, to my mind, demanded as much attention as the actual design.

During the last decade or so, the introduction of synthetic materials such as Mylar and Kevlar has revolutionized the sailmaking industry, especially where 12-meters are concerned. These materials are lightweight but extra strong so they give boats added dimensions not available in cotton or Dacron. But aside from what it's made of, the critical factor in building a sail is getting the exact size and shape right for the conditions in which it will be used. Here's where the real art of sailmaking separates the winners from the losers.

In 1980 my America's Cup sailmaking plans called for a joint effort between Hood Sails and North Sails, then regarded as the two premier sailmakers in America. The way I planned it, North was to take the lead with John Marshall as my mainsheet trimmer. Hood Sails would be there to keep them honest. Ted Hood, the brilliant sailmaker and all-round sailing genius, was gradually phasing himself out of the company and I didn't feel the sails were up to their previous standard.

It was then that I asked Tom Whidden, the president of Sobstad

Sails, to join our campaign as a tailer aboard *Freedom* and as alternate skipper of our trial horse. In his own inimitable fashion, Tommy managed to weasel a Sobstad sail onto the boat before we knew it, and lo and behold, it became our famous number 41. This was a specially cut forty-three-foot, half-ounce spinnaker that we tested against the best North and Hood had developed over two years, and it just blew them away. I couldn't believe it, nor could John Marshall, who as president of North Sails knew a few things about spinnakers. In fact, John was so nonplussed that he insisted we run four additional tests the next day. The results were the same and he was finally convinced. We immediately began ordering more and more Sobstad spinnakers.

By the time we got to the Cup, almost all our spinnakers were from Sobstad. We also let them build some jibs, but they weren't as good. By the end of the Cup summer, Tom was firmly entrenched in our program as a sailmaker, and his reputation as one of the world's top sailmakers was on the rise nationally and internationally.

So while it had been predominantly a North camp in 1980, it was very definitely a North and Sobstad one in 1983. They both made about the same number of sails for us. North started out dominant in the mainsails, but as the summer went on Sobstad sails were used more and more. In fact, in the actual Cup races, John Marshall found himself trimming a Sobstad main some of the time.

For the 1986–87 campaign, we started out using Sobstad as the major supplier and North was the backup. My relationship with Tom was very close, while my main link to North, Pete Bennett, had passed away. I never really developed close ties to North's San Diego loft, and then when John Marshall was replaced as president of the company, my estimation of their business sense was greatly diminished.

I guess some people may be surprised by the extent to which personal relationships determine business dealings concerning something as impersonal as a sail. The major reason for this is that sails, right out of the box, never fit perfectly on a 12-meter. Of course they're sewn together, they have luff tape on them, they have a tack and a clew and a head. But after they're tested, they always have to have adjustments made. A little bit may be taken out here, a little added there.

I liken the relationship between a boat owner and his sailmaker to a man and his tailor. The closer the relationship, the more the two know about each other, the better the fit of the suit. What we have in common with the well-dressed gentleman is that we're both seeking perfection. When Tom built a sail, especially a mainsail, we had to make a lot less adjustments than with any of the other sails we used.

THE COMMITTED

Over the years we've been together, Tommy and I have become closer and closer. I have an enormous respect for his abilities, not just as a sailmaker, but as an all-round sailor. He is an expert tactician and an excellent helmsman. Because of our closeness, I was able to persuade him to join me for the 1986–87 run for the Cup as our sail adviser and tactician. This was great for me as well as Sail America because he happened to be one of my very best friends.

Shortly after the Clipper Cup regatta in Hawaii in 1986, something occurred that could have devastated our Cup campaign. Tom Whidden, the man who for all intents and purposes had built Sobstad sails into a world power in the field, received written notice from his business partner that his services were no longer needed. Tom's partner owned 51 percent of the business while Tom had 49 percent. When I heard about the letter my first thought was that there had been some terrible mistake. Indeed, there *had* been a terrible mistake. Tom's partner had made one of the most foolish decisions of his life. Tom was the heart and soul of the business and he had earned the respect (and a lot of the business) of the world's top sailors. Sobstad had gone from strength to strength because of Tom's genius.

The entire incident was quite a shock to Tom and for a while we were uncertain if he would continue with Sail America. Tom meant so much to our program in so many incalculable ways that I knew we couldn't replace him. There was also great concern that with Sobstad out of the picture (our dealings with the company had degenerated to the point that they approximated a kind of "cold war"), we would lose our primary source of power. If Sobstad and Tom were no longer talking, that meant we might lose our tailor; our intimate relationship with our "fitter" might be destroyed.

During the past two decades, as sailing has become more popular in the United States, sailmakers have perhaps benefited from America's Cup campaigns more than any other type of business. First, there's the large amount of money spent by 12-meter syndicates for sails themselves. But maybe even more important is the lure of being associated with a winner. Winning the Cup under a particular mainsail or jib can translate into millions of dollars for the manufacturer when the kids or the club racers decide it's time for the next set of sails. When the guy with the Star or J-24 or his own custom 42-footer reads all the ads saying such and such sail company brought home a winner, he can't help but be impressed.

That's why the competition for the 12-meter business is so fierce. That's why Sobstad's decision to cut out Tom made no sense. Immediately, our orders began going to North, and those orders were worth many thousands of dollars. Suddenly, we noticed a great improvement in the North sails we were getting. The more business we gave to North, the more concentrated effort we got. They analyzed the situation with Sobstad immediately and saw their opportunity. They also took advantage of two of the world's best sailmakers in John Marshall and Tom Whidden, both of whom consulted with the company on each sail made. This ultimately resulted in Stars & Stripes going from using 85% Sobstad sails in the preliminary series to about 35% in the final series.

By the time we had set up camp in Fremantle, we realized this beautiful little city smack on the edge of the Indian Ocean was a long way from Connecticut where our sails were built. The sheer logistical problems of moving men and material was frustrating, and one of the first areas this became apparent was in our sail program. Trying to design a sail for a boat in Fremantle, have it built in the States, then shipped to Australia, was enough to try even the patience of Job.

Pretty much on a lark, we asked our maintenance crew under the direction of Bill Petersen if they'd take a shot at building some sails in Fremantle. We started them out on a number-three main that had to be replaced. Tom, John, and I got together with our tailers Adam Ostenfeld and Bill Trenkle and we all discussed what we might do to improve the sail. Then Tom sat down with the sailmakers and produced a mainsail that turned out to be perfect for conditions of sixteen to twenty knots of true wind.

That was the birth of our own in-house empire we named "We Be Guessing." "WeBe?" became our private logo and sort of an in-joke, but of all the innovative ideas we came up with, this stands out as a prime example of our guys rising above adversity. As soon as we saw how well the "WeBe 3" performed, we immediately cranked up the program. Next was a light-air mainsail that was dynamite. In fact, it became our first-string light-air main. Then came a jib and another main and a couple more jibs. When the *Azzurra* guys were eliminated, we took over their sail loft right next to us on Fisherman's Harbor. It was a beautiful facility and we had seven people in there sewing up sails at the rate of one every two days. It was a fantastic boost to our program because we didn't have to worry about shipping and delivery and getting through customs. We also realized great financial gains. The "WeBe?" program with free design technology from Whidden and Marshall built sails at 65 to 70 percent of cost. Our labor was on site anyway, we had no overhead, and materials accounted for only about 30 percent of the final cost.

The logo for the "We Be Guessing" sail loft. Betsy Whidden, wife of tactician Tom Whidden, and Luann Parins designed this logo for the custom sails we built in Fremantle.

So as it turned out, we snatched a huge victory from what at first looked to be the jaws of defeat. Tom's dismissal actually worked to our advantage. We were on a roll now. No matter what we touched, it all turned to gold. In fact, Tom Whidden not only restored our sail program but soon attracted an offer to join his former foes at North as their president. Sobstad had really cut their own throats!

If the "WeBe Guessing" incident turned to gold, an area in which we started golden and continued to improve was crew selection. I like to make sure people understand I just drive the boat—the ten guys in front of me are the ones who really make it go. And the guys who came to join Sail America were the best the country has to offer.

Ultimately, selection of each crewman falls to me. As skipper, or captain, it's my responsibility to choose ten guys out of hundreds who have not only achieved—and continue to seek—individual excellence, but ten guys who have the mental and physical attributes to become integral members of a total team effort. Being successful at sailboat racing, particularly America's Cup competition, is to a large degree the function of how well the crew works together. Whether their performance is tested in the routine tasks such as going in and out of a hundred thousand tacks and jibes, or they are forced to react immediately to an emergency situation such as a blown-out jib, the crew's major nemesis is time. Response time is measured in seconds, and seconds often mean the difference between winning and losing.

The three major factors to consider in a successful crewman are attitude, attitude, attitude. What we required of everyone was a total commitment to the commitment. Now there were some guys who joked that they should be committed for their commitment to the commitment, but by and large everyone who made the team did so because they were prepared to dedicate themselves 100 percent to their job. I made it clear to everyone from the beginning that no one would make the team unless he or she put winning the Cup ahead of everything else in their lives: families, social lives, money, sex, religion, friendships. It had to be give all or nothing at all.

I have a family of my own and I guess it could be argued that I have not been the best father or husband in the world. I chose, for better or worse, to commit myself to a particular goal. I'm not necessarily proud of that decision and it certainly isn't something everyone can make, but I made it and I expected everyone on *Stars & Stripes* to make it. Those who did not only survived, but flourished. Everyone on our boat was dedicated 100 percent to excellence, and I believe that same dedication carries over into all of life as well.

My insistence on the commitment to the commitment has led me to believe I may be a bit abnormal and no doubt some people view me as insane. That doesn't bother me because inside I know how I feel, and I also know that if you're trying to take care of everybody else and to be Mr. Nice Guy and the world's greatest provider, the results will not be satisfactory. Part and parcel of the kind of commitment I demanded from the *Stars & Stripes* team was a certain kind of selfishness. Commitment to the commitment demands a very narrow focus. You have to start with a meaningful goal, something of the utmost importance, and then put everything else aside until you achieve that goal.

If you want something bad enough, you will make sacrifices. In 1979 and 1980, it was very important for our program with *Freedom* to maximize the potential of the crew, the boat, and the sails. Kyle Smith likes to recall that he was made to sand the bottom of the boat with 50- or 100-grit sandpaper, instead of a 200- or 400-grade that would have made the task easier. That probably would have done the job, but it wouldn't have done the *best* possible job so we had him use the fine stuff. When he was through, we knew we had a superbly prepared boat. *Freedom*'s hull was as smooth and as fair as it could be.

That was the year the press picked up on the "Dennis the professional" bit. I was criticized for expanding our program to include two years of practice and two boats instead of working for six months to get one boat in shape. But the results of our program was that when we stepped on *Freedom* we did so knowing we had the best boat, the best sails, the best equipment, and the best physical training program. We knew we had done the best we could, that all the testing of ourselves, the pushing of each other to do better, to make the boat go faster, would pay off.

That same attitude was pervasive in the *Stars & Stripes* camp in 1986/87. We set out to have the best boats, the best sails, the best of everything. And in the end, we achieved our goal.

After losing the Cup in 1983, it would have been easy for us to say "the hell with it, it wasn't that big of a deal." But inside I knew it was a big deal and if I was to make a run for it, it couldn't be half-ass. I was thirty-nine years old at the time and the prospect of another three or four years out of my life was pretty daunting. In my own case, the commitment to getting the Cup back had to become supremely important. It would mean continued personal sacrifice, but without that commitment, I couldn't have gotten up every morning at five-thirty and put up with all the bullshit that goes with the twelve-to-eighteen-hour days, seven days a week, for three years.

I found out about commitment when I was a kid. I saw people back then who may not have been the most brilliant Star boat sailors, but because of sheer commitment, they made their boats and themselves ready for competition. They would sand the hulls of their boats incessantly or work constantly on their sails so that they could compete against guys like Malin Burnham and Lowell North.

In 1968 Alan Raffee and I decided to attempt to make the Olympic Games in the Star class. Alan bought one of the world's first fiberglass Stars and, with just six months to go until the trials, we set out to learn everything there was to know about racing the boat. We were only on two wheels and so dumb we didn't even know which way the boat went on the trailer. But it didn't matter because we pledged ourselves to have the best equipment available and to be totally committed. Raffee spent about $50,000 on upgrading the boat, and in 1968 that was a great deal of money to lavish on a Star boat. Lowell and Malin could sail the pants off all of us, but it was obvious to me that our commitment would pay off. We did prove to be the fastest boat in the trials, but in the fourth race we hit a mark that meant immediate disqualification. Lowell North took our boat to Acapulco and used it as his tune-up boat when he won the Gold Medal. The lesson there was that crew work had to be as flawless as boat and equipment preparation. I never forgot it.

Although unlike the Australians we never went in for sports psychologists, there were times when I spoke to the guys collectively and individually about how to lift their game. I asked those who sailed on *Stars & Stripes* to think about their self-image, to imagine the limits of their "comfort zone." I told them they had made it into the program because they were winners, because they had earned the right to be there through sheer hard, relentless work. But to stay at the top, I used to say, they had to continue to see themselves as winners.

I never allowed negativism to enter our thinking. I never criticized them in front of their peers or friends. They were my crew and they knew I would fight like hell to support them just as I expected them to support me. I told them that was what a champion team is all about. We had to help out each other. When something went wrong on the boat, I never yelled or screamed because I knew the guy who screwed up realized better than anyone else what he'd done and that he would set about making it right. Negativism is a very destructive force, especially if it is being directed at you from someone you respect. What we tried to do throughout the campaign was build the guys up with positive feedback. But this wasn't just talk. I believed they had to go out and experience things for themselves. For example, beating a sailor as good as Britain's Harold Cudmore in twenty knots of wind does more for a crew's psychology than a room full of shrinks could do.

Winning breeds winning. The more you win, the more used to it you become, and the more hardened becomes your own view of yourself. The harder we worked, the higher we raised our self-image, and pretty soon we were operating at a higher level than we had experienced before. That's the best part of working on your self-image. Once you raise yourself a level or two into that higher "comfort zone" I want my guys to strive for, you rarely go back. Success feeds on success.

Another part of the psychological buildup had a lot to do with my theory that one's self-image cannot distinguish between reality and a very vivid imagination. I tried to get the guys to imagine how good it would feel to execute the perfect cast-off or the perfect jibe. I asked them to imagine what it would be like to perform to complete perfection. I told them to capture the images of that perfection in their mind's eye. For my purposes, I felt that was in many ways as important as actually going out there and picking off Harold in a close race. I asked them to use their affirmations to raise their self-image in the same way that they used real-life experiences to shape their own image of themselves. My theory is if you can visualize something, you can actualize it.

With the demands placed on them and the pressure to seek perfection, I sometimes wondered why it was that so many great sailors joined *Stars & Stripes*, and why some of the old alumni keep coming back. I've answered that by concluding that the bottom line is people like to win. Even before the Cup showdown, I asked designer Bruce Nelson what he was going to do for the next Cup. He told me he had had a lot of offers, which didn't surprise me, then he looked me in the eye and said, "I want to stay with you." I asked him why and his answer seemed to speak for every guy who has participated in a winning effort. "Well, DC," he said with a grin. "I like the odds."

Those odds are so good in large part because of the superior talent of the people on the team. I've been very fortunate to surround myself with all-stars at every position, whether it be on the boat, in the maintenance shack, on the fund-raising committee, or on our trial horse.

Perhaps no one is a better example of the skill and dedication it takes to earn a spot with us than Jack Sutphen. He is a great natural sailor who has gotten the most out of every boat he's ever had. He grew up in Mamaroneck, New York, smack in the middle of Long Island Sound sailing country, and he used to win everything there was to win at the Larchmont Yacht Club. For years and years no one could touch him.

Involved in every America's Cup defense of the modern era (there were no races between 1937—when the last gigantic J-boat competed —and 1958, the first year 12-meters were used), Sutphen's path crossed mine in 1974. He is the perfect example of "what goes around, comes around." In '74, I was asked to join *Courageous* as the starting helmsman after the crew had pretty much been selected. My coming aboard meant someone had to go, and that someone who got the knife in the back was Jack Sutphen, the tactician. Jack never held a grudge against anyone and his reputation as one of the finer gentlemen in the sport continued to grow.

Jack is someone to whom I owe an awful lot. When, for the 1980 campaign, I needed someone completely trustworthy, mature, and steady to help me with *Freedom*, I asked Jack. He started out by coming up to Newport on weekends and eventually he was there all the time. He's been with us ever since. Jack loves to sail and he's very good at it. He's been my sparring partner, the helmsman of our trial horse, for many years now and he's always been perfectly steady and indefatigable. For hour after hour during our sail-testing drills, Jack never wavers. Although he was a confirmed East Coaster for so many years, when we got *Stars & Stripes* rolling, he and his wife, Jean, moved to California. He undertook the job of coordinating the junior sailing program at the San Diego Yacht Club and he settled right into the life.

Aside from his competitiveness, his major strength is that the guys love him. He is greatly respected as a coach, a teacher, a man who understands the needs of the program and the needs of the individual. Every syndicate needs a Jack Sutphen, but part of the reason for our success is that there's only one.

Ed du Moulin is an old and valued friend as well. He has played major roles in many Cup campaigns, but he was particularly responsible for helping organize *Stars & Stripes* in the early stages. He has also been a long and loyal member in good standing of the New York Yacht Club, for whom he has provided countless services in the 12-meter arena over the years. While Ed was also upset with the way things were handled in 1983, he agreed with Malin that our first loyalties lay with the Club. In October and November of 1983, unknown to me, Ed tried to put together a deal with Bob Stone in which I would have had a role in the Club's challenge. Although I didn't find out about it until the eve of the 1987 America's Cup, Ed had been quietly lobbying for me to be the Club's skipper.

He also did a lot of work on my behalf by trying to persuade the Maritime College at Fort Schuyler to be our tax-free shelter. Ed was a trustee at Fort Schuyler Foundation and he and Admiral Miller wanted to do it, but other trustees were a little shaky about committing the college to the new era of the America's Cup and all that that seemed to entail.

Ed has been a trusted adviser to me for years and a master at organization. He knows how to set things up and, more importantly, he knows how to get things done. With a solid East Coast establishment background, he was able to open a lot of doors for us that otherwise would have stayed shut.

So with guys like Fritz Jewett, Malin Burnham, Ed du Moulin, Jack Sutphen, John Marshall, and Tom Whidden all coming back for another go, I felt Sail America was rich in talent on land. But except for Whidden and myself, as the syndicate began to gain momentum, I still wasn't sure who would be in the boat.

For some guys, my commitment to the commitment routine gets a little old very quickly. Those are the guys who come and go real fast. Others have something to contribute, enjoy the program, and feel they grow and learn. Some might stay for a year or two, or they might even make it through an entire campaign, but when it's over, they decide to move on to other things in life. Then there are the guys who find a larger meaning in the program than simply a boat race. These are the guys who keep coming back, keep giving 100 percent, keep contributing. They have learned what winning means, not just in a regatta, but in life.

I was fortunate to have enough of these guys to form an on-board nucleus that amounted to something like more than a hundred years of sailing experience. That thought was awesome, and awe-inspiring. The press kept asking me what I had in the way of "secret weapons" and I kept talking about my crew. No one really picked it up until the end, but I suppose most skippers continuously praise their crews. In my case, it wasn't false modesty. These guys were world-class sailors from the word go, and in many ways this was never a new campaign but a continuation of one that started years ago.

I knew that if we were going to win the Cup back in 1987, the victory would be a victory for the whole team. Not just for Dennis Conner or Malin Burnham or Fritz Jewett or for our bowman or grinders, but for everyone associated with us. There would be no prima donnas on board our boat, although each man who sailed with me was a champion in his own right. If we were to win, that team of champions would have to allow themselves to be molded into a championship team.

Here are the guys who made it. Many more were on the team and each one deserves a full mention, but I'm sure they know I have no intention to slight them by mentioning the guys who raced.

Scott Vogel is the first man in history to lose the Cup. You thought I was? Scott was our bowman in 1983 and as such he was the first to cross over the line and I've never let him forget it! Of course, since we won it back, he was the first guy to regain the trophy.

I've sailed with plenty of first-class sailors over the years, but I have yet to sail with a better bowman than Scotty. I'm not sure why the guys nicknamed him Boo-Boo, but it couldn't have been for any mistakes he made, because in all the miles we've sailed together, I can't recall ever seeing him make even one.

He is a graduate of the New York Maritime College at Fort Schuyler, and a measure of his determination is the fact that he took a leave of absence during his senior year so he could sail with us on *Liberty*. Following the defeat many men would have gone on to other things, but Scotty had the drive to return to Fort Schuyler and get his diploma.

Scott actually won the spot as bowman from Adam Ostenfeld. Both guys are very good in that position because they are very quick and agile and they react fast. But Scott had had a lot of small-boat experience and I felt he was a little bit better judge of time and distance than Adam. Scott seemed to have the eye. In January 1983 he was just one of the scruffs who worked as a tailer or down in the pit, but he quickly made his abilities known and by September he was on the bow for the Cup races.

It takes a certain finesse to accomplish all the tasks of the bowman. Not only is good judgment a prerequisite for the position, particularly at the start, but the bowman also is one of the key men on spinnaker sets and douses, sail changes, and jibing the spinnaker on runs and reaches. Scott has been more than satisfactory in every category.

He has my complete trust up in the bow. In very tight situations such as during prestart maneuvering, Scotty used to stand at the forestay, right on the nose of the boat, and watch our speed and distance relative to the other boat and the starting line. I take special pride in my own ability to judge time and distance, but it certainly was a comfort to have Scotty up there sending me hand signals.

There were a couple of times when we came within inches of other boats as we crossed tacks, and whenever that happened, I insisted that Scotty stay hunkered down with the rest of the guys aft of the mast. With two boats barreling along at 8.5 knots, it could be curtains for the bowman if we had a little smash.

None of this is said to demean the abilities of Adam. Here's a guy who is at once tough and sensitive. He flew choppers in Vietnam and he's also a sculptor. Adam has been with me in a lot of ocean races aboard many different boats and I know the value of having him on board. As our starboard trimmer during the 1986–87 season, he performed brilliantly.

He came to us after years of sailing and, in fact, I don't know anyone who has more sea miles under his belt. He has competed around the world in every major offshore event. He, Jon Wright, Tom Whidden, and Peter Isler, all members of our crew, sailed together in three SORC (Southern Ocean Racing Circuit) regattas aboard a succession of boats named *Love Machine*.

The discipline that made him a top helicopter pilot in the Marine Corps also makes him a top sailor. He had a total dedication to his job on board, which actually was recently acquired because when we first sailed together in a 12-meter (*Enterprise*, 1979), he wasn't prepared to make the total commitment I demanded. Instead, he went to England and helped build the maxiboat *Condor*. He came back in 1983 and sailed as our alternate bowman.

For the 1986/87 campaign, Adam actually started out in the *America II* camp sailing with John Kolius. He helped to build their boats, but the style and approach of that camp was so different from ours that it didn't take him long to figure out which way the wind was blowing and who would catch it best. In June of 1985 he knocked on my door in San Diego and I was happy to let him in. He had done everything there was to do in yachting except to compete in an America's Cup race.

Bill Trenkle, our port tailer, came to us in 1979 along with Scotty. Like Scott, Bill went to Fort Schuyler. Both were part of a group of enthusiastic young kids who were chosen for the sailing program by Dick Chesebrough, who was then head coach at the maritime college. That says a lot for Chese, who was also with us in 1986–87—his fourth campaign.

Bill is a seaman in the finest sense of that term. He understands from both an academic and a practical standpoint what it takes to make a boat go. Give a job to Bill, any job, and you know it will be done to perfection.

He started out aboard our tender, just learning the ropes. Right away we were impressed by both his enthusiasm and his tenacity. He soon graduated from the tender to second-team pitman aboard *Enterprise*, which was used as our trial horse in 1979/80. We liked him so much we took him on board *Retaliation* when we did the SORC. Several of the guys who had been around awhile recognized his raw talent and told me that if I wanted Bill to campaign for the Cup, I better keep him under wraps. They advised me that the circuit is sort of a proving ground for a lot of sailors and everybody's always keeping an eye out for that special talent that might make the difference between winning and losing. Bill had it and so did Scott, so we needed to guard them from enemy-camp recruiters. I gave Scott a job and Bill was hired as the professional hand aboard the ocean racer *Lobo*.

Protecting your talent is all part of the game. While as a skipper I might quote the old saw about skippers win races, crews lose them, I only believe that on alternate Thursdays. Good crews help win. It's as simple as that and everyone in this game knows it. So no one is too averse to enticing talent by offering double wages. When a guy is making only $75 a week and his skipper is telling him if he wants to win he's got to give up girls, booze, religion, friends, and family, the temptation to leave for more perks can be great.

Bill graduated from Fort Schuyler as a marine engineer and his skills were invaluable in helping to build *Magic* and *Spirit of America*. Later, he did most of the work in rebuilding *Spirit*.

As our port tailer, he had lightning reflexes and very sure hands. Twelve-meter sailors need to have great anticipation, and one of Bill's great strengths was his uncanny knack of knowing what I was about to do with the helm. He had to keep his eyes on the speedo and on the bow, watching the front end move back and forth and adjusting the jib or spinnaker accordingly to make sure we sailed at maximum efficiency.

A good tailer also has to have an eye for fast-sail shapes. He has to know instinctively what's fast and what's not so he can make immediate adjustments in luff tension, sheeting positions, and overall trim. Bill knew all this. I never once had to say a word about sail trim.

Once Bill made it onto the first-string boat, he became sort of a one-man clearing house for other talent. If a guy didn't get along with Bill, he simply didn't last too long. Not that Bill is a hardass. It's just that he sets high standards for himself and he expects others to do the same.

Jon Wright is known simply as J.W. Here's a guy who loves to sail and is a perfect example of being committed. I started sailing with J.W. in 1974 when I joined *Courageous* as the starting helmsman and he was already on board. In 1977 he crewed for Ted Hood aboard *Independence,* and he was with me in the *Freedom* and *Liberty* campaigns. He was by far the most experienced 12-meter sailor in our program.

Being through four America's Cup battles is a great record, but J.W. was a national champion long before he started sailing in twelves. He had a distinguished record at the U.S. Merchant Marine Academy at Kings Point, New York, and in 1971 he was named All-American and College Sailor of the Year. That is an honor in sailing equivalent to the Heisman Trophy for the best college football player.

Jon runs a thriving ship's chandlery business in Rosemont, Pennsylvania, so he was a little wary of making another almost-two-year America's Cup commitment. But the loss of the Cup had left a bitter taste in his mouth and he pledged to help us get it back.

J.W. is a fantastic mainsail trimmer, which means by constantly adjusting the mainsail, he continually monitors our speed. The mainsail is very much the boat's engine, so that while I had my hands on the wheel, Jon was in charge of the accelerator. He also had a sculptor's eye for shape and form. He knew every stitch in every seam in every panel of cloth in the sail over his head. We have been friends for a long time and I've always considered him a sailor's sailor.

An irony in our relationship is that when I was just beginning to sail, I had a Wright Penguin back in the late 1950s. Jon's father built it. I must have been in the tenth grade but I can still recall the sail number—5440. I called the boat "5440 or fight."

Peter Isler came to us a little late after an unfortunate duty assignment with Leonard Greene on *Courageous*. "Pedro" is a graduate of Yale, but instead of heading to Wall Street, he headed to sea. One of the best sailors in the country and recognized as such by the 1976 award as College Sailor of the Year, he was invited to sail aboard *Courageous*, the grand old lady of 12-meters. Peter campaigned her in Fremantle during the World Championships, but she was greatly outclassed by the newer twelves. Nevertheless, he did a good job and he earned my respect.

When it became clear that promises of a new boat were not going to materialize, we did everything we could to lure him to our program. I felt his knowledge of the rules and the ins and outs of match-racing was greater than almost anyone else's, so I wanted him to sail with us. He flew out to Hawaii and we immediately convinced him to come on board as our navigator. He's smart and picks things up fast. He's also a true gentleman, and like most of the guys on board, a quiet achiever.

Kyle Smith was our starboard grinder in 1980 and the port grinder in 1983. He is the standard against which all 12-meter grinders are judged. At six feet five and two hundred thirty pounds, his impressive presence belies his very sensitive soul. When in 1983 we became the first American crew to lose the Cup, Kyle made no attempt to hide his emotions. He cried openly and that's something I will always respect. He took it hard, as we all did, but he derived extra strength from the experience and his role on our team was major.

Aside from the physical skills that allowed him to attack the winches, Kyle's sense of humor helped the rest of the guys get through some tough times. He's from New Orleans and his one-liners laced with his deliberately extrathick Louisiana accent would turn tension into laughter.

If Kyle's ample musculature sometimes leads to false first impressions, those who meet Henry Childers for the first time must not know what to think. At six foot four and weighing in at two hundred forty pounds, Henry is a thinking man's grinder. He postponed graduate work at Harvard in microbiology to join us. He had had a lot of experience in the SORC and we'd heard about him from an associate of Tom Whidden's.

I asked J.W. to fly to Florida to meet Henry. Jon is not an easy guy to impress, but before he left the Sunshine State, he had extracted a promise from Henry to fly to Hawaii for a tryout. Once we saw how big he was and how well he handled himself on board, we never let him go back to the mainland.

Henry is a perfect example of someone sacrificing a lot for our effort. He put aside a couple of years of Harvard grad school to come on board. I'm sure he'll go on to get his degree, but he'll also have something I feel may be even more valuable. Not just the right to say he helped win the Cup, but the knowledge of what led to that victory.

Lowell North recommended we take a look at John Barnitt as a possible mastman, and that suggestion led to one of the best finds of the entire campaign. He had been sailing in the SORC but his experience was not too extensive. He sailed with me at the maxi-series in Newport in 1984 and I had a gut feeling he would work out. I tend to trust my instincts about people and John was positive, committed, clean-cut, all-American. He was my kind of guy.

I took him right into the inner circle of Scotty, Trenkle, J.W., and Adam, and I think the old guys sort of resented it at first. They tend to be hard on a new guy until he proves himself. Barnitt was the youngest guy on the crew, and if that wasn't enough of an obstacle to get over, he is also dyslexic. Since his height makes him ideal for the mastman/sewerman position in which he would manhandle sails to get them on board and then stow them below after they were used, he had to know every sail in our inventory. Usually we would just put a number on the sailbag and anyone reading it would immediately know what sail was inside. However, for John this was all Greek. So he invented his own system based on colors and it worked fine.

Our old hands felt they had paid their dues to get where they were, and they didn't like someone new showing up without first earning his stripes. This is where our crew selection system is taken out of my hands and left to the nucleus I spoke of earlier. During the first few weeks of our program, especially if you're vying for a first-string position, it's a little like a rough Marine boot camp. If you can survive your time slogging it out with the A-team, you'll get a chance to prove yourself over the long stretch. My guys are relentless in their pursuit and if they find a weakness, they'll exploit it until you leave or find a way to counteract it. This is survival of the fittest. It may be a bit rough, but it's a system that hasn't failed us yet.

One guy who made it through that system and ended up as my choice for "man of the match" was our pitman Jay Brown. At the end of the summer he was by far the most improved sailor on the boat. He had crewed for the very successful champion John MacCausland in Star boats. John recommended Jay to J.W. and when they met, J.W. was impressed with Brown's integrity and sincerity. Jay hadn't had a lot of big-boat experience, but he was eager to learn and he had had enough sailing experience so that he picked things up fast.

Jay is a real perfectionist, so much so that whenever he was guilty of even the most minor goof-up—and that wasn't often—he used to plunge into the deepest despair. J.W. usually talked him out of it, or Kyle would crack a joke and Jay would realize the world wasn't going to end.

He had one of the most demanding jobs on the boat. As his title implies, the pitman has to sit in a little dug-out just behind the mast and from there he controls five winches handling the halyards for the jibs and spinnakers. He also has to take care of the spinnaker pole topping lift and the pole foreguy. Apart from all these responsibilities, he also has to be very careful in judging the precise swing of the spinnaker pole during a jibe so that it comes down under the forestay and then sets on the other side in one continuous arc.

Sitting right under the mast, he keeps an eye on the bend in the rig and he also is responsible for regulating the amount of tension in the jib halyard. If all that isn't enough, he also jumps aft and helps the winch grinders whenever he has a chance. Jay was a man for all seasons and he performed more and more ably throughout the competition.

Another of our grinders, Jim Kavle, was quite literally a tower of strength aboard the boat. Twenty-five years old and six feet five inches tall, he weighed about two hundred thirty pounds. Right from the beginning I felt we needed big, powerful men on the winches if we were to cope with Fremantle's boisterous winds and seas. I had known of Jim's reputation as an excellent Star boat crewman and so, early in 1985, we approached him. He'd been building Star boats in New Jersey, but he said he would give us a try.

He became one of the most dedicated guys in the program. At first, although he was big, he wasn't particularly powerful. He set out to change that by working out in the gym day and night. In the end he was the strongest, fittest man on the boat. He is a gentle, soft-spoken guy, but he helped me at times by speaking out when he saw something wasn't quite right. Of the three grinders we had, he was the only one who sailed in every America's Cup race. We liked to alternate the grinders because of the physical demands of the job, but Jim was always ready.

I've already said quite a bit about Tom Whidden, my tactician. He's my closest personal friend and naturally I have the greatest respect for him as a sailor and a loyal colleague. I have complete confidence and trust in him and although it's well known I like to race my own race,

I always relied on Tom's wisdom. His calls were invariably spot on, although I will admit to times when if I disagreed with him, I just acted like I didn't hear him. He has a nice dry sense of humor and he knew when to use it to break tension in the cockpit.

Often when we were racing, I would look around the cockpit and see Tom, J.W., and Pedro and realize we had the world's best afterguard and then look forward and think we also had the world's best crew and I was delighted to see they proved it race after race.

Our helmsman was Dennis Conner. A lot has been said and written about him, but I happen to know he was just the guy who drove the bus. As far as I'm concerned, too much attention is focused on me and nowhere near enough on all the other guys who made that big blue machine hum. Unlike some other recent America's Cup skippers, I want the world to understand that the helmsman is not the be-all and end-all of 12-meter campaigning. He is simply the quarterback, just one member of the team. If the team doesn't play well, the quarterback can't score. It's as simple as that.

So whether a guy had plenty of experience or a lot of credentials or was new but determined, he had a chance to make the team. The team didn't consist of just the eleven guys in the boat, but close to a hundred men and women who worked with us in various capacities over long stretches of time. If running a syndicate is like running a business, it also has its share of similarities to belonging to a family. We all became very close and I think we all believed that every win was a result of a hundred people working, not just one guy steering or another guy making a quick jib change.

I feel I know all these people intimately, and yet I can't say that I've ever had dinner with them individually. I guess you have to maintain some sort of distance, like a general does with his troops. You can't afford to allow personal ties and emotions to cloud your judgment.

So there you have it—America's Cup 101 with Professor Conner. Start out with a goal, assemble an organization, raise the money, tap the best technology your country has to offer, test, experiment with, and try out seemingly crazy ideas, establish a sail-development program, find the perfect training site where you can blend all the ingredients, seek out the best talent available, and then work and work and work.

From the time Fritz Jewett served me my third rum and tonic and said, "Let's talk about the next Cup," until the day I stepped on a plane headed for Perth, Australia, that's the program I tried to follow. When the time came for us to leave, I knew we were ready. We were ready to go get what we believed was ours. We were off to the races.

7

❋

At the Races

B Y the time we arrived in Fremantle, Western Australia, in September 1986, much of the town had changed from when I first visited in 1984. Fremantle's character has been frozen in a delightful Victorian time warp, and having the Cup there inspired a tremendous renaissance. The old buildings were beautifully restored and painted in the strong late-Victorian colors they originally sported in the 1880s at the height of the great gold rush. A hundred years later a new kind of gold rush revolved around a silver cup, and the townspeople were determined to show off their home to the world.

With help from the government and private industry, miles of waterfront had been converted to accommodate the seventeen syndicates vying for a place on the starting line come January 31, 1987. Before then, however, these teams would have to endure four months of preliminary races to determine who would move on first to the semifinals, and then to the finals of both the Challenger and Defender series. The America's Cup competition is one of the longest and most grueling in all of sport. Before the 1986–87 event was concluded, more than three hundred and sixty races were run starting October 5, 1986, and ending on February 4, 1987. Add to that the thousands of hours spent training, and it's a very long haul.

I can't say enough about the Australian people and the tremendous reception they gave us. Compared to Newport, it was like night and day. The Aussies actually liked us. They enjoyed having the event in their own backyard, whereas in Newport we were made to feel like we were intruding on the townspeople's little bit of paradise. In Newport people were always asking when we were going to leave. In Fremantle they asked us to stay as long as possible. The fishermen, whose harbor we more or less took over, used to come by our docks and give us fish and lobsters and crabs. In Newport, they felt we were taking fish out of their mouths.

It was a wholly different attitude in Australia. The people were always warm and friendly. Often, we even got the feeling that we were more popular than the Australians who were defending the Cup. We certainly had a much higher, warmer public profile. The four Australian teams were quiet and kept pretty much to themselves behind locked compound gates. I guess they didn't want to cause any incidents that might detract from the purpose at hand. We certainly weren't looking for any extra excitement either, but on several occasions we opened up our dock space for an open house. The local people loved this, and I think a few such gestures did a lot of good for Australian-American relations.

We were made to feel right at home as soon as we got there. In fact, the climate, the ocean setting, the carefree attitude of the people, all reminded me a lot of Southern California. The fact that we were 12,000 miles from home was never really forgotten, but I don't think any of our guys were really bothered by it. Apparently, the same was not true when the Australians used to come to Newport to challenge. I think they felt the changes in climate, culture, and people more than we did. Of course, I used to feel the same way going from California to Newport!

We settled into life in Fremantle pretty quickly, but we had to attend to a million details before feeling truly prepared for our first race on October 5. Our team was still not functioning as the flawless, well-oiled machine we would have to be to win the Cup, but I considered that an advantage. This competition is a long haul and I didn't want the guys to peak too soon. As was said many times during our summer in Australia, the America's Cup is a marathon and those who are good only in sprints will be home by Christmas.

In my mind's eye, I kept envisioning the America's Cup just out on the horizon, basking in the vivid green-and-blue light reflecting off the Indian Ocean. There it was, almost within our grasp, but between us and it stood sixteen boats, all no doubt with the same vision. I wondered if that damn Cup remembered me as well as I remembered it.

Certainly there were sixteen other skippers just as determined as I was to win the trophy, but I doubted it would mean quite as much to any of them as it would to me.

None of the other skippers was really a stranger to me. If I hadn't actually met them, I had certainly heard of them. The sailing world tends to be fairly insular and most of us travel to the same major regattas. A lot of us have sailed with each other at one time or another. There is a bond that develops between sailors, a mutual understanding of what it takes to move a boat through water. Men who sail small boats do so for a million different reasons and they tend to share the same unspoken fears and realizations about the power of the sea. In many ways, the ocean is the great equalizer. Egos diminish in the face of a 40-knot wind and fifteen-foot waves.

But despite the fact that we may know each other and are friends on the dock and in the pub, we are all still fierce competitors who give no quarter as we approach the starting line. At forty-four I was one of the older guys in this America's Cup. When I looked around I saw the "new breed" of 12-meter skippers the press liked to make such a big thing about. Guys twenty-five, twenty-six, twenty-eight years old in command of boats representing $10- and $12-million syndicates. The word in the press was that the youngsters were more capable of enduring the long hours in the expected stiff winds and boisterous seas than us old guys. Well, it sounded good but I think they forgot that the experience a Dennis Conner or Buddy Melges or Harold Cudmore or Tom Blackaller brings to the game has its own special merits.

Before we came to Fremantle, we already had a fairly good idea of what to expect from the competition. In fact, our "Hawaii strategy" allowed us to gather a lot more intelligence about the opposition than we felt they had acquired on us. While all syndicates had their own sources, our guys seemed particularly good at separating bar talk from hard, substantial fact. This, coupled with the results from the 12-meter World Championships held off Fremantle during the previous February, gave us an idea of what we were up against.

We didn't enter the Worlds for a variety of reasons and that seemed to upset a lot of the Cup aficionados. We were said to be "in hiding," afraid of competing, scared we'd find out we were slow. Actually, the major reason for not entering was simply time. By February 1986 we were well into our training and sail-development program, and to take a month out to transfer boats and crew to Australia would have been a serious disruption. Costs were also a consideration, as were the possible benefits. At that stage I wouldn't have wanted to show all my cards, so winning the regatta wasn't of prime importance. However, not winning could have had a negative impact on our fund-raising attempts. After weighing all the pros and cons, it just didn't seem like a very intelligent thing to do. Besides, by not going we kept all the competition guessing about what we were doing there in Hawaii, and the press gave us such a strong play that by not going we actually received more publicity than if we had.

The Worlds did provide us with some interesting notice on other boats. I guess it wasn't too much of a surprise that Bondy won the regatta with *Australia III*. However, the surprises were the number two, three, and five spots. In second place was one of the two fiberglass yachts that New Zealand had entered. Three things about this impressed me. First was that this twenty-four-year-old kid named Chris Dickson seemed to be as good as the rumors said he was. Second was the fact that the boat did well in both light and heavy air. And last, I was a bit surprised that a rookie effort from a small nation could perform so well. Obviously, the Kiwis were a force to be reckoned with.

By finishing third, I felt *America II* sort of shot itself in the foot. They succumbed to the same trap we wanted to avoid. I doubt their backers were too happy with the results. After all, these were the guys who had built two boats before anyone else, who had spent more time training in the same waters than anyone else, and who had more money than anyone else. On paper, you would have had to say they would win the regatta. But by losing to a relative newcomer like *New Zealand* and by beating the 1983 boat *Australia II* by only a fraction more than one point, *America II* appeared suspect in several areas. Actually, if one considered their blown-out spinnaker, their ripped mainsail, and their man overboard, the third-place finish wasn't that shabby. But that type of stuff doesn't go over too well in boardrooms. America likes winners and that means number one, not three.

Finishing fifth in the Worlds was *French Kiss*. We had heard they were well funded by the instant photo company KIS, and that the group was determined to make a good showing in the 12-meter game. They had bought *Enterprise* and *Freedom* to use in training and they had hired Phillipe Briand to design a new boat. Briand had had many successes with IOR boats and he had designed the winner of the Whitbread Round-the-World Race, *L'Esprit d'Equipe*. At the helm was Marc Pajot, a successful skipper who had done well in the world of commercially sponsored multihulls. *French Kiss* won two of the seven races and proved she was a very good boat in heavy air.

Like us, an unknown quantity in September was the Kookaburra syndicate. This interesting group was started and principally funded by Kevin Parry, a business rival of Alan Bond and a hard-nosed, self-made millionaire. The story making the rounds was that Parry had attended a luncheon in Perth one day when Bond was discussing the need for the business community to get behind his effort to keep the Cup. Parry volunteered his help but Bond snubbed him. So Parry said, "The hell with you. I'll go it alone meself," and he formed his own syndicate. His major stroke of genius was selecting Iain Murray to put the program together. Murray is one of the best sailors in Australia, a world champion in several classes. He had also volunteered his help to Bondy but was told where he could put the sharp end of the boat. Both Parry and Murray were out for revenge.

The Kookaburras had put together an impressive program complete with three new boats and lots of razzle-dazzle computer technologies. Murray helped design the boats with John Swarbrick, and dockside rumors said the boys had done well. Although they didn't enter the Worlds either, our intelligence sources indicated the rumors weren't off the mark.

Although I'd never met Murray, I certainly knew about him. Several of the other skippers I did know well and I also had a pretty good idea of how their boats might perform. Harold Cudmore, sailing *White Crusader* for the Royal Thames Yacht Club in England, has been an aggressive, accomplished helmsman for years. Although he might have a penchant for vociferous chewing-out when there was a crew screw-up, he tends to get the best from both boat and crew. He's also a damn good match-racer.

Cudmore was involved in 1983 with the British challenge bankrolled by Peter de Savary. Peter and Harold mixed about as well as oil and water and Harold was soon replaced. He surfaced later as a trial-horse skipper for Australian John Bertrand, who gives him credit for helping him with his starts. Cudmore is too good to go unnoticed for long, and when the Royal Thames began putting together their 1986–87 effort, they gave Harold complete control of the sailing program.

I was interested from the beginning in the British campaign because their designers, Ian Howlett and David Hollom, had had an ironic involvement in the infamous "keelgate" episode of 1983.

When the New York Yacht Club finally got around to attempting a protest over *Australia II*'s keel, we learned that the keel committee of the International Yacht Racing Union had issued a secret dispensation to the British yacht allowing "winglets." Howlett, who also designed *Lionhart* (1980), had been experimenting with a wing keel prior to the 1983 races and the syndicate had queried the IYRU on the legality of such a keel. However, Howlett was thwarted in pursuing a breakthrough because he did not have the same type of testing facilities as Ben Lexcen had in Holland and thus couldn't accurately forecast how the wing keel would affect the boat's performance.

But even though Howlett was involved again and their design team had use of the facilities at British Aerospace and British Airways, I didn't feel their boat had the legs to go the distance. However, I did feel Cudmore would win his share of races. I just wanted to make sure that share wasn't going to come out of my hide.

Of all the people I have raced against during some thirty years, there's one guy who has given me the most trouble. When I think of the Ted Turners, the Ted Hoods, the Lowell Norths, the John Bertrands, the Bob Baviers, none of them stick in my mind like Tom Blackaller. Tommy has been nipping at my heels for something like twenty years now. The press has played up the supposed feud between the two of us, but I'm not sure there's anything more to it than media hype. I've tried to be low-key in my remarks about Tommy, but he's sort of a bombastic type and I've been his favorite target for quite a long time now. At first all the verbal crap got to me a bit, but then I realized Tommy knows how to use the media, who are perfect dupes for him. Playing the same game could only get me in trouble, so I just shut up. Tommy never has, but then all I have to do is point to the record.

That record includes a lot of head-to-head battles the two of us have had on the water. He's good, he's always been good, but I've always been able to get the measure of him. But back in September there was a lot of talk about his *USA*, the revolutionary new boat he was bringing to Fremantle. *USA* was the product of designer Gary Mull, who had started out with us. Mull had access to the best technology Silicon Valley had to offer, as well as the top brains associated with U.S. defense projects. We had a pretty good idea what the design was. In fact, we had played around a bit with the front-rudder idea ourselves. If that was what Blackaller was bringing to the Cup, we'd have to keep a close eye on him.

Although *America II* finished third in the Worlds, I wasn't about to dismiss them. I really wasn't convinced their design would prove much of a breakthrough, but Kolius is a good natural sailor and I knew I couldn't ignore anyone who had spent as much time and money on their boats as this syndicate had.

So going into the first week of races, I felt that on the Challengers' side the major players would be *New Zealand*, *Stars & Stripes*, *America II*, *USA*, *French Kiss*, *White Crusader*, and possibly *Canada II*. Frankly, I didn't feel anyone else had much of a chance.

America's Cup racing really isn't like most sports in that "on any given Sunday" a usually shabby team can rise up in one glorious effort and beat the favorite. That does happen on occasion, but history has shown that one boat is usually superior to the others and that's the boat that wins. 1983 was a bit of an anomaly, not because the faster boat didn't win, but because it took the full seven races to do so. The upset wasn't that *Australia II* beat us. The real upset would have been if we had won.

That said, it was still left for us to beat these guys I felt didn't have much of a chance. Since there were thirteen Challengers who made it to Fremantle, there were six boats that I felt would be home by Christmas.

Of the other Americans, *Courageous* plainly had no chance at all, and I felt Buddy Melges's *Heart of America* was too underfunded. However, Buddy is one of the great sailors in the world and I suspected he would indeed pull off an upset or two. Considering what happened, we were lucky we weren't the victim of their great upset. *Eagle* was skippered by Rod Davis, an Olympic medal winner and an experienced match-racer. However, they too had insufficient funds and their boat was a product of a one-man (Johan Valentijn) design effort. After seeing the results of our design team's work, I was more convinced than ever that this approach would produce the best boats. Of the boats I mentioned above as being strong contenders, only *America II* and *Canada II* came from the drafting table of one man.

Among the foreign ranks, I placed *Challenge France* and *Italia* in the same category as *Courageous*. *Azzurra* had done very well in 1983 for a first-time effort, but the poor showing (tenth) in the Worlds had dispelled much hope for this Italian group.

The first day we actually sailed in the Indian Ocean was September 11, 1986. Up until then all our design work and sail developing had been strictly tests. As we sailed out to the America's Cup course, I could see a number of the other contenders. I decided it was now or never.

"Let's hook up with some of these guys and see what we've got,"

I said to the crew. A few smiles of excitement and anticipation spread through the boat as we came up alongside *Azzurra*. Within only a few minutes we blew them away. Then we went after *Italia*, *Eagle*, *French Kiss*, and *White Crusader* with similar results. That was an important day. Our confidence grew a great deal.

On the eve of the first series, the atmosphere of cordiality among the syndicates was replaced by one of tension. In the pubs around Fremantle, the realization seemed to be dawning even on the racer chasers and bilge bunnies that the America's Cup was finally going to begin. We'd all been working toward this for the best part of two and a half years and I think everyone was anxious to get going.

The night before the racing began, the mood in our camp was one of guarded optimism. While we knew the competition was a marathon, we couldn't shrug off the feeling we needed to do well in the 100-yard dash. Some people may have thought the October series wasn't that important because the winning boat in each race collected only one point. But that theory soon proved to be dead wrong when *America II* failed to make the semifinals because it ended up one point behind *French Kiss*.

With only a few hours remaining before the start, I thought about the competition once again. Some boats appeared to be more ready than others and most boats seemed to have a particular wind range in which they were especially competitive. I believed that the October series would be largely determined by the weather. Since most of the boats had been designed to take advantage of the heavy air expected after December, light air in October might make for some surprises. At the time I thought the winner might have a record of 9–3 or 10–2, and I also thought whoever won in October would not win the Cup.

As far as *Stars & Stripes* was concerned, I didn't feel we were completely together yet. I certainly don't like to lose any race, but at that point I felt realistically I had to expect to lose a few in which the other boat was just plain faster or the other guys did a better job. Another factor that nagged at me a bit was that just prior to the first race I had had to attend to fund-raising duties back in the States. While I was gone the guys took the opportunity to ensure the bottom of the hull was smooth. Still, I didn't much like the idea of being away at that particular time.

The America's Cup regatta of 1986/87 was set up in two main divisions with the Defenders on one side and the Challengers on the other. The Challengers' races, called the "Louis Vuitton Cup" races, consisted of five different rounds—three round robins, a semifinals, and a finals. The first round was held between October 5 and October 19 and the winner of each race was awarded one point. Five points were earned by the winner in the second round robin, which began on November 2 and was over on the 19th. What proved to be the most critical round was held from December 2–19, and each victory was worth twelve points. The semifinals were scheduled as a best-of-seven series in which the number 1 and 4 positions raced each other while number 2 met number 3. The finals, between the winners of the semis, was also scheduled as a best-of-seven series. That winner would go on to meet the winner of the Defense series in the actual America's Cup Match Race. The Cup would go to the first boat to win four races.

All races on both sides were "match races," in which only two boats would compete. This type of racing, different from "fleet racing" in which many boats compete on the same course at the same time, puts a different and probably more important emphasis on strategy and tactics vis-à-vis your opponent.

The course had been laid out in an area called "Gage Roads," just off Fremantle. It is an approximately 10-nautical-mile stretch of water between the mouth of the Swan River and the beach suburbs of Perth to the north. A breakwater of sorts is formed by the coral reefs and two islands, Rottnest and Garden, which are a few miles offshore.

Since 1970 a standard Olympic triangular course of 24.3 miles has been used in Cup competition. The course for the twenty-sixth America's Cup had been changed by the addition of two legs that made it more compact so the overall length grew to only 24.5 miles. Now there were three weather legs, three downwind legs, and two reaches.

The first leg is always sailed into the wind, so the race committee would set the starting line perpendicular to the direction of the wind and then anchor the first mark 3.25 miles directly upwind. Since yachts can't sail directly into the wind, their route was a zigzag caused by tacks, or what sailors call "beating." Twelve-meter yachts actually sail closer to the true wind direction than any other sailboat, but still the angle is only about 32 degrees.

On the beat, or windward leg, the boat's mainsail and the headsail, which is called either a "genoa" or "jib," are sheeted in tight. This is referred to as being "close-hauled," which means both sails are as close to the center of the boat as possible. As the wind blows, the yacht heels over, and because a boat sails the fastest when she is as flat as possible, the crew will gather on the windward rail to try to balance her.

After rounding the first mark, a spinnaker is set for the downwind square run. This occurs when the wind is directly in back of the yacht.

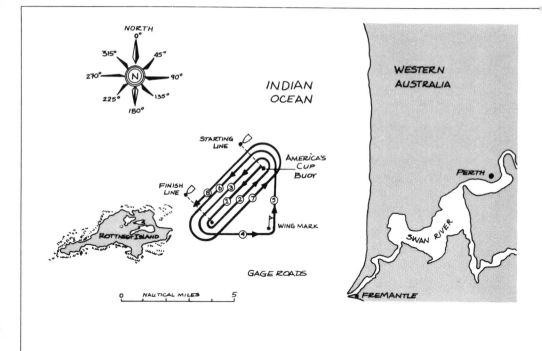

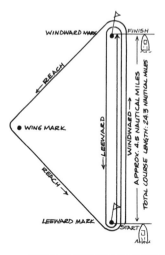

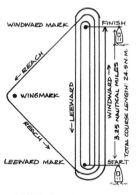

1983 AMERICA'S CUP COURSE
NEWPORT, RHODE ISLAND

1987 AMERICA'S CUP COURSE
FREMANTLE, WESTERN AUSTRALIA

TOP: The America's Cup race course is located in the waters known as Gage Roads between Fremantle and Rottnest Island, Australia. The prevailing wind (the "Fremantle Doctor") usually comes in each afternoon from the southwest as hot air rising over the land draws cooler ocean air inland.

BOTTOM: After 1983 each leg of the America's Cup course was shortened and two legs were added but the total length of the course stayed about the same. This change placed a premium on skillful boat-handling and tactics.

Also, the jib is dropped and the mainsail let out so it is roughly perpendicular to the yacht's centerline.

The third leg is a repeat of the first, followed by the two reaches. Each reaching leg is 2.3 miles long. These are the other two legs to the triangle and are sailed with the wind coming from abeam, or over the side. Thus the reach is sailed between close-hauled and running downwind.

When the two reaches are concluded, the yachts head into the wind for the sixth leg, back downwind for the seventh, and the final leg is a beat to the finish line.

Because as many as three different races were held each day, several different courses on Gage Roads were used and not each was 24.5 miles long during the first three rounds. But the full-length course was used in the semifinals, finals, and America's Cup races.

On October 5 we were a little lucky to draw *Italia* as our first opponent. I didn't think we'd have much trouble, and I also thought it would be a good opportunity to get everyone into the racing mode and experiment with a couple of things as well. We had prepared for light winds, but on the way to the course we encountered a number of small cells with relatively heavy rain and substantial increases in wind velocity. The forecast was for light and variable winds in the morning becoming west sou'west by eleven A.M. and increasing from 8 to 10 knots.

With that forecast in mind, we had on board five half-ounce spinnakers and two three-quarter-ounce spinnakers. These "light" winds increased from 14 true to 25 true within a half-hour of the start, and we had to scramble to take on additional sails. We exchanged the sails we would have used in light air for ones more suited to the conditions, but were left with no time to test the sails.

During the starting maneuvers, *Italia* engaged us in a circle exercise that we turned to our advantage when we jibed and ended up in control. Both boats crossed the line about even but we had more speed and we were on the favored end. Anyone paying particularly close attention to the performance of *Stars & Stripes* in the first leg of that first race could have determined our major strength and our tactics for pretty much the rest of the entire competition. Our boat had been specifically designed to go fast in a straight line. I wasn't really interested in a boat that was highly maneuverable. What I requested from our design team is what I got—a straight-line devil.

Italia hung in there to leeward and we hoped they'd drag race with us for a while instead of throwing in a lot of tacks. They fell for our strategy and in the first five minutes we had gained three and a half boat-lengths. If we hadn't known before, we could be pretty sure now —*Stars & Stripes* was indeed a flyer.

We turned the first mark a minute ahead of *Italia* and from then on we gained at every mark. The winning margin was a healthy 5:49, so we knew right away we were going to be tough.

It was a good first race, not just because we won by so much but because we had a chance to get our competitive juices flowing. It was also the first time in three America's Cup opening races that we didn't suffer gear breakage. In 1980, in our first race against Ted Turner, we jibed and the traveler broke. In the first race in 1983, the bicycle chain on our steering came apart and we had to steer the entire race with the trim tab. Against *Italia*, I was pleased we had a good wind and no ill effects.

Other races that first day indicated who was looking good. We expected *New Zealand* to be fast and they proved they were just that in an impressive win against *Heart of America*. I commented that night that my bet was *Stars & Stripes* would meet the Kiwis in the finals of the Challenger trials (the Louis Vuitton Cup). I'm on record as saying that that night, but I'd actually predicted the same thing about a month before.

French Kiss, *Canada II*, and *White Crusader* also looked good. The real surprise was to see Harold Cudmore come from behind three times to pass *USA* on the beats to windward. It appeared that in choppy seas and medium winds Blackaller had trouble steering with his forward rudder. Although *America II* won, the key to the race was that *Canada II* was able to gain twenty-nine seconds on the first beat in conditions we would see in December and January.

In the second race we beat *Azzurra* by more than three minutes and the day after we pounded *Eagle*. In our fourth race we met *White Crusader* and, prior to the contest, I was concerned about them. Our scouting reports, from guys who were in rubber duckies following the British boat around the course, was that Harold might stay with us on the upwind legs but he'd probably have trouble downwind.

The day started out with very light winds and as we were tuning up before the race, I requested our lightest jib. I also noticed that the wind was quite erratic, so I felt whoever was in the right place at the right time would catch a shift and that might be the race. Windshifts are extremely important in sailboat racing, particularly in match-racing. If the wind is coming at you from a certain direction, then moves left or right, the course the boat needs to sail to the next mark is altered because of the angle at which the wind now strikes the boat.

The committee had set the starting line for the wind coming out of the southwest at 205 degrees. But right before the ten-minute gun the wind became very light and shifted to 250 degrees. The shift resulted in *Stars & Stripes* being dead upwind of Harold, who was at the port end. He would have had a tremendous tactical advantage in a normal match race start. To catch him, I would have had to go directly downwind on a run.

Tom Whidden stayed calm and said, "The wind is too fluky to try anything here. Right now the right-hand side of the line is favored, but I think the wind will build and shift again."

He was right. With a minute to go before the gun, the wind suddenly freshened from about 7 knots to about 16 true. Harold was up to weather at the start, but we had a bit more speed on so we gained bearing almost immediately. We both needed to change our light headsails, which were way too full for the building breeze. The crews scampered to change jibs, and here is where Harold made his big mistake.

Normally, changing a sail is done during a tack. It is easier to drop one sail and raise another as the boat goes through the wind. This is standard operating procedure. However, different situations call for different actions. I noticed as our guys were setting up the new jib that the windshift had resulted in placing our boats within a few degrees of laying the mark. On the bow, Scotty was looking at me and then over to *White Crusader*. He could see the Brits were ready to tack and change sails. I looked back at him and shook my head slightly. I knew he was wondering what the hell I was doing, but I had my eyes on the compass and if I was right, Harold was going to tack himself right out of the controlling position. I looked back at Scotty and said quietly, "Change sails."

Scotty's been through enough with me to know instantly what we were doing. I called for a straightaway set, which meant the guys had to get one sail up and the other down while we were sailing right into the wind. As they went to work, Harold tacked and his crew completed the sail change without incident. We were not so fortunate. When the new jib was almost in place, the head popped out of the headstay foil. Because of the tremendous amount of tension we had put on the backstay to aid our trim of the lightweight jib, the headfoil simply parted and the jib came adrift. A normally one-minute sail change was turned into two minutes, but Cudmore had missed his chance. By the time we completed the jib set, Harold had tacked back, but now he found he had given up his tactical advantage. We were to leeward and ahead, practically laying the mark. I knew Whidden had been right about the shifts, so I was determined not to alter course but wait for the wind to return to 240 degrees. When it did, it allowed us to sail within 5 degrees of the mark. We had gained considerably on straight-line speed despite our sail mishap, and at the mark we were able to tack and cross in front of *White Crusader*.

Although Harold had made what might be considered a tactical error, he doesn't make many and we certainly hadn't won the race yet. That guy knows how to sail and he dogged us around the entire course. Neither one of us showed much brilliance downwind, but *White Crusader* gained ten seconds on each of the two reaches. We had a little more speed on the beats and we stayed in front to win by one minute fifteen seconds. The victory was sweet, but ruining a $17,000 Mylar light jib by carrying it in the 16 knots of wind hurt a bit.

Our fifth race in October was against Tom Blackaller and it turned out to be one of the most exciting races I've participated in. Again the day started with winds light and unsettled. The committee postponed the start for an hour until some sort of steady breeze developed. It finally filled in at about 290 degrees and as we entered the starting arena, we hooked up with *USA* and the two boats began circling each other. This was our first head-to-head look at the revolutionary boat with the bow rudder. My first impression was that Tom kept the boat out of tight circles. I suspected he might be having some steering problems because you'd expect a boat with a bow rudder to maneuver well. It looked like when he did turn sharply, the boat just about stopped.

With a minute fifteen seconds to the gun, we were chasing *USA* back to the committee boat. We found ourselves underneath them, trying to force them over the starting line. As we came up into the wind, we yelled, "Coming up, coming up." He ignored us. "Coming up!" No response. *"Coming up, damn it."* We were within three feet and I had the option to tap him and foul him out. But I've seen too many protests go either way. No matter how right you think you are, I maintain you have no better than a fifty/fifty chance in the jury room. If I think I can win a race on the water, I'll pass up the possibility of losing it on land.

We were both on port tack and I was to starboard, about to be squeezed into the committee boat. My options were to jibe or tack under his stern. I probably should have done the latter, but I chose the former and in doing so was thirty-four seconds late across the line. We did have the favored end, but we were a good four boat-lengths behind. We tried some straight-line speed, then we tried a few tacks to see if he would cover. He didn't, which meant he was pretty confident of his own speed. The wind was still shifty and right before the first mark we caught a 40-degree lift, but he ended up with the perfect controlling position. When we got to the mark, Tom had been there first about fifty seconds before us.

The shift turned the run into a reach, and I noticed that as Tom rounded the leeward mark, he went quite wide and made some leeway, meaning he slipped sideways. We executed a good rounding and ended up about a boat-length to windward, but still considerably behind. I think the leeway problem USA had can be attributed to the low wetted surface due to the keel configuration. USA was the only boat to come to Fremantle that did not have a wing keel. What this boat had underneath was a large, torpedo-shaped mass of lead. It seemed to me that when the boat was not up to speed as when she rounded marks or came out of a tack, the leeway problem occurred. That was a result of not having enough lateral resistance. The idea behind the bow rudder and this keel configuration was that the bow rudder was supposed to produce enough lift to make up for the lack of lateral resistance from the keel. In other words, they were willing to take the trade-off in the belief that the gain in lifting ability of the rudders would outweigh the loss in side force from the keel itself.

On the second beat our tactics gained us a lot of ground. Again, the wind shifted to the left, which meant we overstood the mark on our present course. We now had to make additional maneuvers to reach the mark before we could round it. Tom was on our right and we suckered him into tacking below our line by aiming below our normal course. When he tacked below us, we were able to come up above him and have clear air two boat-lengths to weather all the way to the mark. In doing so we cut his lead from 280 yards to 140 yards.

Once again the wind had shifted so much that the second reach became a run. We kept on his stern down the entire leg and ate up a little more ground. At the leeward mark, we had cut our deficit to thirty-four seconds. We needed to get him in a tacking duel, but our position on the course after a couple more windshifts was such that we needed to get back to the middle to gain some maneuvering room. Tom gained another boat-length before we started tacking in earnest.

As I said, we noticed in the prestart dancing that USA didn't turn too well, so we thought we could take advantage. We threw five, six, seven tacks in a row at them and the lead began to diminish. We were

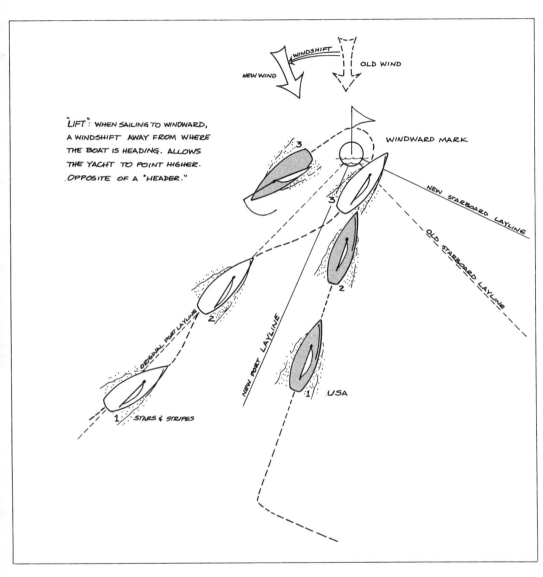

Within the figure:

WINDSHIFT

OLD WIND

NEW WIND

"LIFT": WHEN SAILING TO WINDWARD, A WINDSHIFT AWAY FROM WHERE THE BOAT IS HEADING. ALLOWS THE YACHT TO POINT HIGHER. OPPOSITE OF A "HEADER."

WINDWARD MARK

3

3

NEW STARBOARD LAYLINE

OLD STARBOARD LAYLINE

2

ORIGINAL PORT LAYLINE

2

NEW PORT LAYLINE

1 USA

1 STARS & STRIPES

Round Robin I, October 1986, vs. Tom Blackaller's *USA,* second beat. Windshift and tactics allow *Stars & Stripes* to reduce *USA*'s lead: *Stars & Stripes* (1) trails *USA* but forces *USA* (1) to tack short of the layline by changing our course so we are heading short of the mark. Blackaller, who is ahead on the opposite tack, assumes our course change is meant to let us fetch the mark; he unwittingly tacks and now he too is heading short of the mark. Our position allows us to then point back up, and foot to the mark more rapidly, and reduce his lead.

putting it to him so he broke off to the right and with a quarter mile to go, he made a dash for the finish line. We went left where the breeze was stronger and after two more tacks, we had closed to within a half boat-length.

The next few moments were, to me, what makes sailboat racing so exciting. At that point the race could have gone either way. What would determine the winner? Tactics? A windshift? A mistake? Boat-speed? It was a toss-up.

He was on port tack coming upwind to the favored port end, where the wind was stronger, of the finish line. He needed to make one more tack to get over the line. He did the right thing by tacking a little short of the layline so that we would have to tack under him, leaving him in control. But as we approached I felt we had a chance to cross his bow. It would be dicey, but at that stage, it was our only hope. About three or four boat-lengths from the line I made my move—I went to leeward to steer across his bow and he altered course to windward to block me. I saw his jib go light so I called him for changing course: he had the right of way and therefore was not supposed to change course within close proximity to our boat. I luffed and he luffed and *Stars & Stripes* had just enough way-on to get over the line about three feet in front of *USA*.

I consider that race one of the greatest I've ever been in. As things turned out, it was one of the most critical of the summer, even though only one Challenger series point was at stake. It was critical because of the psychological impact of winning and losing. It was the type of race that you remember forever if you win, and one you can't forget if you lose. Tommy is tough and has been through this before, but I knew that a race like that could eat away at his young crew's confidence. Already, the image of themselves as losers began to take shape.

For the guys on *Stars & Stripes*, the race was a turning point. We had trailed around the entire course, but our guys never gave up. Although they're pros who have been in a thousand races, the lesson of giving 100 percent until the finish line is crossed was brought home once again. Even on the last tack, it's possible to come from behind. I didn't say anything, I didn't need to, but I looked at the faces of Adam and Tom and Billy and Pedro and Barnitt and I knew we'd all raised our game another notch.

The win was particularly gratifying because Tommy and his boys were not our favorite drinking buddies. In fact, I'll say it, they were downright nasty and rude on the water. Any time the two boats got close, the boys on *USA* would open up with a stream of invectives and

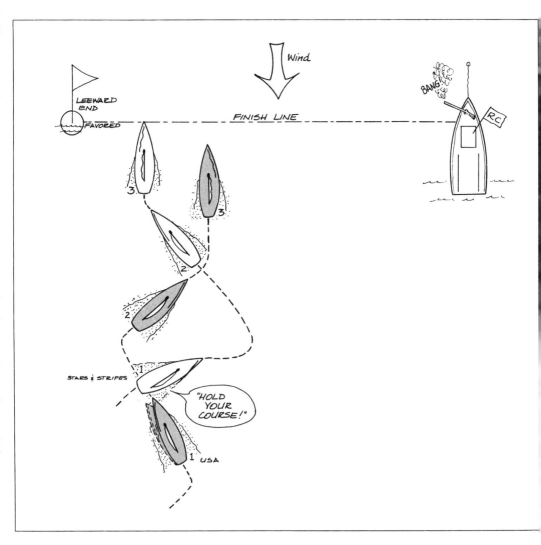

Round Robin I, October 1986, vs. *USA*. *USA* tacks a little short of the lay line that would take it to the pin end (1). *Stars & Stripes* steers across *USA*'s bow (1) and calls *USA* for changing course. Both boats continue toward the line (2–3) and when each luffs up (4) *Stars & Stripes* wins by three feet.

epithets. They'd yell and shout and hit their winch handles against the aluminum deck, all in an effort to disrupt us. Tommy thinks that he can rattle Dennis, that he has a way of psyching out DC. What he tends to forget is that while his boys are reliving their kindergarten years, our guys are sailing our own boat. We never respond, never give them the satisfaction. Breaking concentration is a two-way street, especially when it's the other guy who starts it.

There were two other races in the October series, officially known as Round Robin I of the Louis Vuitton Cup, which were of special note. In the eighth race we came up against *America II* and in the eleventh race, we met the Kiwis. If our win against *USA* was an important lesson in never giving up, our loss against *America II* illustrated how vulnerable we were downwind.

The conditions of the race were similar to what we could expect more and more—lumpy, confused seas with swells to six feet and a sou'west wind at about 12–15 knots. Frankly, this was a race I wanted badly because of all that had occurred between Dennis and the New York Yacht Club over the past three or four years. John Kolius wanted it too, of that I was sure. He wanted to prove himself against Dennis, to show what he could do with a boat he believed was at least our equal. I'm not sure who felt the most pressure; the old man fighting to retain the crown or the kid battling to show the world his time had come.

With five minutes to go before the start, Kolius began chasing us toward the committee boat. We tried to blow him off by maneuvering close to the boat, but *America II* stayed on our hip as we circled. Neither of us was very aggressive, and with seventy-five seconds to go we both luffed up bow-to-bow about 300 feet from the line. The seconds ticked away. After letting our boats inch along into the wind, we both ran down the line and Kolius won the start by two seconds, but we were to windward and so had the favored side. We started out drag-racing, but after about three minutes, it seemed *America II* was gaining a bit. In match-racing, a good indicator of who is ahead on the first leg is to see who tacks first. The guy trailing usually initiates the first tack, so when we did, a great war whoop went up from *Scotch Mist*, the New York syndicate's official spectator boat. However, the shouts of glee soon died in the wind when *Stars & Stripes* began to hit her upwind stride and we rounded the first mark with a solid lead of thirty-three seconds.

On the first square run, *America II* showed her superior speed going directly downwind by gaining back sixteen seconds. In this type of racing, the boat behind has the controlling position on the runs because her sails catch the wind first. Immediately downwind of the trailing boat's sails the air is turbulent and weak. If that boat is close enough to the leader, that boat can dictate the tactics by maneuvering, for example, to deny the leader clean air. *America II* kept clawing back and there wasn't too much we could do. We tried a few jibes to shake her off, but Kolius was too smart to allow us free air.

On the second upwind leg our speed was a little better so we gained back some time and when we turned into the first reach, we had a twenty-five-second lead. *America II* whittled that down to fourteen seconds by the second reach and we stayed even on that leg. The third beat was a copy of the first and second with *Stars & Stripes* gaining once again. But Kolius knew he had better speed on the run in light air and he really cranked up *America II*. She just kept coming at us and I felt a little helpless. She caught us near the last mark and rounded it ahead of us by ten seconds. From there, all she had to do was cover us and not make any mistakes. The race went to *America II* by thirty-three seconds.

Although I wanted that race, I didn't feel any great sense of loss. I had known for some time that *Stars & Stripes* needed to somehow find some downwind speed if we were going to win the America's Cup. But I was pleased with our upwind speed, which I believed would be a far more important factor in the long run. We had sailed well and I didn't detect any problems with our crew work. Kolius had sailed well and the better boat—that is, the better boat on that particular day—had won.

When New Zealand showed up at the 12-meter World Championships with two fiberglass boats, it created something of a sensation. Word immediately spread about the "plastic fantastics," and when they both performed well, novices began questioning why no one else had ever thought of the idea. While many, many boats have been built of fiberglass, the New Zealanders were the first to do so in a 12-meter.

The theory behind the benefits of fiberglass construction is that it allows the boat to be stiffer and lighter. These are extremely desirable characteristics. Stiffness—particularly in the conditions we all expected and later experienced on Gage Roads—was sought by most designers preparing for this regatta. One of the disadvantages of conventional aluminum construction (which nearly every boat except *New Zealand* had) is that in heavy seas the boat would bend. In effect, the bow and stern rise up a fraction, lessening the tension on the forward and aft mast stays. Thus, when the sails slackened just a hair, they would spill wind—not much, but just enough to disrupt the steady flow so that there was no strong, consistent force against them. To address this problem, our design team developed a special longitudinal framing system for our aluminum boat that they thought would be even stiffer than glass. Fiberglass had been considered for 12-meter construction for decades, but it was never used for several reasons, chief among which was probably cost. Another was that aluminum can be continuously changed and reshaped, cut and welded as the boat is optimized during a campaign while fiberglass is not so malleable.

The ingeniousness of the Kiwi design program lay not so much in their use of fiberglass, but in their use of the same mold to build two identical boats. These became floating laboratories, for every time any change was made to either, the other stood as a test. Change the rig on one, you know immediately if it makes the boat slower or faster. Same with a new keel, different sails, more ballast, less equipment, whatever. The Kiwis had done Dennis one better! I began the concept of "leap-frogging"—that is, using trial horses to test different concepts —but the tests couldn't be 100 percent accurate because the boats always started out different. But with two identical boats, there were no inherent differences, so what you saw was what you got.

The major reason fiberglass is used for building ocean racers is that a lighter structure is possible. But this is not legal in twelves, where glass construction must be the same weight as aluminum. From what I saw in Fremantle, I wasn't sure New Zealand's glass boat was carefully enough measured to ensure the hull was as heavy as required. All design and construction in the 12-meter class is supervised and continuously monitored by Lloyd's Register of Shipping, the great maritime concern in England. They have established specifications that must be adhered to in the construction of any 12-meter. Many aspects of the boat are covered by these specifications: weight, rigidity, length, girth, size of scantlings, and so on. They also control the specific gravity of the ballast and the types of materials that can be used in the hull and deck.

When we arrived in Fremantle and *Stars & Stripes* underwent her official measurement, we noticed that the measurement did not include inspection of two points we believed to be critical in determining if a boat, made of fiberglass, was a legal 12-meter. These two points were the calculation of the exact lengthwise weight distribution and the vertical center of gravity to ensure they were identical to the aluminum standard as the rules require. The next day Malin Burnham

wrote a letter to Commandante Gianfranco Alberini of the Yacht Club
Costa Smeralda, the Challenger of Record with jurisdiction over all
matters concerning the Challenger races. The letter read, in part: "We
request that the Lloyd's surveyor take core samples of all composite-
construction yachts to ensure that the laminate meets the 'as built'
Lloyd's specifications."

By the time we were scheduled to meet the Kiwis on the race course,
more than a month after Malin wrote the letter, the press had blown
our so-called protest way out of proportion. In an attempt to resurrect
the controversies of 1983, this issue was labeled "glassgate" and Sail
America was portrayed as trying to get the Kiwi boat disqualified
because they were winning all their races and winning in grand style.
The truth is that we asked for a clarification on this matter before the
competition had even begun. We had every right to do so under the
rules and when we did, we had no idea the New Zealanders would be
undefeated going into our race.

What we wanted to make sure of was that the fiberglass construction had not enabled the Kiwi boat to be built legally light in the ends.
While the weight of the entire boat might meet specifications, if that
weight was packed in the middle leaving the bow and stern lighter
than other 12-meters, the Kiwis would enjoy an enormous illegal
advantage. A boat light in the bow would take the waves on Gage
Roads a lot easier than a conventional twelve. Without the proper
weight, the bow would not be submerged as much as a bow with
weight. Thus the waves would not slow down the Kiwis as much.

The scribes went to work saying here goes paranoid Dennis again.
They wrote that since we didn't come up with the wing keel we tried
to get that declared illegal, and now that we didn't have a fiberglass
boat we wanted the Kiwis tossed out. They charged this incident was
reminiscent of old New York Yacht Club tactics of changing the rules
to protect the Defender.

I didn't help our case any when at a press conference (the issue was
being discussed ad nauseum) I piped up with my most regrettable
quote: "The last seventy-eight 12-meters built around the world have
been built in aluminum so why would you build one in fiberglass
unless you wanted to cheat?" Even before the words were out, I
regretted them. I've eaten my share of shoe leather over the years for
things I've said, but there are still times I can't keep my foot out of
my mouth.

"Glassgate's" final chapter was a meeting where twelve of the thirteen Challengers (Blackaller failed to attend the meeting) voted on a proposal drawn up by Sail America to amend Rule 24 to permit accurate resurveying of all hulls. The motion failed by one vote. Our last real recourse was gone.

I still feel pretty strongly about this issue, but I suppose my concern is more philosophical than practical. I was disappointed in the results of the "secret" ballot not so much because I believed the Kiwi boat was illegal or that they purposely tried to cheat, but because I felt this type of control on glass boats would be necessary to ensure the future of the 12-meter class. I wanted to establish a sense of fair play by which core samples would have been taken from all the boats. Notwithstanding the Lloyd's certificates that the New Zealanders were given, I think anyone who has had anything to do with fiberglass construction knows that it is impossible to verify density and weight distribution in a glass hull without taking core samples.

Regardless of what was going on on land, we knew that to win the Cup we'd have to beat the Kiwis on the water. When we met them for the first time, their boat, which was variously called *New Zealand*, *Kiwi Magic*, and *K-Z 7*, was undefeated. They had beaten *America II*, the only boat to beat us so far. The race looked to be a real shoot-out.

The starting gun went off in 22 knots of wind, which certainly was our type of weather. *Stars & Stripes* liked robust conditions and on the first leg, she performed well. Again, the boat had been designed to produce straight-line speed and here was a perfect example of why I had made that a priority. The Kiwis were used to rocketing out in front on the first beat and then staying there for the rest of the race. Looking at *Stars & Stripes*'s stern was a completely new view for them. When we rounded the first mark one minute seven seconds ahead, I felt we had established our speed superiority and that the Kiwis might not have known what hit them.

But the race wasn't over, and I had to admire the way Chris Dickson and his crew kept coming after us. Like my guys, Dickson had a boatful of believers who weren't going to quit until they crossed the finish line. Although on that day we had better speed both upwind and down, Dickson put on a charge during the third beat that almost caught us. The Kiwis picked up a minute on that leg and as we rounded the mark, our lead had shrunk to just eighteen seconds. We picked up another thirteen seconds on the square run to give us some breathing room as we headed for home, but Dickson kept coming. We applied a loose cover on the final beat as our speed held up on this leg.

We got to the line forty-nine seconds in front of the New Zealanders to hand them their first defeat. That loss was the last those guys experienced for the next twenty-eight races.

I was impressed by Dickson, his boat, and his crew. I felt that night that we would come up against them in the finals, but obviously there was a lot of racing before then. We had to score enough points in Robin Round II (five points for each victory) and Round Robin III (twelve points for each victory) to get into the semifinals before we could start thinking about whom we might meet in the finals. Even so, I had a premonition it would be a *Stars & Stripes/Kiwi Magic* finale.

At the press conference, Dickson showed a little of his humor and style. I'd been asked to give my comments on the race and after I gave a rundown, Chris took the microphone and said, "It was painful enough losing the race and just as painful to listen to it all over again. Actually, I thought *Stars & Stripes* looked a bit light in the ends." After the laughter subsided, I smiled as I said, "We'll take core samples." I appreciated Dickson's humor. It took a little of the sting out of the way the press had handled "glassgate."

Round Robin I ended with *Stars & Stripes*, *New Zealand*, and *America II* at the top of the heap with 11–1 records. The three of us had lost only to each other, so at that point it looked like we were the class of the fleet. But I still felt there were some surprises in store for those who counted out boats like *USA*, *White Crusader*, and *French Kiss*. And I was still skeptical about *America II*.

Between the first and second round robins, most boats went into the shed for alterations. The only time throughout the regatta substantial changes could be made was between rounds, not during racing periods. It seemed everyone had a little different theory as to how to prepare for what we all thought would be heavier winds and bigger seas in November. *Heart of America* added 1,000 pounds of ballast, while *Eagle* removed some of hers. *America II* shipped in from Connecticut still another keel costing about $20,000 to build and about $120,000 to air-freight. Other boats had rudders changed, rigging moved, and sail area increased or decreased all in an effort to find the optimum mode.

Stars & Stripes was reballasted and twenty inches were added to her stern overhang. We still needed increased speed in lighter winds and some help on the square runs, but our aim in adding ballast and length was to increase our waterline and stability for heavier air. We were very comfortable against the others in the heavy air in October, but we felt these changes would take us even further in the right direction. Unfortunately, if anything, they slowed us down even more in the lighter winds that prevailed in the opening races of the second round and we didn't really need the extra heavy air speed.

I also found myself in a bit of a tactical mess between the rounds. We were still hurting for money and I was asked to return to San Diego for a few fund-raisers. Before I left we had the draw for Round Robin II and it couldn't have been more favorable. Our first race was scheduled against *Challenge France* and then we had a lay-day. This relatively easy setup meant that I could spend some time pressing flesh for bucks in the States and return a couple of days before we were to meet *Challenge France*, which had won only two races in the first dozen.

However, what I didn't anticipate was the announcement by the *Courageous* syndicate that they would drop out of the competition. That meant that there would be a new draw and with the number of contenders reduced to an even twelve, there would be no automatic lay-days. So while I was in San Diego, news arrived that our first race would be against *USA*—news that didn't particularly cheer me. I returned to Fremantle just two days before the race, which didn't give me much time to get over jet lag, to gauge how the changes affected *Stars & Stripes*, and to prepare for Blackaller and his boys.

But even with this minor change in plans, I could never have foreseen the near-disaster that the November races brought.

8

●●●●●●●●●●●●●●● ★ ●●●●●●●●●●●●●●●

Waiting for
the Doctor

●●●●●●●●●●●●●●●●●●●●●●●●●●

WHEN we met Blackaller and the "banshee boys" for the second time, the conditions were miserable for us. The wind never got over 10 knots and most of the time it was in the 4–7 knot range and very shifty. I wasn't totally used to the feel of the boat after her changes, I was frustrated by the weather, and now I had to go through the blue movie/drums-in-the-jungle routine the *USA* crowd featured in their weak attempt to rattle us. I wasn't particularly overjoyed with the afternoon's prospects.

During the prestart, I noticed that *USA* was turning a little better than the first time we raced her. I figured they must have worked on their steering system between the rounds and maybe they had done something to the keel and rudders. It also may have been that Tom was getting more used to the boat.

In any case, we got the start by two seconds, but *USA* was going a little faster to leeward, in clean air. We both started up the course on port tack, looking for shifts and trying to get the boats up to full speed. *Stars & Stripes* seemed to have a little better sail trim and we definitely got the better of the shifts. About nineteen minutes after the start, we crossed well ahead of *USA* and I began feeling maybe the afternoon wouldn't be so bad after all.

But then our luck changed. Tom caught a massive wind shift, as much as 30 to 35 degrees, which we didn't catch. That allowed him to make the layline without any further tacking, while we had to tack twice to reach it. Since *USA* didn't have to maneuver—they were headed directly for the mark—*Stars & Stripes* lost more time. Whenever you tack you slow down, and if you tack and your opponent doesn't, you invariably lose time. This change of fortune cost us the lead and ultimately left us fifty seconds behind. We had a real race on our hands now. The light air was killing us, and I knew *USA*'s keel and rudders would produce less drag downwind than our keel configuration. All we could do was keep our heads down, work like hell, and hope for a break or two. Three would be better.

If the psychological makeup of our guys and their skipper had been different this might have been the perfect time to begin some sort of war chant like "Remember the first race, remember the first race." We don't go in for that type of stuff. My men know what they have to do, what's expected of them, what I believe is necessary to win. A cheerleader I'm not, but I will admit that first race against *USA* did cross my mind more than once.

There was no doubt *USA* was showing some real speed in this race. Blackaller was more comfortable with the steering, the crew work was good, and the boat seemed to like the conditions. We just kept after them.

On the run, *USA* maintained her lead but we started picking up a second here and a second there. This was somewhat encouraging for us because *Stars & Stripes* hadn't previously shown much on the runs. She certainly didn't like the conditions, and *USA* should have added on time because of the drag factor. As Blackaller said later at the press conference, "*USA* is faster downwind because we're not dragging all those silly wings through the water."

Actually, at the bottom mark we got back eleven seconds because we hit a few shifts perfectly. Now we were thirty-nine seconds behind and it was time to shift gears. We excelled on this second beat. The guys did everything right; every tack was a lesson in perfection. They whipped the mainsail and jib from port to starboard and back again with maniacal frenzy. *Stars & Stripes* went in and out of each tack without much loss of speed and then accelerated quickly. We got the shifts, maybe every one of them, before *USA* saw what was happening. We were always in the right place at the right time. All this, the hard work and the good fortune, paid off handsomely. We caught

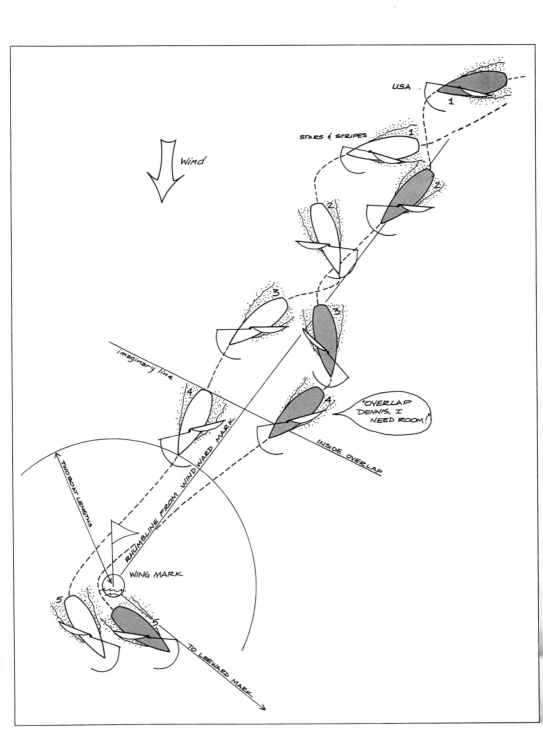

Blackaller near the mark when we got a good puff and we were able to pass him to windward, inside of him. The third mark was ours by fourteen seconds.

On the reach, *USA* started coming back. Tommy began throwing jibes at us, and we had to cover. There was no doubt *USA* was quicker in these maneuvers than *Stars & Stripes*. Their steering had definitely been improved.

With about 600 feet to go to the wing mark, Blackaller had worked himself into an attacking position. Remember that the boat behind, if it is within striking range, has the advantage on off-wind legs. *USA* was within striking range and Tommy made his move. First he steered high on our stern quarter, placing him closer to the wind as he approached from behind and forcing us to go with him, off the layline, to keep our wind clear. When we were a little out of position, *USA* jibed short of the mark, forcing us into a sequence of two protective jibes. *USA* was quicker, she accelerated faster out of the jibes, and at the wing mark Blackaller grabbed the inside overlap.

The inside overlap is nirvana to the match-racing helmsman, as well as the source of many protests. The racing rule that covers this situation is the International Yacht Racing Rule 42.1. An inside overlap occurs when the trailing yacht crosses an imaginary line between his bow and his opponent's transom and is able to come between the mark and the opponent just before the yachts approach the mark. The operative words here are "just before." The rule states that the outside yacht must give an inside overlapping yacht room to round the mark. But it also states that the yacht claiming the inside overlap has the onus of proving she achieved that overlap more than two boat-lengths from the mark. We thought a rule had been broken and so raised a protest flag.

During the second reach, *USA* did everything right and just walked away from us. She built her lead to fifty-five seconds and looked to be in perfect position to put the hammerlock on us. We weren't dead yet as we bit off eighteen seconds on the third beat, but that's about as close as we could get. Blackaller covered our every move from there on out, and won the race by thirty-nine seconds.

Our last hope, the jury room, was no more forgiving than *USA* had been on the course—we lost both a lot of sleep and the protest. We

Opposite: **Round Robin II, first race, November 1986. After successive jibes (1–2–3), *USA* (4) grabs the inside overlap and is now entitled to room at the mark to round as the inside yacht.**

were unable to convince the jury the inside overlap occurred closer to the mark than the prescribed two boat-lengths. In fact, the official findings from the jury in their Protest Case Number 13 read, "At more than three boat-lengths from the mark, US 61 established an inside overlap after a series of gybes by both yachts. Outside the two-boat-length circle US 61 achieved a mast-abeam position, and so hailed. US 61 also hailed for room at the mark. The yachts then rounded the mark overlapped with US 61 inside. US 61 then warned US 55 that she still had her continuing rights under the earlier mast-abeam position. US 55 bore away and protested. *Conclusion:* No rule infringed by either yacht. *Decision:* Protest dismissed." The incident further proved my theory that no matter how right you think you are, your chances are never better than fifty/fifty when you try to win a yacht race on land.

So with one loss in one race in the second round robin, we had the unenviable task of facing the Kiwis on the second day. Our fortunes had certainly changed in the past two weeks. This was supposed to be our lay-day after an easy win against *Challenge France*.

Our "lay-day" turned out to be cool, wet, and windy, just the opposite of the day before. The weather in Fremantle fits that old saying about New England: "If you don't like the weather, just wait a minute." The past twenty-four hours had been a perfect example of that. The "Fremantle Doctor," the southwest wind that usually comes in off the sea after noon on hot summer days to cool the city off, was howling on this day at about 23 knots true.

There was a nasty, choppy, short sea and the air was cold and wet with thunderstorms banging around overhead. The conditions reminded me of the annual Fastnet Race off the coast of England, which seems to always attract the worst weather.

We got to the course about an hour before the races were scheduled to start. Our race versus the Kiwis was actually the third after *America II* against *Azzurra* and *French Kiss* vs. *Heart of America*. We tuned up against any boat we could find and we blew them away—*Azzurra*, *Canada II*, *French Kiss*. We began getting psyched up. Our loss the day before hadn't bothered us at all because we knew our boat just wasn't designed to do well in light air. Today we had our type of wind and we could feel *Stars & Stripes* kicking up her heels.

We were ready. The guys were psyched, the boat was fast, the skipper was eager. Then *America II* drove by the committee boat to request a postponement of her race because of a breakdown. The committee granted the request, which meant our race would be delayed as well. During the first three round robins, because of the number of Challengers in contention, as many as four races were run on three different courses each day. They were usually started about twenty minutes apart. I didn't like this delay. If we were pushed back too far, we stood the chance of racing in dying winds. Nothing could be worse than going against the Kiwis in light air with leftover seas. Their boat, light in the ends or not, would eat us alive in that type of weather.

We drove by the committee boat and began razzing the members. Working on the principal you see in American sports when the coach constantly complains to the referee or umpire in hopes of just one favorable call, we started yelling, "What are you guys doing, waiting for the winds to die? Why are you permitting delaying tactics today? Should we go back to shore and buy some lights for our night race?" The committee seemed a bit flustered and, after a brief meeting, they signaled *America II* that only a fifteen-minute delay would be allowed.

But once they got *America II* and *Azzurra* off, the committee was faced with another request for delay, this time from Buddy Melges on *Heart of America* who had experienced some gear breakage. When *French Kiss* was told of the request, they refused the delay. We cheered them on. But then just one minute before the ten-minute gun, the committee called us on the radio and informed us the representative from *French Kiss* had now agreed to the delay. This news was met with anything but good cheer aboard *Stars & Stripes*, yet apparently our razzing tactics had paid off. The committee agreed to allow our race to start.

As *Stars & Stripes* and *New Zealand* prepared for the race to begin, the wind increased to 26 knots. I had the guys set the number-five jib and just about the time it was hoisted, the wind dropped to 22. When it didn't pipe up again, we realized we were about to enter the starting arena under the wrong jib. Panic broke out on the foredeck as we scrambled to change the number five to a number four. The five was dropped, we entered the starting area, and Dickson sensed our vulnerability and immediately came after us.

So there we were with no headsail and the *KZ-7* chasing the *US-55*. He showed no mercy, just as I wouldn't have when I was twenty-five (in fact, today was Chris's birthday). We were in a precarious position. The kid had all his guns loaded while the old man was still searching for the right holster. *New Zealand*, with her greater speed and maneuverability, had a perfect opportunity to put herself in position to foul us out. She could achieve this by obtaining right of way and then, with her greater speed, maneuver into position where we couldn't avoid a collision. I ran downwind and *KZ-7* pursued. He came at us, we barely avoided him, and then he turned for us again. The foredeck was exploding in frenzy, my guys trying to get the new jib up. Dickson came at us, the guys raced to the mast, grabbed the halyard, yanked it down as the sail went up. Halyard around winch, tailers pulling, grinders flailing their arms in a circular motion, trying to find the speed of light. The jib was finally set and we were up to speed, able to wriggle off the hook at just the right moment.

Now the shifts starting coming. With two minutes to go to the gun, the wind went left 30 degrees, favoring the left side of the course. Both the old man and the kid pointed their bows toward the pin end and the race was on. *Stars & Stripes* ended up to leeward and ahead of *New Zealand*. We had right of way. The old man had turned the tables and now the kid was in trouble. He could have driven underneath me, but he knew we were close to the layline for the top mark, so if I drove him lower he would eventually have to tack to lay the mark. The left side, where we were, was so favored that even if *New Zealand* had won the start by a considerable margin, *Stars & Stripes* would still have been in control.

As it was, we won the start because of perfect timing. When I got in the position I wanted, I was moving a little too fast for the time we had left before the gun. I simply luffed up to slow down a little, and Dickson tried to force us over the starting line or to fall below the layline. But when we cranked in the sails and got up to speed, we hit the start right at the gun. Official time: *Stars & Stripes* won start by three seconds.

Dickson's only move was to tack and he took it. The wind soon shifted again, so we tacked and crossed the Kiwis by three boat-lengths. So far we had sailed flawlessly, caught the shifts, positioned ourselves perfectly, and had our speed working for us. We were looking very good.

Then everything changed. I checked the compass, looked for the mark, then asked Pedro (Peter Isler), the navigator, if what I thought to be true was so. He sighted the mark and confirmed we were only about 5 degrees from laying the mark. Normally, I would have protected the left side because it was favored, but now, because we were almost on the layline, I took the right side and let Chris have the left. Then the wind turned further and further left until Tom Whidden told me it had gone so far left that we had overstood the mark. Both *Stars & Stripes* and *New Zealand* tacked and we found ourselves now reaching for the mark at 30, 40, 50 degrees due to the shifts.

Suddenly disaster struck. Huge seas were coming at us from the direction of the mark and enormous waves began breaking over the bow. Tons of water started cascading into the cockpit, which soon filled up. At one point I was standing knee-deep in the stuff. The water slowed us down and *New Zealand* came abeam. Our boat felt water-logged. I couldn't figure out why all the water wasn't draining, but I did know the boat wasn't performing like it should.

The wind had now shifted so far we actually needed a spinnaker on the first beat, but we weren't organized and the spinnaker didn't fill. *KZ-7* immediately took advantage by getting on top of us and taking our wind. The weather wasn't getting any better either. Squalls were coming through now with wind gusts of up to 30 knots. Finally we got our chute set and then a gust hit the kid and ripped his spinnaker to shreds. We quickly attempted to seize the moment, but *Stars & Stripes* just wasn't cooperating and we couldn't get through the Kiwis' lee. They set another chute and soon that blew out too. We were being given chance after chance, but we couldn't get by. It was like a night-mare. I just couldn't figure out why we couldn't get going.

Later, we discovered that when the wind had shifted so much to turn the first beat into a reach and we took on all that water, some computer chips from our wind instruments had floated out and got clogged in the cockpit drains. We continued the race with thousands of pounds of water ballast on board and never got rid of it.

Even with all the extra weight, we began clawing back. When we came onto the reach, which the wind shifts had now turned into a run, *KZ-7* rounded the mark about eight boat-lengths in front, but the boat was a little low. When we came into the reach we had a near-perfect chute set and were able to get up on the Kiwis' wind. Slowly we began gaining, gaining, gaining. Then the kid made a rare mistake. Instead of fighting us off his wind, he jibed into even deeper trouble. I think he got confused because all the shifts had turned the course inside out, but by the time he recovered and jibed back, I had established mast-abeam on him. This term, also a favorite among match-racing skippers, is pretty self-evident. Technically, mast-abeam occurs when the trail-ing boat's mast is abreast of the helmsman on the leading boat. The trouble in this case was that with the wind so far aft, *New Zealand* ended up with an inside overlap on us at the mark.

As we finished our starboard reach and rounded the wing mark to begin the course's port reach, our foredeck crew had raised a new jib out of the sewer and had placed it on the deck, ready to be hoisted in case we couldn't hold a reaching spinnaker in the fluky wind. As

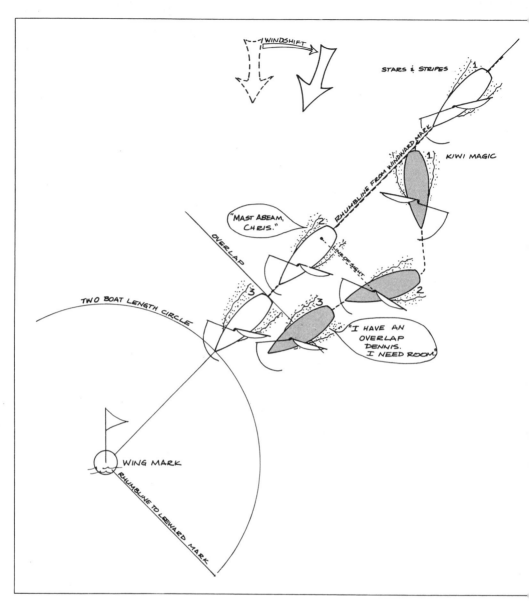

Round Robin II, third race, November 1986. Mast abeam versus inside overlap: *Kiwi Magic* (1) is leading *Stars & Stripes* (1). The Kiwis jibe to starboard (2) as *Stars & Stripes* (2) continues straight toward the mark and gains a "mast abeam" position. (That is, the boat to windward establishes a position where its skipper, sighting from his normal position at the helm, is abreast of the leeward yacht's mast.) Therefore *Kiwi Magic* (2–3) is forced to bear off even though under *other* circumstances the leeward yacht (the Kiwis) would have right of way. But, since the boats are almost at the mark, *New Zealand* can be said to have "inside overlap," And so now *US-SS* must allow *KZ-7* the favored inside position as the two boats round the wing mark.

1. Top Gun. My favorite hat. It was blown overboard during the last Cup race.

2. Malin Burnham, champion sailor, close personal friend, and chairman of Sail America.

3. John Marshall is a fine sailor and administrator. He oversaw the design effort.

4. Left to right, the naval architects of *Stars & Stripes:* David Pedrick, Britton Chance, and Bruce Nelson.

6. Tactician Tom Whidden and I at the post-race press conferences.

5. Jack Sutphen, trial horse skipper and longtime friend.

7. Fritz and Lucy Jewett, two of the first supporters of my bid to win back the Cup.

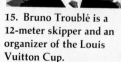

11. Trading looks with Chris Dickson, 25-year-old skipper of New Zealand's *Kiwi Magic.*

8. Harold Cudmore, the expert skipper of Great Britain's *White Crusader.*

9. John Kolius, helmsman for the New York Yacht Club's *America II.*

10. Tom McLaughlin, head of the *America II* syndicate.

15. Bruno Troublé is a 12-meter skipper and an organizer of the Louis Vuitton Cup.

14. Robert Hopkins was a liaison between the sailors and the designers of *Stars & Stripes.*

12. Iain Murray, skipper of the Defender of the America's Cup, *Kookaburra III.*

13. Kevin Parry, who organized and backed the *Kookaburra* syndicate

16. Here, Henri Racamier, head of Louis Vuitton, presents the Challenger trophy.

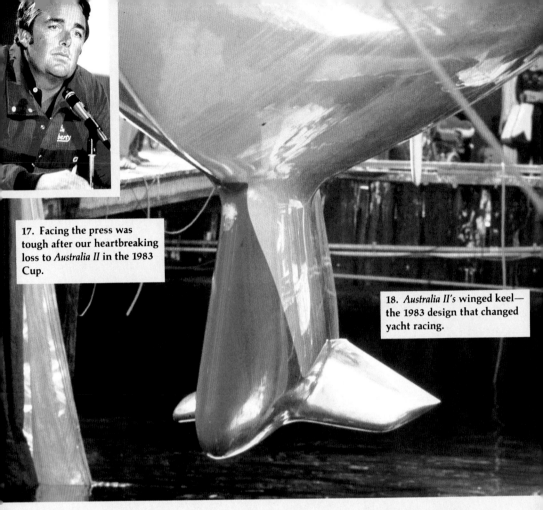

17. Facing the press was tough after our heartbreaking loss to *Australia II* in the 1983 Cup.

18. *Australia II's* winged keel—the 1983 design that changed yacht racing.

19. The class of '87: the challenging skippers, photographed at the Yacht Club Costa Smeralda race headquarters. Seated left to right: Aldo Migliaccio, *Italia*; Mauro Pelaschier, *Azzurra*; Tom Blackaller, *USA*; Harry Cudmore, *White Crusader*; John Kolius, *America II*; Chris Dickson, *New Zealand*. Standing left to right: Dave Vietor, *Courageous*; Dennis Conner; Buddy Melges, *Heart of America*; Marc Pajot, *French Kiss*; Yves Pajot, *Challenge France*; Rod Davis, *Eagle*; Terry Neilson, *Canada II*.

20. For eighteen months before going to Perth, we trained in Hawaii.

21. *Stars & Stripes* training against Great Britain's *White Crusader.*

22. The Aussie fans were great sports throughout the races. Here they give us all a rousing sendoff as *Stars & Stripes '87* (foreground) goes out to train against our trial horse, *Stars & Stripes '85.*

23. *Stars & Stripes '85* crew members give the "mushroom salute."

24. A scouting party. We often sent out our key people to observe rival yachts—their sails, tactics, and performance.

25. *Heart of America* loses a spinnaker and a crewman overboard during the America's Cup trials (see arrow).

27. Riblets: Here you can see the glossy sheets of grooved plastic that we applied to the hull to reduce friction in the water.

26. *Stars & Stripes*, sailing close to the wind.

29. *Kookaburra III* tacks ahead of *Australia IV* in the Defender trials. The Kookas won from Alan Bond's syndicate the right to defend the America's Cup.

28. *America II* reaches the finish of its last race.

30. *Stars & Stripes* drops its spinnaker before rounding a leeward mark in the semifinals against *USA*. Blackaller trails us; his red and white spinnaker can be seen on the right.

31. Here's *Stars & Stripes* coming from behind to overtake *USA*.

32. *Stars & Stripes* (right) leads *USA* (left) on a reach during the semifinals.

37. Live ballast. In Fremantle's strong winds the crew often had to hike outboard to help keep the boat upright as we sailed to windward.

38. Alan Bond's syndicate hid the shape of their keels by covering *Australia IV* (left) and *Australia III* (right) with these green plastic security skirts.

33. *Facing page, top:* Tactician Tom Whidden (left), myself, and mainsheet trimmer Jon Wright (right).

35. *Middle:* In *Betsy,* our tender, we had a support boat big enough to carry every spare part and sail we could possibly need before a race.

36. *Bottom:* Months of training in the heavy seas of Hawaii prepared us for the big waves of Gage Roads.

39. Helmsman Tom Blackaller (right) with his afterguard on *USA.*

40. *Stars & Stripes* leads New Zealand's *Kiwi Magic* downwind during the Challenger finals.

41. *Above: Stars & Stripes* has just rounded the weather mark and is heading downwind during the Challenger finals. White-hulled *New Zealand* is about to do the same. By defeating *New Zealand,* we won the Louis Vuitton Cup and earned the right to challenge Australia's *Kookaburra III* for the America's Cup.

42. *Below:* Australia's *Kookaburra III* trails *Stars & Stripes* through the middle of the spectator fleet before the first race of the America's Cup.

43. Two loyal supporters of *Kookaburra III.*

44. Scott Vogel (in midair) is hauled out to clear the afterguy prior to a spinnaker pole trip.

45. Starting maneuvers prior to Race Two of the America's Cup. *Stars & Stripes* is in the foreground, *Kookaburra III* seeks a controlling position on our stern.

46. During the early part of Race Three for the America's Cup, we ducked behind the stern of *Kookaburra III* and, when the gold Australian boat tacked to cover, we had enough speed to power through their lee.

47. *Kookaburra III* and *Stars & Stripes* sail to windward, hip to hip.

48. *Above:* Concentration.

49. *Facing page:* Spinnaker change. Top to bottom: Peter Isler is ready to take in the spinnaker sheet, I'm driving the boat, Jon Wright trims the mainsheet, tailer Adam Ostenfeld (red cap) trims the guy, tactician Tom Whidden (white cap) has stepped forward to aid grinder James Kavle, tailer Bill Trenkle (all in white) has moved forward to keep an eye on the current spinnaker's trim, pitman Jay Brown (seated) pulls the new spinnaker halyard off the winch, grinder Henry Childers assists, and mastman John Barnitt is on the foredeck helping Scott Vogel prepare the new spinnaker.

50. *Stars & Stripes* wins the America's Cup. This is the moment of truth as we cross the finish line first in the fourth and final race.

Victory

51. After we won, the rest of our crew joined us on the boat.

52. Thousands of people cheered as we entered the harbor under sail.

53. Tracy Aron waves the Stars and Stripes.

54. The crew threw me in. I made sure I was near a raft.

55.

56. The victory celebration at the dock with a fine mist of Moët champagne.

57. Alan Bond and Warren Jones of the *Australia IV* syndicate along with Alan Crewe, Commodore of the Royal Perth Yacht Club, look on during the award ceremony.

58. The crew gathers to receive the America's Cup.

59. I waited four years for this moment.

60. The Prime Minister of Australia, Bob Hawke, hands over the Australian bush hat that he bet against a cowboy hat from President Reagan.

61. San Diego: my hometown victory parade.

62. *Stars & Stripes* supporters. My wife Judy is in the middle row on the right.

63. At the White House with the America's Cup, President Reagan, the hat he won from Prime Minister Hawke, and the crew of *Stars & Stripes*.

64. The ticker tape parade New York's Fifth Avenue w Mayor Ed Koch, Maureen O'Connor, mayor of San Diego, and Donald Trump.

we turned, I tried to jibe around the Kiwis' stern so we could attack from the windward side. But just as we went into the maneuver, an enormous wave smashed into us and ripped the jib right off the foredeck, broke the sail ties, and washed $15,000 worth of sail right into the ocean. I said, "Holy crime in Italy," or something along those lines. "It's too bad to lose the jib but I'm sure glad it wasn't attached to the boat." But just then the boat practically stopped dead in the water, as if someone had slammed on the brakes. The jib had indeed been attached and as it went under, it acted like a huge sea anchor. Scotty leaped to the cleat where the line was attached and hacked at it with a knife. While he cut it loose, I called for our number-five jib, from which we had changed at the start. Unfortunately, the jib wasn't in the turtle because of all the initial confusion, so suddenly half the crew ran forward to get things sorted out.

The guys did a fantastic job and despite all the problems, the second reach was good to us. We rounded the mark only six seconds behind. This was one hell of a race. Both crews were exhausted by now, but neither would rest for a minute.

The Kiwis started pulling out again and before too long they held a five-length lead. But just as it looked like they might run away with the race, fortunes changed once again. Their mainsail came off the track and they had to lower it, then get it up again. Their crew work was superb, but we had gained three boat-lengths.

On the run, all the water in our boat was too much to overcome and we simply weren't competitive. They got back what we had just gained, and when we went into the final beat, they were half a minute in the lead. Our only hope at that point was to institute a tacking duel in an attempt to cause their mainsail to pull loose once more. But the ploy didn't work and because of their maneuverability and our boatful of water, we lost more ground.

But still, the race wasn't over yet. We had the last windward leg ahead of us. About two-thirds of the way to the finish line, their mainsail finally did come out of its groove. Once again, their crew hustled forward to repair the damage and we went after them with everything we had. Full credit goes to the Kiwis' crew work. It was impeccable. But the slight pause in their march home allowed us to pick up a couple of boat-lengths.

Our last resort was to split tacks and hope for a windshift. We went left, they went right, and lo and behold, there was a shift. Unfortunately, it was 20 degrees to the right. They came about onto starboard tack, the shift allowed them to fetch the finish line, and they crossed fifty-eight seconds before we did. The kid pulled it off in a magnificent race and all the old man could do was doff his hat and say, "Good on yer, Chris, and happy birthday."

On the scoreboard, *Stars & Stripes* was sinking fast. Two races before we had been tied for first. Now we were suddenly tied for sixth. While most of the other boats were gobbling up five-point victories, we had added nothing to our first-round score of eleven points.

Our third race promised to change that. Finally we were coming up against *Challenge France*, who still had only two wins to her credit. We had fairly strong winds again, up to about 17 knots, and we were very confident we'd finally get on the scoreboard for this second round.

It really wasn't much of a match. *Stars & Stripes*, in these conditions, was just too powerful for the Frenchmen. We might have pulled off even more of what sailors like to call a "horizon job"—that is, leaving your opponent so far behind all he sees of your boat is a little dot on the horizon—but we jammed the luff on our jib in the feeder so the sail's forward edge froze on us. Hoisting a jib while going downwind can be tricky because it's fairly easy to get two layers of material caught in the feeder, or sail track, which is a metal "tunnel" through which the sail's luff edge travels. That's exactly what happened, and as we approached the mark we couldn't get the jib up and we couldn't get it down. The guys yanked and goaded and kicked, but it wouldn't budge. Finally, we just cut the sail off and stowed it below. That meant that we rounded the mark with no jib up and were forced to use a smaller jib than needed. That type of thing often loses races, but fortunately our opponent wasn't one of the top competitors.

We won the race by 4:51 and it felt good to get back in the win column. That momentum propelled us to substantial victories in the next four races. The winning margins illustrated the superiority of *Stars & Stripes* against the less-competitive boats: *Heart of America* (4:50), *Italia* (5:15), *Eagle* (6:29), and *French Kiss* (2:34).

The eighth race, in which we met *Azzurra*, was noteworthy because it started in another dying wind, and *Stars & Stripes* just wasn't going to get out of bed unless she felt more than 15 knots blowing. We expected the southwesterly "Fremantle Doctor" to make its housecall a little after noon. But apparently it was still on the golf course because the wind stayed out of the east. During the race, as the Doctor tried to make its way to the race course, there were massive windshifts as the easterly finally died out.

Azzurra was a good light-air boat and although we got the start and powered by her, she began gaining on us quickly and our lead of 180 yards was cut to 80. The Italian yacht, known around the docks somewhat uncharitably as "The Blue Rock" because of her speed charactistics, apparently chose this race to try to shed that label. Today she was more like a rolling stone going downhill. As we went into the reaches we were a minute behind, and by the time we got out of the reaches we were two minutes behind. I could see the headlines declaring *Stars & Stripes* would be headed home for Thanksgiving.

Then the Italians made their first mistake. When they rounded the mark, they were able to lay the line on starboard. They tacked, which was the right thing to do, but when we went by their stern on our way to round the mark, we saw that the sea breeze was finally going to fill in, that is, strengthen from the southwest. They should have known that also, and when we did round, they should have tacked again to cover us because we were about to get the stronger wind. Instead, they felt they were going straight for the mark while we were at right angles to it, so they falsely believed they had the far superior position. The breeze did build, which gave us the good position and forced *Azzurra* to pinch up, which slowed her down while she tried to keep on the layline. With our breeze and their slower speed, we gained about a minute.

There was another massive shift of almost 100 degrees, which meant we sailed a sort of great circle route to the next mark. Now that the sea breeze had come in and was up to 17 knots true, *Stars & Stripes* decided she would get out of bed after all and put on a show on the last beat. Rounding the mark, we were about nine and a half lengths behind. With the entire crew concentrating as hard as possible, *Stars & Stripes* was going like a banshee. We closed to eight lengths, then seven, then five, then three. We finally passed *Azzurra* near the finish line and won by a mere thirty-seven seconds. Thanksgiving would have to wait, much to our relief.

With three races remaining in Round Robin II, *Stars & Stripes* was in third place behind *New Zealand* (who hadn't lost since we beat them in the first round) and *America II*. That position was perfect. We had come to Fremantle intent on being one of the top four boats at the end of the three round robins, not necessarily on being in first place. The number of points didn't matter beyond having enough to get into the semifinals.

Our last three races of this round were with *White Crusader*, *Canada II*, and *America II*. All three were strong competitors, and all three were in the hunt for a semifinal berth at that point. While I was confident we could beat each of them if the wind favored us, November had been such a fluky month so far that I wouldn't have wanted to predict anything. I was a little surprised that with so many days of light and very shifty winds, the race committee hadn't postponed more races. There were still nine lay-days left in the round, and I felt that more judicious use of them would have resulted in better and more fair races.

A perfect case in point was our race against *White Crusader*. It should have never been started. In the morning the wind was blowing 15 knots out of the east, similar to the day before when we raced *Azzurra*. The race committee had apparently learned something from that race because it postponed today's race, waiting for the Doctor to arrive. At one o'clock the easterly had died completely. But the Doctor must have been golfing once again because at two there were only 3 knots of breeze, and at three there were only 4. By four o'clock we should have all been at the Norfolk (a favorite Fremantle drinking establishment frequented by both racers and racer-chasers) having a beer. But the committee decided to change the course to just 9 miles, instead of the full America's Cup course of 24.3 miles. With nine lay-days at the ready, I thought this was a ridiculous decision.

Like it or not, we had to race. During the starting sequence, the wind shifted 30 degrees to the left, and I could see that Harold Cudmore was no more pleased with the situation than I was. We got a nice start a little in front of his bow and forced him to the right. We stayed left and got another shift, and after two minutes we tacked and found ourselves laying the mark. Harold was to leeward on the outside of a 7-degree lift, gaining bearing and hauling the mail. He gained 17 degrees of bearing, allowing him to point more directly at the mark than he had before, but because we had quite an advantage as a result of being two minutes to his left, we went most of the way to the mark relatively even. Toward the end the wind died where we were but he found enough to get him around the mark forty-four seconds in front of us.

Although the second leg was supposed to be a run—where we may have had a chance to attack—the wind had shifted to make it a reach. *White Crusader* picked up a lot of time on the leg, and by the time we rounded the mark to head for home on the shortened course, we were facing a deficit of one minute seventeen seconds. On the beat back up, we threw tack after tack at Harold, hoping to get him out of phase (tacking out of sync with wind shifts), cause a gear breakage, or disrupt him in any way we could. But Harold has been around quite awhile and as one of the better match-racers in the world, he doesn't fall for much. He covered us well and breezed home with a 2:18 victory.

White Crusader probably would have won on the longer course also, but we would at least have had a fair shot at her. I still get annoyed when I think of that day. Starting a race at four o'clock on a shortened course in 7 knots of wind is no way to run a regatta, especially the America's Cup. Commandante Alberini must have agreed with me because the next day I received a personal note of apology from him. He said he was upset with what had happened and assured me they wouldn't use the short course again.

From *White Crusader* we went to *Canada II*. While we had beat her by two minutes and change in the first round robin, she had shown she was no pushover. Designed by Bruce Kirby, the same man who designed the phenomenally popular *Laser*, *Canada II* wasn't a new boat but an update of *Canada I*, which had raced in 1983. She was in the lower half of the twelve-boat pack, but she had shown bursts of speed and had beat *French Kiss* in the first round. I believed she should be considered dangerous.

The race began in 11 knots of wind. We won the start, and then on the first beat we were a little faster and gaining. Then about six minutes away from the mark, our mainsail came off the hook. The car that takes the mainsail headboard up the mast is affixed with a Teflon slider that smooths the path for the car. Apparently, the lock at the masthead caught only the Teflon slider and not the metal car. The Teflon was attached to the main carriage by four self-tapping screws, and when we started trimming the main, the pressure just sheared those screws right off. The result was that the car slid down the mast about six inches and we had to limp the rest of the way to the mark with a drooping mainsail.

While we were crippled, *Canada II*, with Terry Neilson at the helm, overtook us and rounded the mark thirty-one seconds in front. When we rounded, we hoisted Boo-Boo (Scott Vogel) 90 feet up the mast where he secured himself by using a sail tie. He used the gantline (a line at the top of the mast used for hoisting the main) to pull the main over the outside of the Teflon and then he tied the main tight. We were back in trim, but we had lost about six boat-lengths. *Canada II* had piled on another thirty seconds on the run, so now we were about a minute behind.

The wind picked up about a knot when we were on the second beat and I felt our boatspeed was at least equal to theirs, if not a little faster. Neilson did a nice job of covering us, but near the end of the leg, they let us get to the left right near the mark where we got a nice lift and cut their lead in half. During the two reaches we carved off another seventeen seconds because we had a little better chute, and we had also executed a very nice jibe at the wing mark.

When we rounded the second leeward mark, we were only twenty seconds behind. We were right back in the race. On the third beat we tried to initiate a tacking duel, but they failed to cover as we went to port. Our speed was a good deal more than theirs (officially we recorded 6.13 knots Velocity Made Good to their 6.01), and soon we found ourselves right on their hip. We tacked again, and when we came together we had overtaken them. *Stars & Stripes* led around the mark by eighteen seconds.

We both hoisted our spinnakers, and then halfway down the leg Neilson had gained enough to be right on our stern and to leeward. That meant that when we needed to jibe to starboard, he would be in perfect position to get on our wind.

The tactic I used here is one of my favorites—the fake jibe. Neilson not only took it hook, line, and sinker, he swallowed the fishing pole as well. We squared up with our stern directly into the wind and began trimming in the main, giving the appearance we were about to jibe. Since he was right on top of us, he could see our every move, but I had already warned our guys that this was only a charade. As the main flew across the boat, I yelled "Trip!" supposedly alerting my bowman to trip the end of the spinnaker pole to allow the spinnaker to go from one side to the other as well.

Canada II, believing they would cut us off at the pass, jibed furiously, hoping to get our wind. But as they went through the maneuver, we hardened back up on port and took off in the opposite direction from the Canadians. Presto, they no longer were on our wind. It was a slick move, but it was a shame to use it in a race we eventually lost.

As we rounded the leeward mark the wind went from about 14 knots to 8. We only had an eight-second lead, and as we put up our light number-one jib, we were holding on by the hairs of our chinny, chin, chins. They had the speed now (4.71 Velocity Made Good to our 4.64) and they just kept coming, coming, coming. Near the finish they crossed us by a boat-length and a half. A few minutes later they won one of the biggest races of their lives. We felt we had done a nice job, but in the light stuff it seemed we were driving a truck and they had a Ferrari.

Going into the final race, we had accumulated thirty points in this round and added to the eleventh from the first round. Our forty-one

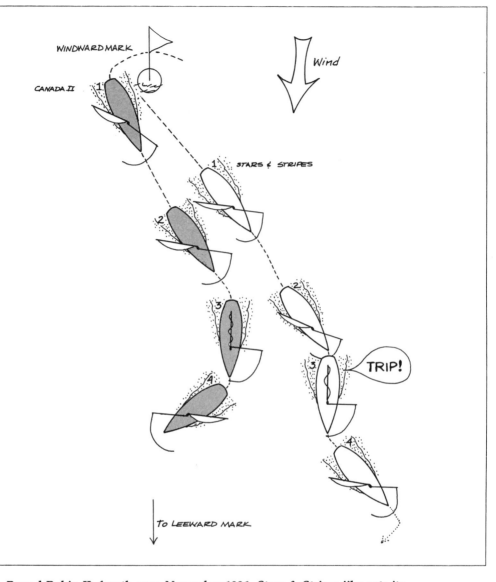

Round Robin II, fourth race, November 1986. *Stars & Stripes* jibe-sets its spinnaker to port (1) 18 seconds ahead of *Canada II* (1). Halfway down the leeward leg, I initiate a fake jibe (2–3) by bringing the boom across the centerline of the boat and loudly calling for bowman Scott Vogel to trip the spinnaker pole. *Canada II* (3) prepares to cover *Stars & Stripes* (3) and quickly completes a jibe to starboard. But *Stars & Stripes* returns to her port jibe, heading off (4) as we had secretly planned. Now we have clear air since on a run downwind the trailing boat (which was *Canada II*) gets the wind first, and so can give the lead boat weak, turbulent air by sailing just up wind of her.

points put us in fourth place. Our last race was against *America II*, which had beat us in the first round and had lost only twice so far, both times to *New Zealand*. Even so, I was confident we could beat them because I sensed those chinks in their armor were about to surface.

The wind was about 22 knots true and the seas were building as we went into the prestart, the time between the ten-minute and start guns during which both boats must enter the starting area. The boundaries are actually imaginary lines forming a triangle with the starting line as the base. *Stars & Stripes* was moving very well and I knew our guys wanted this one badly.

Kolius got the start by nine seconds, but on the first leg we overtook him pretty easily and stayed in front for the entire race. Getting to that first mark with the lead is critical in match-racing—the boat that does so wins something like 90 percent of the time. The story of this race was that we had the speed on the windward legs, *America II* had the speed on the off-wind legs, but because we had the controlling position, we were able to stay in the lead by using sound tactics. Tommy Whidden called another good race and our lead grew from forty-eight seconds at the first mark to one minute fifty-seven seconds at the second windward mark. The official time for our victory, which moved us into third place, was 1:31.

Round Robin II had started out pretty bleak, but ended up rather bright. Although we had five losses, we were still in the top four and that was our goal from the start. I was glad to see the end of November racing because I believed the winds would be more in keeping with the norm—heavy—in December. Of the eleven races we participated in in November, only five were in conditions suited to our design. I looked forward to December. I knew we would do well.

9

●●●●●●●●●●●●●●● ★ ●●●●●●●●●●●●●●

Clockwork

●●●●●●●●●●●●●●●●●●●●●●●●●●●●

GOING into Round Robin III, the top boats were *New Zealand* (sixty-six points), *America II* (fifty-six), *Stars & Stripes* (forty-six), and *French Kiss* (forty-five). *USA* and *White Crusader* were tied for fifth, just one point behind the Frenchmen. The winner collected twelve points now, so the importance of each race was apparent. The number of points awarded the winner of each race in the three round robins had escalated from 1 to 5 and now 12, indicating the premium put on races in Round Robin III.

In our first encounter of the third round, we met *Canada II,* which was greatly improved but still not enough to come close to *Stars & Stripes*. With 19 knots of wind at the start we had the conditions we liked.

We put on our fastest jib, our good main, and we were ready. We went off the line on port tack with them ahead and to leeward. We couldn't sail our own race from there because, under the rules, we had to stay clear of the leeward boat. So we tacked to starboard. They tacked to starboard on our hip, and in five minutes we had gained another boat-length. Now we sailed into a little header. They tacked. We tacked and now we were catching the freshest part of the wind. Pretty soon that meant we were four boat-lengths ahead, then seven, and then nine. They tacked again and we followed.

As we stretched our lead to eleven boat-lengths, we discovered a

121

whole wad of kelp on our rudder. We poked that off with a kelp stick, but in the meantime it cost us about eighteen seconds. After cleaning it, we got rolling again and they fell back a little.

They gained a little on the run, but on the next beat the wind came up a little more and they were out of touch with us. When that happens, the boat astern is unable to do as well because there really aren't too many ways to force any action.

We gained on both the reaches, so as we headed into the wind for the third beat our lead was 1:43, and by the leeward mark we were almost three minutes ahead. On the final beat we poured it on and won by 3:46.

It had been a conservative, easy race for us once we got several minutes ahead and the pressure was off. The win basically put the Canadians out of the series. The way I saw it, they would have had to beat us to qualify, and I didn't think they could do it twice in a row.

The second race of the series was against *America II* and a lot was at stake. It had developed into one of the most eagerly awaited matches of the summer.

We knew we were in for a real blow when we faced the boat from the New York Yacht Club so we put on our heavy-air gear, changed to our heavy-air boom, double-checked everything, went out to the course nice and early, and then wham, the boom came apart down aft with a big horizontal split. What a way to start a big race!

We got the sails down, got the boom off and replaced it with the spare boom off the tender. The guys did a fantastic job in changing the whole thing in just fifteen minutes. It was the first time all summer that our entire program had really come together. It worked like clockwork.

By now it was about eleven-thirty and with an hour and a half to the start, already the breeze was piping in. We checked with Chris Bedford, our weather guru, who said he was absolutely sure it was going to be windier than he had expected, so with that in mind we changed from our medium-heavy main to our heavy-heavy main, which was around fifteen inches short on the foot. Our experience in Hawaii had proved this was the perfect sail for a breeze of 25 and above. We weren't overconfident, but we were praying for the race to start because we knew we were going to be fast.

We believed the left-hand end of the starting line would be favored because due to wind shifts it was closer to the first mark. It was all very conservative with no circling whatsoever. We came around the committee boat, jibed on port, and sailed away from John for three and a half minutes.

With about five minutes to go before the gun, we jibed and headed at him. He jibed to our leeward side and then we powered over the top of him back to his leeward side and got the favored left-hand side, to leeward of *America II*. We now had controlling position and forced him to tack away. We were going 9 knots and when we hardened up, we had a three-boat-length lead immediately. Kolius was going a little higher and slower, and we just sailed on the numbers the computer gave us as the ideal course and speed. Pretty soon the lead was six lengths and that turned to eight. *Stars & Stripes* was moving today.

We rounded the first mark with a comfortable 1:36 lead. At that stage it was blowing 26 true and since I felt the race was all but over, we just sailed conservatively from there on.

We both set big spinnakers for the run and *America II* picked up about five seconds. On the second beat we used a little smaller jib which causes less heel than a larger jib. *Stars & Stripes* was flatter in the water and therefore faster. and gained more than a minute. For the reaches we set a small, heavy chute, and to make sure we didn't break down we hardly pulled the boom vang on and hardly touched the mast. We didn't even think of opening the zipper most 12-meter mainsails carry today. This device allows more sail area and is usually used on downwind legs. It may have added a bit of speed on the runs, but many boats experienced problems with jammed zippers.

At that point, in that kind of wind, it was a matter of keeping the boat together. The wind was gusting and the seas were building. *Stars & Stripes* was smashing through waves and great mists of spray surrounded us.

We executed a slow, methodical takedown and set the jib early coming into the mark. Everything we did was calculated to keep the guys on board and to minimize the possibility of breakages. Because Kolius was feeling the pressure so far back, he left his spinnaker up too long in trying to get the last bit of speed he could. The result was that he went around the mark without his jib up. That gave us another thirty seconds to add to our lead.

On the run things fell apart for *America II*. A big wave washed one of their guys over the side. The man-overboard drill was quickly executed by dousing their spinnaker and turning all the way around to fish the swimmers out of the drink. Obviously that cost them a lot of time and I imagine the crew must have been pretty upset. The dry members were probably thinking, "What are those guys doing in the damn water? This is the most important race of our lives. How'd this happen?" Kolius was probably worried about facing heavies when he saw Bill Packer's *Scotch Mist*, used by the New York

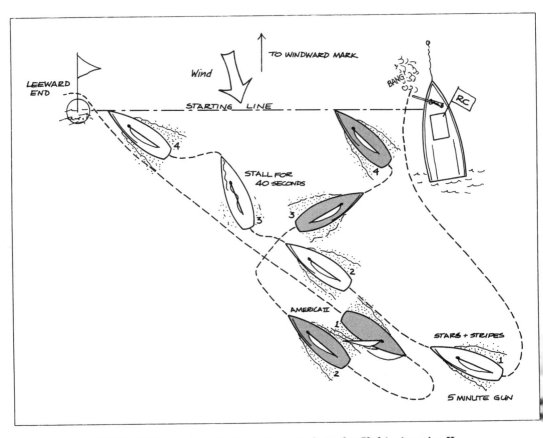

Round Robin III, December 1986, vs. New York Yacht Club's *America II*.
Starting maneuvers. One of the basic truths in racing is that one prefers to
cross the starting line on starboard tack, which gives one right of way. If you
cross on starboard, the buoy marking the port end of the line will be to
leeward, and so that is called the "leeward end" even if a windshift has placed
that end closest to the wind.

When the starting line for this race was set, it was as usual (a) set
perpendicular to the direction of the wind and (b) perpendicular to the shortest
distance (called the rhumb line) to the first mark. But, as often happens, the
wind shifted (see diagram). This meant the boat starting at the leeward end
would be able to sail a quicker route to the mark on the first beat to
windward.

With five minutes to go before the start, *Stars & Stripes* jibes around (1) and
heads toward *America II* (1). *America II* also jibes to starboard (2), but *Stars &
Stripes* powers over her (2) into a controlling position. *America II* tacks to port
(2–3), then tacks back to cross the starting line at the committee boat (4). *Stars
& Stripes* continues on starboard, heads into the wind and luffs up to stall for
40 seconds (3), then bears off to a close-hauled course (4) to cross at the
favored leeward end at the starting gun.

syndicate as their VIP spectactor boat, headed back to the dock early in a huff.

By this time we were over a mile ahead so we took our chute down and sailed the rest of the run bare-headed. You don't get extra points for finishing a race a mile ahead. Our thirteen-minute (!) win would count the same as a one-second thriller, so we just concentrated on good and safe seamanship. Besides, at that point we probably could have beat them even without a mainsail.

My attitude is usually to keep pouring it on, but you have to be smart about these things and to keep pushing would not have been smart. If anything, I wanted to keep going on the lifts and wait until we were headed before tacking, regardless of what *America II* was trying. But the smart money says you keep going with them. You don't add too much to your lead, but you make sure they can't pass you. I had to control my normal instinct that demands, "When they're down, jump on them."

Crew morale was especially high after that win but I try to control my highs and lows, so for me it was just another day at the office. There really wasn't very much to it. I made a good choice of the mainsail and we got a good start, but after that there were a thousand people who could have sailed that boat. She was a machine. *Stars & Stripes* was coming into her own. I just got her speed to 8.3 knots and off she went.

With that smashing victory we earned second place. The third race pitted us against *New Zealand*, number one in the standings and still unbeaten since we had taken them on October 17, some forty-eight days before.

This was the closest, most exciting race of the series so far. The wind was blowing between 23 and 25 knots, which meant in many ways the conditions were similar to both our other races with the Kiwis.

Stars & Stripes was to leeward of *New Zealand* as we approached the starting line, which meant they had to stay clear of me wherever I steered. I tried to luff and force the Kiwis over the line early, but they had a little more room than I anticipated that allowed them to move immediately into a controlling position. We went into a flurry of short tacks that ended with the Kiwis having to break off with a fouled jib sheet. That allowed us to find clear air, and from then on it became a boatspeed test for the rest of the first leg.

The two boats looked pretty even. In fact, our Velocity Made Good (VMG)—which is a precise measurement of speed over distance taking into account such factors as current, leeway speed, and course sailed

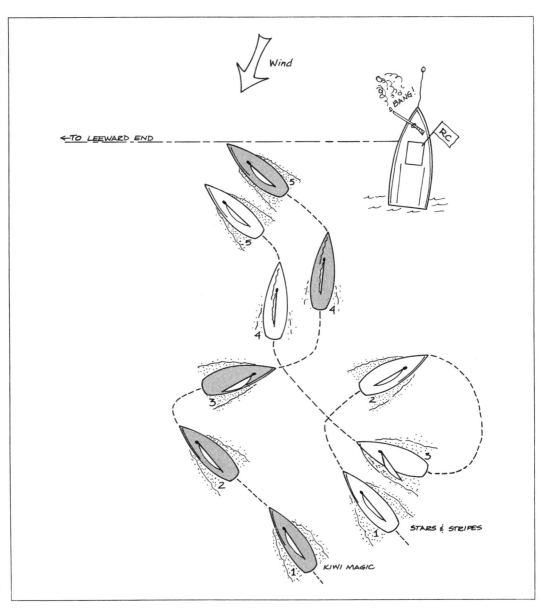

Round Robin III, December 1986, vs. New Zealand's *Kiwi Magic*. Approaching the starting line early, *Stars & Stripes* does a circle to kill time (1–3) as *Kiwi Magic* tacks across and gains a controlling position.

—was an identical 6.31 for the entire beat. Approaching the mark we tacked on the leeward bow of *KZ-7* so we would be on the starboard layline. We anticipated a tack from them, but they kept on going and drove over the top of us.

They made it to the mark first by fifteen seconds. We had a good spinnaker set and again we got to leeward of *New Zealand*. We felt our speed had increased downwind, which was very refreshing. As we continued the run, we caught up and soon established an overlap and with it grabbed the controlling position.

Now *New Zealand* pulled in their mainsail in order to slow down so she could attack across our stern. Both boats jibed onto port tack with *Stars & Stripes* now in the lead. The breeze was at about 25 knots and *New Zealand*'s Kevlar spinnaker halyard snapped at the turning block, which allowed us to get a few more boat-lengths ahead. They repaired their damage quickly, but we stayed in front almost the whole run. Then as we approached the mark, needing to douse the spinnaker and raise the jib, our guys had difficulty on the foredeck. The spinnaker was slow in coming down. The Kiwis charged after us and established an inside overlap near the buoy which forced us to let them pass inside of us as we both rounded the leeward mark. They took the mark by ten seconds.

We initiated a tacking duel and it took us almost half the second beat to shake ourselves free. *KZ-7* seemed to be tacking a little bit better than we were. Their speed was just about equal to ours. The two factors meant New Zealand stretched their lead to thirty seconds at the weather mark.

Neither boat gained nor lost anything on the two reaches. My guess is that there wasn't a boat-length added or lost for the entire 4.6 miles.

The heat was really on. Both boats were sailing superbly, no mistakes, no problems. If we eased a bit ahead now, they got it back later. This was the way we progressed up the third beat as well. We sailed virtually all the way up that leg in clean air, but we weren't able to haul them back much. *New Zealand* was the lead boat and if the lead boat sails well on the shifts, she will maintain control. *KZ-7* covered our every move and held us off.

With two legs to go, we were still twenty-nine seconds behind, but on that last run we got *Stars & Stripes* moving very well. We got on the Kiwis' wind and reduced their lead to just twelve seconds. But as we headed into the mark we couldn't establish an inside overlap and I was unable to pull any tricks. Once we had rounded, they just kept tacking

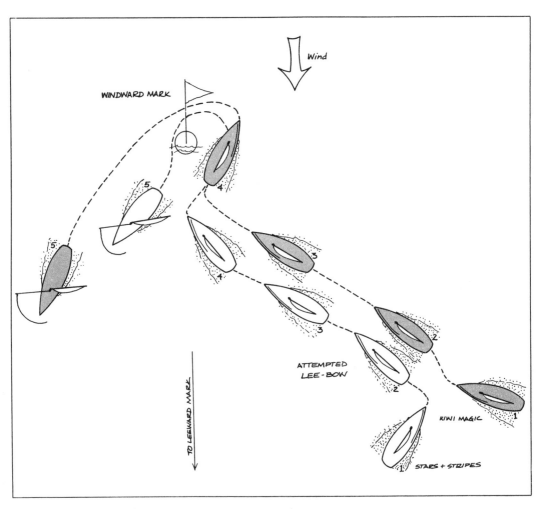

Round Robin III, December 1986, vs. New Zealand's *Kiwi Magic*. *Stars &
Stripes* tacks to try to lee-bow *Kiwi Magic* (1–2) near the starboard layline. To
lee-bow your opponent you position yourself on his leeward side with your
bow ahead. Disturbed air from your sails spills aft and to windward, slowing
any boat in its path. In this case, however, *Kiwi Magic* (3) already has enough
way-on to power over *Stars & Stripes* (3). Both boats tack to round the mark
(4); *Stars & Stripes* (5) trails *Kiwi Magic* (5) by 15 seconds as they begin the
next leg.

to cover us and maintained complete control all the way to the finish line. Their race by thirty-two seconds.

The next race was against *Challenge France* and it was a blow-out. The start was in a good 20 knots of wind and our goal was to hold together and not to foul out. There was no question by now we were the much faster boat—they still had only two wins to their credit—so we just needed to concentrate on a safe, solid performance.

We were pretty conservative in selecting a number-five jib, usually used in winds of 25 knots. If we had been up against a really competitive boat we would have worn a larger number-three jib.

From the moment *Challenge France* went over the starting line too early, until we finished ten minutes and forty-eight seconds in front of her, there was never any question who would win.

We came up against the revamped *Heart of America* in our fifth race. As Buddy Melges said, they had "added tiplets to the winglets." These were added to increase stability. But even with this new wing keel and its high-aspect tips, we still felt very confident.

The start was fairly even. We were to leeward. Right away it was clear that we had a little edge in speed. We figured the advantage was about one boat-length in five minutes, and sure enough, fifteen minutes into the race we were almost four boat-lengths ahead. It took us thirty-three minutes to sail the first leg, and we rounded the weather mark six boat-lengths, or thirty-eight seconds, ahead.

On the run he gained ten seconds in the building breeze and closed to twenty-eight seconds at the leeward mark. The second beat saw pretty much the same loose-cover scenario in which we gained another twenty seconds. The reaches were fairly even but at the second leeward mark we were almost one minute ahead. I knew the race was over, barring any breakdowns.

The only excitement of the day came at the end of the run when we had problems getting the jib up. The feeder spread apart and the jib came out halfway up. That meant we had to drop the jib and go around the mark with it lying on the deck. But at that stage, we had over a minute lead and that's quite a long way when it's blowing 20 true. The challenge was to keep the boat going and the guys on deck while we got the jib back into the feeder and gingerly hoisted it up. Our lead was down to twelve boat-lengths by the time we got things going again. But we stretched that out to nineteen at the end of the beat. The official time was one minute thirty-two seconds.

Although our race that day was pretty straightforward, there was a bit of an upset when Blackaller, our next opponent, managed to beat

White Crusader. Harold Cudmore had a problem at the third leeward mark, which looked to be a knot in the port jib sheet. This prevented the jib sheet from being brought all the way in. *White Crusader* had been leading by twenty-two seconds, but she rounded the mark only nine seconds in the lead. The jib problem caused a terrible tack and that allowed Blackaller to put a slam-dunk on Harold. *White Crusader* had to play catch-up for the rest of the windward leg and Blackaller squeezed out a three-second victory.

That night, anticipating the race against *USA,* we all felt it was the last time we would be meeting Blackaller for at least three years. There was a sense of relief, not because we were afraid to go out there and race the guy, but because we wouldn't have to put up with his antics anymore. We would be able to avoid incidents like the one in Newport in 1980 when he tore around and around our circular driveway at Seaview Terrace in his van, kicking up gravel, terrifying and trapping in the middle the Whidden' kids and ours, ages one and a half to ten years old. We wouldn't have to put up with Paul Cayard and Russ Silvestri shouting obscenities. And we wouldn't have to put up with Peter Staulkus in the chase boat lobbing half-full cans of beer into *Stars & Stripes* while we were racing. Blackaller went out of his way to try to make life difficult for us all right. Once, in a tight match we were having against *White Crusader*, Blackaller just barged onto our course and tacked right on top of *Stars & Stripes*. Another example of his "psych jobs" was to take a hacksaw and cut an opponent's boat during a major regatta. He did that to my Star boat during the World Championships for the class when they were held at the San Diego Yacht Club.

His idea was that whatever he and his boys could do to upset us— whether moral or not, right or wrong—that's how he would play the game. I figured out a long time ago the worst thing I could do would be to respond to that kind of provocation. For seven years he has pushed, looking for a weak link, but never once have I come back at him.

I view actions like these as expressions of jealousy. He was in the Star class fifteen years before I was, but I won the Star Worlds first. He's never won the SORC, the Congressional Cup, or an Olympic medal. He's entered the America's Cup three times and each time he failed: *Clipper* in 1980, *Defender* in 1983, and *USA* in 1987. He looks at three failures and sees me on top each time. I think he's frustrated because he thinks he's a much better sailor than I am and he may well be—I'll let the record speak for itself.

CLOCKWORK

Anyway, we went out against *USA* on December 8. The wind was light during the morning, and we were worried we were going to have another light-air race or possibly none at all. But around noon a big wave of wind came in and we were towed out to the course. It built up steadily from 17 to 21 true and by the time we got around to making our mainsail call, it was blowing 22 knots. We went right to the sail we liked and figured we were in for a great race. We had formed a game plan calling for a conservative start in the standard position—to windward up the line.

We went across the start fairly even and he was going fast. Neither of us gained on the other for a long, long time. Then we went out to the left-hand layline, got a little header, and he was to leeward. We tacked and he tacked and it became clear he was pointing higher into the wind and faster. *USA* beat us to the mark by nineteen seconds. On the run, he gained a little more as the wind died some, and the race committee changed the course hoping they had correctly aligned the leg to run into the wind, but their change was actually 20 degrees in the wrong direction. That meant that the next beat was in fact a fetch, which occurs when you can reach the next mark without tacking. We layed the mark on starboard and rounded it thirty seconds behind *USA*.

But now the first reach had turned into a run so we were able to attack and cut the lead to thirteen seconds. Because the committee had canted the course the wrong way, the second reach was a close fetch in which we used a jib. There wasn't much we could do but follow in the wake of *USA* and we remained thirteen seconds behind.

Up the third beat he found some more speed and pulled out by another thirty-five to forty seconds. Now he had a fifty-four-second lead, which we got down to forty-eight on the run. We picked up six seconds on the last beat so the final margin was forty-two seconds. It was a fairly basic race. He got the lead, didn't make mistakes, didn't break down, and got the victory.

After losing four races in each of the first two rounds, Blackaller had been upset by *Italia* and *Heart of America* in this third round, but his win over us tightened up the standings. Twelve points goes a long way and he was right back in the hunt for a semifinal spot. *USA*'s performance all summer was a surprise to a lot of people. I don't think anyone really expected it.

During the race we noticed Tom had installed a new forward fin-rudder. We questioned this but he claimed his other was broken so he got the measurers to approve a new one. We took the view that the

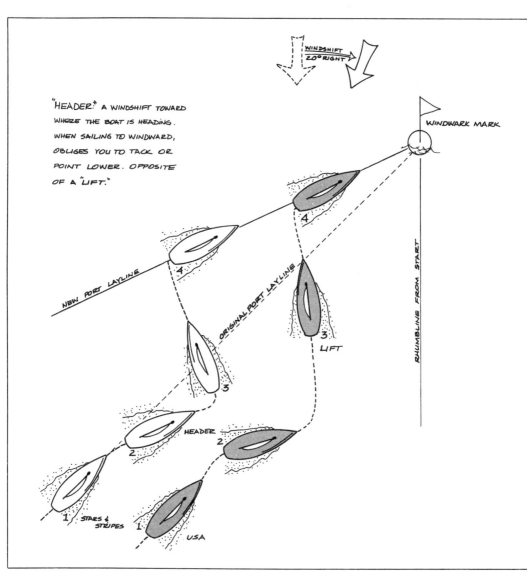

"HEADER." A WINDSHIFT TOWARD WHERE THE BOAT IS HEADING. WHEN SAILING TO WINDWARD, OBLIGES YOU TO TACK OR POINT LOWER. OPPOSITE OF A "LIFT."

WINDSHIFT 20° RIGHT

WINDWARK MARK

NEW PORT LAYLINE

ORIGINAL PORT LAYLINE

RHUMBLINE FROM START

LIFT

HEADER

STARS & STRIPES

USA

Round Robin III, fourth race, December 1986. *Stars & Stripes* and *USA* are nearer on left-hand layline, steering toward the mark. The wind shifts 20 degrees to the right, heading both boats at (2). When they tack (2–3), slight differences in the way the wind hits both boats allows *USA* to point higher into the wind and sail faster (3). *USA* tacks for the mark ahead of *Stars & Stripes* on the new port layline (4) that the header created.

measurer had no right to give him such permission. Malin wrote a letter to Commandante Alberini blasting the decision, but it didn't do much good.

The following day, when Blackaller beat Harry Cudmore by just three seconds, the British syndicate launched a protest that went on for about eight hours. John Marshall served as a witness. We thought they had an excellent case. They claimed that substituting a rudder, specifically in races three through seven, was an infringement of the Race Conditions. The jury, however, voted that *USA* had damaged her rudder, had contacted a measurer immediately to inspect the rudder, and when he did, he concluded the rudder was damaged and couldn't be repaired in time for the next race. He then authorized *USA* to reinstall the original rudder used in Round Robin I. Thus, the protest was dismissed.

We tried to help Harold in this protest by allowing John Marshall to testify for him about a conversation that Brit Chance had had with Tony Watts, Chairman of the International Measurement Committee. We had asked him whether we could change rudders in the middle of a series and we were told no, absolutely not. Now what *USA* had on her hull were rudders, one at the forward waterline and one aft. Blackaller may have called them "appendages," but in fact they were rudders.

Tony Watts was adamant. He said under no circumstances could we change our rudder, but when it came to Blackaller those circumstances seemed to change. I think the jury just backed down after eight hours of discussion and decided they didn't want an international incident over throwing *USA* out of four races.

On the day we raced *Eagle*, there was some doubt about whether or not the committee would allow a start. The forecast called for winds in the 26- to 38-knot range, which gets to be pretty scary stuff. But when we got to the starting arena, the wind was blowing about 23 true so it wasn't as bad as expected.

We had a short-footed mainsail up and although the wind was blowing pretty good, we put up a number-eight jib. Normally we would have used a four or five jib, but I thought we could beat *Eagle* even with the shorter head sail. I knew we'd be underpowered with the smaller main and head sails, but I felt it was okay for this race.

We forced them over the line early so we had a good jump from the beginning that we built on over the entire course. The wind continued to build and at one point was in the 30- to 35-knot range. *Stars & Stripes* performed magnificently in the rough stuff and so did our guys. Look-

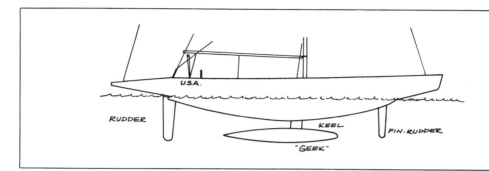

Diagram of Blackaller's *USA* showing underbody with rudder, keel with "geek," and forward fin-rudder.

ing back, I don't remember any momentous turning point in this more-than-ten-minute victory. But I do think this race really showed off the pure power of our boat and well illustrated the mastery of the crew. A statistic from the summer sticks in my mind: From this point to the last of our races, we sailed a hundred twenty-one legs on the course and led at all but fourteen marks.

Perhaps the only incident of note in the *Eagle* race was caused by Rod Davis's frustration with our insurmountable lead. As we sailed down the second run and he was still going up the second beat, he sailed toward us on starboard tack and tried to foul us out of the race. He chased us around a little, but we escaped him easily. I guess he felt this was his only hope; in fact, I had done the same thing in the 1983 Cup series when in one race *Australia II* had an insurmountable lead.

Our ten-minute margin meant we were in high gear and we just powered through the last four races of Round Robin III. In succession we beat *French Kiss* (2:07), *Italia* (3:37), *Azzurra* (4:11), and *White Crusader* (4:12). At the end of the first three rounds, our record stood at 27–7, good enough for second place overall and a berth in the semifinals. In first place was *New Zealand*, whose only defeat was the October win we got off them. Somehow Blackaller got into third place, which meant we would face him in the coming round. *New Zealand* would race number four, *French Kiss*.

The third round was the undoing of *America II*. They suffered five critical losses and ended up just one point short of making the final four. Their biggest upset was at the hands of Buddy Melges in *Heart of America* in the first race of the round. Buddy sailed a near-perfect race and won convincingly. That race effectively knocked *America II* out and

CLOCKWORK

with her, a hundred thirty-five years of the New York Yacht Club always having a boat in the final races of the America's Cup.

For us, we had about nine days to prepare for Blackaller and his banshees. I suppose it was somehow fitting the two strongest boats in the northern hemisphere both came from California and the two skippers were Dennis and Tom. If nothing else, it certainly gave the press a lot to write about. Every day brought new stories about the "archrivalry" between me and the *USA* helmsman.

History has a way of repeating itself. To get into the Cup finals in 1980 and 1983, I had to beat Tom. I was excited about the prospect of making it three in a row.

10

★

Pressing
Concerns

URING the three round robins, the press conference following each race featured different guest stars. Whichever skipper had won, or whoever was in a particularly exciting or noteworthy race, was asked to appear before the Fifth Estate to offer his own words of wisdom. Now that the Challenger series was down to just four boats, the four skippers had to appear at the Fremantle Port Authority building, the site of the press conferences, every night.

My relationship with the press has always been cool because from the beginning I didn't feel I was getting a fair shake. Then in 1979, things turned really frosty. I found myself up against Ted Turner, the megastar hero of the 1977 Cup Defense. Here was Captain Outrageous, everyone's pin-up. Women loved him and men wanted to be just like him. His victory aboard *Courageous*, and the way he handled the media, created a lot of popular interest in the sport. Turner had style, charm, charisma, wit, personality, money, power, glory. Dennis Conner was just a poor carpet salesman from San Diego making $30,000 a year and trying to win the America's Cup.

I knew Turner well enough to know he functioned best when he was the underdog, so I decided not to get in a verbal duel with him. Ted is probably the most articulate guy I know, while I'm your old-fashioned tongue-tied type. I could never compete with Turner in the press so my plan was to neutralize the media. At best they would never be on my side, but I was determined not to allow them to be a negative factor. Frankly, I knew *Freedom* was a better boat than *Courageous*, and I knew we were far more prepared than Ted and his crew. There was little doubt we'd kill them, but I certainly wasn't going to say that.

When we raced Turner in the first race of the Defender Trials, we purposely wore a 1977 mainsail and jib. He beat us. In the second race, we put on better sails and won eighteen races in a row from him. When I faced reporters after that first win, I told them what a great thrill it was for me to beat one of my great sports heroes. When we kept winning, I continued with: "Gee, I'm just thrilled to death to be here and have the opportunity to be on the same water with Ted." The more we won, the more I used that line. I think Ted got frustrated because he couldn't do much on the water and he wasn't getting any reaction from me on land.

That's when Turner uttered his infamous quote about Dennis being a professional and taking all the fun out of the sport for everyone else. The media swarmed all over that one, and they have used it over and over ever since. My reaction was just to pretend I thought it was a compliment. "Gee, Ted, thanks. That's nice of you to say such a thing about poor, dumb Dennis."

The real Dennis would have probably said something like, "Why do you think I've been working my butt off up here in Newport for two years while you've been home in Atlanta making millions of dollars? Hey Ted, I've put together the best 12-meter team in the world and I'm working at trying to be the best I can. That's why we're beating you." By taking the opposite approach—by saying, "Oh, Ted doesn't mean those things"—I felt I was taking the venom away.

Just as I was learning how to deal with Ted, along comes Tom Blackaller. Now he became the darling of the media. Tommy was always good for a colorful, outrageous quote. He could always be counted on to slam someone. To get Tom talking, all you'd have to do was point a microphone at him and away he'd go.

I realize I wasn't exactly going out of my way to cultivate the media. It wasn't until the 1986/87 campaign started gearing up that I saw the importance of a media image. While we were in Australia, the folks back home had to have good news about our campaign to ensure their continued support. That's why we hired Lesleigh Green, the best PR professional in the business. She had performed the same function for Alan Bond in 1983 and we were thrilled when she came aboard. Lesleigh knew all the Australian media and most of the American writers as well, so she was able to keep up a pretty constant flow of DC stories in the newspapers and on television.

Warren Jones, who had been such a thorn in our side in 1983, was back again in the Bond syndicate, this time trying to spread the "Big Bad Dennis" line he had conjured up. But it backfired. The Aussie people thought I was okay, the guy bouncing off the canvas. In their eyes I was a regular guy who wasn't so big and bad after all.

I knew we needed the money and if that meant Dennis turning himself into a dancing bear, Dennis would do it. I had to dance for the media so our message could be heard back home. When the media threw peanuts, I had to swallow them. I believed the media would be a definite factor in the final results so I had to play my cards differently.

I may have tried harder to get the media to see the real me, but I didn't change my essential attitude about them. After seeing them in action once again, I must report that my convictions persist about their frequent laziness and lack of understanding of the sport or the people in it. There are a dozen very good reporters, and they were in Fremantle throughout the entire event. A lot of others would just fly in for a few days, sit in the air-conditioned splendor of the media center, watch the races on TV, and then steal everything the commentators said and write up the questions asked by the few pros.

The following is an example of how dangerous press inaccuracies can be. On Christmas Day, 1986, I was a guest at the home of Alan and Eileen Bond. Eileen produced a newspaper clipping (dated Monday, December 15, 1986) from the *London Times*, a paper I'd always thought of as one of the most authoritative in the English language. The headline on the sports page screamed: CONNER'S CREW RETURNS HOME WITHOUT THE AMERICA'S CUP. NEW YORK MISSES FINAL FOR FIRST TIME IN 135 YEARS. The story, under the byline of the paper's Fremantle correspondent, read: "Dennis Conner is out of the America's Cup—so, for the first time in a hundred thirty-five years, the New York Yacht Club will not be involved in the final round of the most famous trophy in yachting. Conner created a 20-million-dollar syndicate pledged to return the Cup to New York where it had rested since 1851 until the Australians won it three years ago. He was the favourite to keep that promise when the elimination trials started ten weeks ago, but now he has failed to reach even the semifinals to decide the Challenger."

Reading that was what I imagine reading my own obituary would be like. I couldn't believe a paper could be so completely inaccurate, especially not one with the reputation of *The Times*. But I read those words with my own eyes. I was terribly annoyed—not only because some fool newspaperman was totally wrong again, but because of the serious potential harm to our financial situation. What if a would-be backer of *Stars & Stripes* sat down to his morning coffee in a London hotel and read that in *The Times?* Never mind that we actually had the second-highest point total at that time. He'd say, "Oh well, so much for Conner. Guess I'll give my million dollars to someone else."

Toward the end of December, I received a half-hearted apology from Tom Clarke, the *Times* sports editor. He claimed the mistake was not the fault of the correspondent in Fremantle, but of some editor in London. He said the error had been corrected in the paper the next day, but by then the damage was already done.

That note was followed by another from David Miller, the paper's chief sports correspondent. The note shows the lengths to which newspaper guys will go to weasel out of journalistic responsibility. In it, Mr. Miller apologized for the error, characterizing it as "the sporting howler of the century," but added: "it was not my responsibility for I was in Switzerland at the time." His note went on to say:

> The newspaper, in its coverage the next day, carried a substantial retraction/explanation. The error occurred when, late at night on one of the later editions, there was a decision to reshape the introduction and in a temporary brainstorm, the person concerned, in a Freudian slip, made your name synonymous with the NYYC. May I say that we were probably more embarrassed than you. Fortunately, I understand that the error missed our main international edition. There is the opportunity, now that I am here [Fremantle] for the semifinals, to carry a major feature regarding *Stars & Stripes* that would further put the record correct. To this end, I would like the opportunity of speaking with you for five or ten minutes during one of the lay-days. I will call at your dock tomorrow to establish what little may be done to appease your wounded soul and to shed a little of our culpability.

I am not a guy who gets mad and stays mad, but on this occasion I *was* good and mad. My anger made me want to sue those guys for every nickle they had. But when I spoke to my lawyers, they asserted that under British law a defamation action has little chance of success unless an element of malice can be shown. I decided not to push it, not to give the media wolves a chance to howl. I hoped that given a little time, maybe they would start to get it right.

That was a mistake. Reporters just went right on making incredible blunders. A Melbourne cricket writer, who apparently had never even been sailing, devoted an entire feature to tearing me apart through an analysis of the *Concise Oxford Dictionary*'s definition of the word "sportsman." The fact that this guy had never met me, nor had he even sought an interview with me, didn't seem to matter. The result was just plain stupid, as well as insulting. In Australia, as in England, it seems the media can commit character assassination and get away with it.

But that wasn't all. A couple of reports were printed that illustrated their writers' professional incompetence. On December 13 we raced *Italia* and won by 3:37. It seemed like a pretty easy win to everyone except Neil Smith, a syndicated columnist with the *Sunday Times* of Western Australia. According to Smith, *Italia* passed us on the run. Apparently he was watching a different race because everyone who saw it knew the closest *Italia* ever got to us was about thirty seconds.

The same reporter wrote that Blackaller beat Kolius around the weather mark in a race they had. It never happened. When it came to covering the America's Cup, it often seemed that any resemblance between reporting and the actual events was strictly coincidental.

If dealing with the media is the worst part of any America's Cup campaign, then raising money runs a close second. It's no fun having to call people up and beg for dollars. There was a time, not so very long ago, when all the America's Cup funding came from private sources. These days it's more like 60 percent corporate and 40 percent private.

I traveled throughout corporate America banging on doors, trying to get the big guys to sit up and take notice. Some of them could see that this was more than just some crazy Conner dream, but most just sat there puffing on their fat cigars.

It wasn't just a question of my putting together some nice glossy proposal and setting off with a briefcase and blazer. I had to go out and *sell*. I had to be the creative one. I had to come up with some really wild schemes to grab their attention.

One of my best ideas was to go to George Steinbrenner, the principal owner of the New York Yankees. My offer was to paint the transom of the boat in Yankee pinstripes and call her *Yankee*. I had a drawing showing the boat and I was ready to give the baseball man my pitch. But Steinbrenner never saw me, so all was for naught.

Then I thought to go to Donald Trump, and if he gave us $2 million we'd call the boat *Trump Card*. I could see the name and Atlantic City (home port of the Trump casinos) in five aces on the stern. If I had scored with Trump I would have gone to the other Atlantic City casino operators and had them kick in another $9 million.

Trump wouldn't see me either but, determined not to be put off, I simply sat down in his outer office and played the old waiting game. He had his secretaries try to shoo me away but I told them, "Look girls, I know he's in there. I'm not leaving until I see him, so you have two choices. Either let me see him or call the police." Finally, they gave up and let me into his office.

I told Mr. Trump I wanted to stage a 12-meter match-race regatta off Atlantic City and that I'd get Alan Bond to bring over the America's Cup winner, *Australia II*. I tried to convince him that such a race would upgrade Atlantic City's image as well as bring in business. After all, Las Vegas had introduced a motor race to help improve their image.

Trump seemed genuinely interested, but I knew I'd lost him when he told me he would think about it and call me back in a few days. To make a long story short, it just never worked out. Much later on, he did come on board as a major backer, and after we won, he helped arrange and pay for our ticker-tape parade in New York City. Donald Trump turned out to be a really nice guy and a good friend.

11

oooooooooooooo ★ oooooooooooooo

Bye, Bye Blackaller

VER the years Tom Blackaller and I have raced against each other a good many times. Whenever we have, the competition between us has been especially intense. He does everything he can to rile me up and I do everything I can to ignore him. Truth is, we probably both get to each other a little. Add that to the obvious importance of winning the first race in the best four-out-of-seven semifinal series to become the Challenger, and you'll get some idea of the tension DC was feeling aboard *Stars & Stripes* prior to the start of the first race. Fortunately, when the gun goes off so does any nervousness or anxiety.

There were few maneuvers before the start of the first race. That was probably because neither one of us had a lot of confidence in our turning ability. Basically, we wanted *USA* to be to windward as we went across the line, so we managed to stay ahead and to leeward. We got up to the line early and forced Blackaller off. Everything worked precisely according to plan, but then something happened. Either the wind shifted or was filling in fresher on the right, or he was just plain fast. Or it may have been all three because *USA* was going very well today, pointing closer and closer toward the next mark on the course, and gaining bearing and holding height.

At one point Tom was three and a half boat-lengths ahead on the first beat. It was sickening. I was thinking, "HolycriminItly, he's fast."

BYE, BYE BLACKALLER

I could see my life going down the rathole because of another adventuresome design.

When we finally tacked and went over at him, we found he was definitely ahead. A short tacking duel ensued during which we gained some ground. When he found he couldn't tack with us, he opted for a straight-line speed contest. It didn't take long to establish our superiority in that. I'm not precisely certain why we gained on the tacks, but probably it was due to the nature of the two boats. Our wing keel helped us turn a little quicker than his forward rudder.

He got to the windward mark three lengths ahead and then stretched the lead another few boat-lengths on the run. He was so confident that he turned around and waved good-bye to us. He had some nerve. I wanted to shout, "Remember what happened in our first race, Tommy-boy," but I held my tongue. Down at the very end of the run downwind, he came toward us on port jibe trying to get between us and the mark, but I ran by his lee just as he was crossing. That must have been very frustrating because I was blanketing his wind. He didn't know what to do. He just froze. I don't know why he stayed there, but by the time he decided to harden up and get out of there, we had made a nice gain. We were within three or four boat-lengths at the leeward mark and ready to strike.

On the second beat we once again gained through better tacking. Our crew were working their butts off and their efforts paid off. We went around the windward mark fifteen seconds behind and after the two reaches, there was no change. At the leeward mark we were fifteen seconds behind again. There was no passing lane. He was doing a nice job covering us and there was no way for us to get by. But by the end of the run, the wind had strengthened so we came right up on him and drew almost even on the outside. The official time was nine seconds, but when we went round on the outside and got set for the windward beat, we were no better off. We tacked, he tacked, and we started to gain, so he ceased that strategy. We were on starboard and he was on port, and both of us straight-lined for a bit. He came toward us and tacked to windward up on our hip and then got lifted. Holycriminltly! We went from something like one length behind to three lengths in the wink of an eye. Whatever gains we had made, we seemed to give right back.

Tom Whidden wanted to tack him down but I overruled him, saying, "No, we'll never get by. Let's just hang in here and see if we can't get a little header before we go over." Five minutes later, we did indeed get a little gift from above. We were headed and I tacked. This

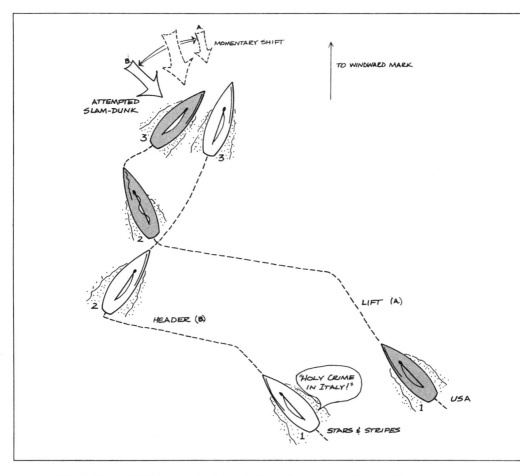

MOMENTARY SHIFT

TO WINDWARD MARK

ATTEMPTED SLAM-DUNK

LIFT (A.)

HEADER (B)

"HOLY CRIME IN ITALY!"

USA

STARS & STRIPES

Blackaller in *USA* has tacked to windward up on our hip and is one boat-length behind (1) when she gets a lift that puts her ahead of *Stars & Stripes* by 3 boat-lengths. Blackaller then crosses ahead of *Stars & Stripes* (2), attempts a slam-dunk, but misjudges his timing. As he tacks in a header, (2-3) *Stars & Stripes* powers through to leeward.

time we were nose-and-nose and the wind direction held steady.

Here's where Blackaller made his big mistake. He came across to try a slam-dunk but misjudged it, and I hardened up beautifully right underneath his transom doing better than 9 knots. We just powered right through to the other side. I guess it took no more than ten seconds to grab the lead. The race was all but over.

Like our first race with *USA*, this was one of the most exciting contests I'd ever been in. We squeaked out a victory because of Tom's mistake, but I didn't feel too sorry for him. I remembered his cocky wave on the first run.

Before we finished the race we experienced some unpleasant drama aboard *Stars & Stripes*. We suffered a rip in the foot of our jib, which could easily have extended through the entire sail. If that had happened, *USA* certainly would have regained the lead and won the race easily. Fortunately for us, the jib held together and we went across the line for a nine-second win. Like our first race with the San Franciscans, we trailed the whole way. Again, there was no give-up aboard *Stars & Stripes*. If the young guys on *USA* had found our October encounter hard to swallow, this first race of the semifinals must have devastated them. I never looked back once after we crossed the line, but some of our guys said they saw Blackaller climb out of the cockpit and sit down on the afterdeck with his head in his hands.

The start of the second race was similar to the previous day's. This time the left-hand end of the line was definitely favored so we battled hard for it and got it. However, we were over early by just a fraction of a second, by no more than three feet. It was a bad mistake by Dennis. *USA* had given us too much trouble in the four previous races to hand them a large head start. But by the time we turned *Stars & Stripes* around and got back across the line, Blackaller was off to an eighteen-second lead.

But our situation wasn't as bad as it could have been. Because the wind shift had made our end of the line so favored, we were only a couple of boat-lengths behind. After a couple of tacks by us both, we got into a straight-line speed duel during which we were lifted and, as a result, pulled even. At the mark we had pulled in front by sixteen seconds.

Blackaller clawed back a little on the run, but on the second beat we received what must have been a message from heaven in the form of a 15-degree lift. We went from one length ahead to six in just eight minutes. The race was really over then and there because we only had to apply a loose cover for the rest of the beat, and during the reaches not much time was gained or lost. As the wind was changing directions, our lead gave us the advantage as we could pick up the shifts first.

The rest of the race was just watching for shifts and covering *USA* carefully. We won by 3:02 in what I call a "standard no-brainer."

Now we were halfway to the finals and I felt Blackaller and his boys were pretty disheartened. I have an idea Tom was checking out the sports pages to see when the next auto race was. When he isn't sailing, he likes to race cars.

As we headed out for the third race, we discussed the forecast. It was for heavy air, so we had left the dock prepared for a strong blow. But when we got to the course, the wind was only 18 or 19 knots true.

We controlled the start, and as we crossed the line we were one boat-length ahead. After a straight-line drag-race for ten minutes, our lead was three lengths. When Blackaller began tacking we stayed with him. During one of the tacking exchanges we were able to lay a perfect slam-dunk on him, and as we parked on his beam about a boat-length away, I could see the frustration in his face. Our boat was faster, our crew was better. He didn't like it.

At the windward mark, we had about five or six boat-lengths on him, and we maintained the lead through the run as *Stars & Stripes* had good downwind speed in heavy air. As we began the second beat, I made the decision to sail more conservatively because there wasn't too much Blackaller could do from his position in that weight of wind. The tactics were simple: When he had a lift we tacked to cover and when we were lifted, we let him go and rode it out.

We rounded the second windward mark 1:24 in command and kept the same distance on the two reaches. By the time we rounded the last mark and began the final beat to the finish line, we were more than two minutes ahead so I took my foot off the accelerator, so to speak. Although our race had turned into a bit of a yawn, the race ahead was very exciting and we broke concentration to watch. *New Zealand* and *French Kiss* had begun their third race of the semis twenty minutes ahead of us on the same course so they were nearing the gun. The Kiwis had trailed for most of the race, but on the last beat they had initiated a furious tacking duel and, with a few minutes left, had managed to stick their nose in front.

We ended up on the line 2:23 in front of Blackaller with just one more win needed to get into the finals. The overall performance of *Stars & Stripes* that day was very pleasing. Between Round Robin III and the semifinals, we had changed the lower part of the keel, lowering ballast and extending the wings. John Marshall felt this would make us faster in both lighter and heavier air. John expected the change to be more noticeable in light air, but actually, just the opposite happened. We were faster when the wind was over 15 knots, and may have been slower in lighter air. The changes had reduced our normal weather helm, and it turned out this made the more efficient keel most helpful in heavy air. So, convinced we were entering a period of heavier wind, we felt increasingly confident.

It began to seem like God really was on our side. Whatever we did turned out well. Since coming to Fremantle we had made a lot of small, subtle changes in *Stars & Stripes*: a new rudder and rig adjustments, a new, lighter mast, additions to the wings, and twenty inches to the stern. Separately, these changes probably didn't have much effect, but together, they definitely improved our speed. A very dejected Tom Blackaller comfirmed this at the press conference that night.

> During the third round robin, I thought *USA* was about a tenth of a knot faster than *Stars & Stripes*. But now he's [Conner] jumped from a tenth of a knot behind to a tenth of a knot ahead. That's two-tenths of a knot velocity made good. He's pretty tricky, you know. While there's a lot of finger-pointing and baloney about changes made, I'd have to say that to get two-tenths of a knot of extra speed, Conner would have to add 2,000 pounds of ballast. He's got those funny stubby little wings that don't go out to the side of the boat. . . . They look like his daughter Shanna designed them.

The truth is that we sailed along making little gains on *USA* here and there. We grabbed every opportunity we could. Our biggest gains seemed to come when their boat got screwed up in a wave and their forward rudder came out of the water. When I watched the videotape replay, I saw *USA* leap sideways whenever it was hit by a medium sea. Every time that happened, we gained a little, and all those half-boat-length gains added up to about twenty seconds on every beat.

After the third race, the official measurers requested that both *Stars & Stripes* and *New Zealand* report to the measurement pen for a spot check. I asked Ken McAlpine, the Australian measurer, if we were allowed to have a representative at the measurement and he said yes. At the last minute, I went over to the Yacht Club Costa Smeralda race headquarters and substituted my name for our rep, Robert Hopkins, because I thought it might be a good psychological ploy for me to be seen inspecting their boat up close. They looked amazed and not a little disturbed to see me drive up to the pen in a rubber raft.

I found Chris Dickson and congratulated him on his race, then offered him a cold Budweiser I'd brought. He seemed uptight and refused to take it. I gave it to their project manager, Laurent Esquier, who had been with us in 1983. When I left, I noticed the Bud still sitting there at the side of the dock.

Our measurement check immediately followed the Kiwis', and Roy Dickson, Chris's father, returned my visit. He was determined that the measurers be as tough as possible on us. I was trying to look calm and nonchalant, but I was starting to sweat a little because our hull sat quite deep in the water. This was no doubt caused by all the wet sails and water in the boat. We'd just finished a race in 22 knots of wind, and every nook and cranny was wet and every sail soaked.

In those circumstances the rules allow you to replace the wet sails with dry ones as long as they are the same size and number. We completed the transfer and stood by for inspection.

Actually, we passed quite easily, probably because measurer Tony Watts fell head over heels into the water. He had been down on his knees in a little rubber boat when he suddenly lost his balance and went right into the harbor. Everybody along the docks was trying not to laugh because we didn't want to get offside with a measurer, but poor Tony sure looked funny floundering around in the drink. It was about six o'clock and as he climbed back into the dinghy, already it was pretty chilly. *Stars & Stripes* passed her inspection very quickly.

While this was happening, I made the mistake of pointing out that if the six jibs we were carrying were all soaking wet and as a result each was 20 pounds heavier, then six times 20 pounds equals 120 pounds, so we could probably take on another jib and still make the weight. McAlpine said he thought that would be pushing it but I insisted I was right. By opening my mouth, I caused us to be flagged back into the measurement pens the next day. They wanted to see if I had added that extra jib.

On that same day, *Australia IV*, which had made it into the finals of the Defender trials against *Kookaburra III*, had broken out one of her specialty sails. This very large, very full sail is called a "gennaker" because it's a cross between a genoa and a spinnaker. *Kookaburra* immediately protested the way it was flown, but in the next day or two *Kookaburra* showed up with a gennaker of its own. *Australia IV* had initially used it out of desperation. They had lost the first three races to *Kookaburra III* and it was apparent the boat just wasn't going to win. At the time it seemed hard to believe that Bondy was about to be eliminated. Suddenly, it dawned on us that we were drawing very close to the end of the entire America's Cup summer.

Our final race against *USA* occurred on a very interesting day weatherwise. The forecast was for the Doctor to come in at 12 to 14 knots, then very slowly build to about 20 knots. Our sail inventory included one main we liked to use in 14 knots of wind and another we felt was good in 16. The race committee postponed the start until the breeze kicked in, during which we waffled on which sails to use for the anticipated conditions. We finally chose our light-air sail and, in fact, the boat was filled with light-air jibs and spinnakers. We didn't have any spinnaker over 45 feet for the reaches, so we hoped the breeze would stay light.

It didn't. Right before the start it began blowing hard and we were caught with our pants down. We had a number-two mainsail up, but we changed that to a number three, and then changed once again to a number four. We hadn't planned this too well.

There we were going into one of the most important races in the series with the wrong sail up and the wrong gear on board. The biggest spinnaker we had was already too small. Our screw-up was our weather team's fault. In Lee Davis and Chris Bedford, John Marshall had picked the best in the business, but today the crystal ball must have been on loan. I trusted those guys and acted on the information they gave us. It's like having a navigator on board who tells you to come up 5 degrees and you don't believe him so the next thing you know you're piled up on the rocks. I believe you have to listen to your specialists.

Wrong sails or no, the race was on. We wanted to guard the right-hand side today, so with a minute to go before the start we tacked and headed for the committee boat. We got the start by about a second, and then both of us straight-lined for the first part of the leg. *Stars & Stripes* gradually worked out a half-length lead, then one length, then a length and a half. It looked like it would be a close race. Tom exerted some pressure by initiating a tacking duel, but I felt this was just the type of racing we needed to prepare us for the finals.

During the tacking duel we held him off until our jib caught on a fitting at the top of the spinnaker-pole track and developed a six-foot rip. That ended the tacking duel. Fortunately, we were on the left layline so we just aimed straight for it and tried to make it to the mark on boatspeed. Tommy was right next to us so he didn't overstand the mark and he didn't have to pay any price for being behind, as usually occurs when another tack is needed to make the mark. When we rounded the mark, *Stars & Stripes* was in the lead by twenty-six seconds and we lost only a couple of those on the run.

On the second beat, the wind had increased to the 22- to 25-knot range. Our main was not working properly and *USA* was our equal in speed. We held on by covering his tacks, but on the reaches our sail-selection mistake cost us because we didn't have a big enough chute up. Turning the leeward mark, Blackaller was breathing down my neck from only a boat-length and a half behind.

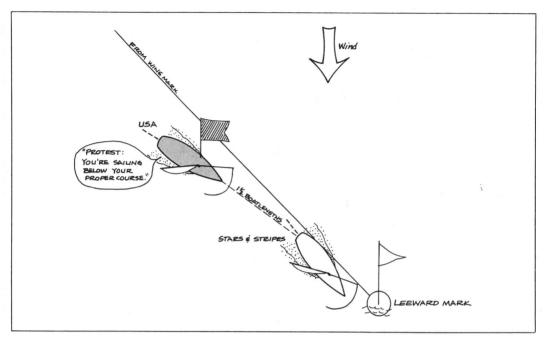

USA, trailing *Stars & Stripes* by one and one-half boatlengths, tries to protest *Stars & Stripes* for sailing below her proper course while in the process of rounding the leeward mark. According to Rule 39, a yacht on a free leg of the course shall not sail below her proper course when she is clearly within three of her overall lengths of either a leeward yacht or a yacht clear astern that is steering a course to pass to leeward.

As we rounded, *USA* raised a protest flag claiming we were sailing below a proper course. This can happen when the lead yacht tries to force the opponent farther away from the mark. However, our telemetry readings indicated our rudder angle throughout the race, so we were easily able to prove we were sailing a proper course.

As soon as Tom got on the third windward leg, he tacked. We had a ten-second lead at that point and we knew *USA* would throw as many tacks at us as they could. The wind had increased still again, and although we had our smallest sail on, we were still overpowered. The main wasn't working correctly, the boat had too much helm, we were heeling too much, and Blackaller was coming after us with fire in his eyes.

Usually, one side of the course is favored because of windshifts or its closeness to the next mark, but today I couldn't figure out which side we should protect. The shifts were small and there wasn't much phasing one way or the other. Eventually we chose the left, but that turned out to be a mistake. *USA* had more speed on now and they got a shift we didn't, so they pulled ahead for the first time in the race. Our computer indicated he had as much as a length-and-a-half lead at times. When we came together on opposing tacks, Blackaller was clearly ahead. The situation was almost identical to the first race, only one leg earlier. Blackaller tried another slam-dunk, the same maneuver that had lost him the opening race. As then, we were able to duck him, but it was as close as we could come without hitting.

The heat of the moment triggered the banshee boys, and the invectives started to fly again. While my guys went about their business, *USA* erupted in war cries. Paul Cayard screamed, "Mast-abeam," but it was an improper call on several counts. First, the rule states that the helmsman must make the call, not the tactician. Secondly, *USA* did not have mast-abeam. Their helm was fourteen feet behind our mast. Bill Trenkle had good cause to remember the position precisely because Cayard, in his usual style, made the call, raised his middle finger, and started in on the obscenities. Bill remembered everything about the incident and would have been a strong witness at the hearing, but they decided to drop the protest after the race.

We were back on the right side of the course now and as we slowly pulled even with *USA*, then edged in front, Blackaller tacked to the left, leaving us in controlling position. We continued on the same bearing until we got a little knock, a little breeze forcing us away from the wind on which we tacked and found ourselves with a lead of about half a boat-length.

While it was still close, I felt we had just won the race. Blackaller's slam-dunk tactic hadn't worked for the second time in a row and we were able to grab the lead back. I could almost feel the tension build aboard *USA*.

At the third windward mark we had the same twenty-two-second lead we had had the second time at the mark. We both jibe-set our spinnakers and *Stars & Stripes* had a very successful run, keeping *USA* back at about the same distance. The last beat was all ours as we doubled the lead to finally defeat Blackaller and his boys by forty-three seconds. We had made it to the finals.

After *America II* was eliminated, several of their members offered us support and the syndicate itself let us use some sails and equipment. At the press conference signaling the conclusion of the semifinals, Blackaller was asked if he would support us now that *Stars & Stripes* was the sole American boat left in the competition. He sort of waffled, and made no congratulatory statement to *Stars & Stripes*. There was no hint of the traditional handshake that might have been expected at this point in the regatta.

Obviously, Tom Blackaller was a very bitterly disappointed and unhappy man. His attitude was in stark contrast to the spirit of cooperation shown by guys like Bill Packer, Tom McLaughlin, and Larry Leonard in the *America II* camp. In many ways, these guys had more reason to be disappointed in their performance than Blackaller. At least Blackaller had a fast boat.

On the other side of the semifinal draw was the series between *New Zealand* and *French Kiss*. Our time was spent on our own efforts so we didn't study these races very closely, but it was obvious that the Kiwis were superior. Like us, they won the series four–nil and they were only threatened in that third race, which we watched from our position on the same course.

The final leg of the *Kiwi-Kiss* third race was one of the most exciting beats all summer. Marc Pajot had demonstrated some excellent sailing up to that point and it earned him a nineteen-second lead at the last leeward mark. But the Kiwis, with a smaller and more maneuverable boat, were able to gain the advantage in the inevitable tacking duel, and the New Zealanders overtook the Frenchmen near the finish line and won by thirteen seconds. That come-from-behind win seemed to exemplify the power of the Kiwi program. Going into the finals, *Kiwi Magic* had cast her spell over every competitor—save one—who came to Fremantle. She had raced thirty-eight races and she had won thirty-seven of them. She went into the finals to meet the only boat that had beaten her.

12

★

Kiwi Tragic

THE first race of the finals to determine who would face the Australians in the America's Cup was scheduled for January 13. Despite the number, I felt lucky. In fact, I was perhaps a little overconfident. I remember a conversation with a friend in my office the day after we knocked Blackaller out of the semifinals. I'd seen this guy on and off over the past few years, and every time we talked he told me I was going to win the next Cup. There just was no doubt in his mind.

"Well, DC," he said, smiling broadly as I fed the Fremantle gold fish I'd had with me since I first arrived in Australia, "looks like I've been right all along."

"Think so, huh?"

"Hell, man, ever since you came into my office two years ago with that hundred-page computerized program detailing your Challenge, I knew this day would come."

"So you think we're on schedule?"

"From what I saw of your 4–0 sweep against Blackaller, I'd say you're ahead of schedule."

"You think they were fast?"

"Yeah, I think they were fast."

The guy had always been so confident and he was right. *USA* was fast and they had given us some trouble. My friend's enthusiasm was contagious, and, caught up in the euphoria of the moment, I got a little carried away:

"Well, let me tell you something. We just won the America's Cup."

Almost as soon as I said it, I wished I hadn't. Talk is cheap. There were still a minimum of eight races before anyone would win the Cup. But I felt we would beat the Kiwis and I was sure we'd take whomever the Aussies threw at us, which right then looked to be *Kookaburra III*. Still, I needed to keep those feelings inside. It doesn't do any good to rile an opponent on the eve of a big race.

However, word did get out that I was pretty damn confident of our abilities. The local press ran a couple of stories about how I'd been telling docksiders that we only had eight races to go before bringing the Cup home. In the press conference the morning before the first finals race, Chris Dickson was asked to comment on this.

"There is no possible way *Stars & Stripes* is going to beat the Kiwis 4–0," Dickson answered indignantly. "I'd like to think she is not going to beat the Kiwis at all. All we can go on is the history of the racing in this America's Cup. The Cup is all about winning yacht races, and the simple fact is that one boat has a better track record than the other."

There was no arguing with Chris on that. They had beaten us two out of three, and their record to date was the best in a Challenger Trials in the history of the Cup. However, *USA* had beaten us two out of three also.

Both skippers were asked how we thought the races would shape up. My reply was: "If *Stars & Stripes* is going to be successful out there, she is going to have to be faster upwind in a straight line. The Kiwi boat maneuvers very well and tacks very well, and it will be difficult for us to come from behind in a tacking duel. If you want a crystal-ball scenario, I can see *Stars & Stripes* having a bit of an edge in a straight line and playing the windshifts when she is ahead. If the Kiwis are ahead, they cover very tenaciously and are hard to pass. It is like having a top fuel-dragster that should go a little faster in a straight line than a turbo-charged Porsche that is good at everything, including the turns."

Then we were asked what changes we had made to our boats. Dickson answered first that *Kiwi Magic* now had a lighter mast and more lead in the keel. He said they had also increased the size of the sail area by moving the forestay forward. They had lengthened the spinnaker pole too.

I kept my answer very low-key. We hadn't made many changes

either, just a little here, a little there, like adding two inches to our wings. Then Chris piped up, "Dennis forgot to mention he's got a new rudder." The audience laughed, but Chris was just warming up. It was the start of a carefully planned attempt to rattle me.

A news conference was to be held later in the morning at our dock. John Marshall was going to explain an addition to the hull of *Stars & Stripes* that we felt would help our speed. When I announced our own news conference at the earlier one, a journalist asked if this concerned some "secret weapon" we might use. Dickson was ready to pounce.

"Maybe I could answer that one for you. Okay, Dennis?"

I knew what was coming because Chris's father had been at the measurement earlier that day. He'd seen our boat and received information about what had been done to her. I just sat back and let the kid have his moment.

"Maybe what they're going to tell you at that conference is that they have a little bit of a plastic boat themselves. I think they're planning on telling you about a plastic coating they've got from the 3M Company. It really doesn't make it a plastic boat—it's on the way but it isn't fiberglass. All the boats have tried different coatings and *Stars & Stripes* has this particular coating that comes in self-adhesive sheets three feet by one foot."

By now the entire press crowd was rolling with laughter. I guess they thought this was some kind of super-spy work because I doubt they were aware that Roy Dickson had heard the whole story just a few hours before. Chris was obviously enjoying himself.

"It's .007 of an inch thick and has little V-shaped grooves in it. I suppose I shouldn't go too far with this, I should leave something for later. But *Stars & Stripes* had this coating on in the third round and we beat them then, so I don't think this 'secret weapon' is secret, nor will it provide huge lifts in boat speed."

Chris had most of it right, but he did make a tactical error. We had actually added the "riblets" on December 24 and 25, so they weren't on when we last raced him. The press, of course, went wild with the plastic boat versus the plastic coating, and how the kid had put one over on the old man.

Here is John Marshall's technical explanation of the riblets:

"Britton Chance was the point man on the riblet program. He had excellent contacts with the 3M Company. Early on we had identified the principle components of drag on the boat. You have to take drag bit by bit to get rid of it. The key elements of drag are wing-tip vortex drag, wave-making hull drag, rough water drag, and viscous surface

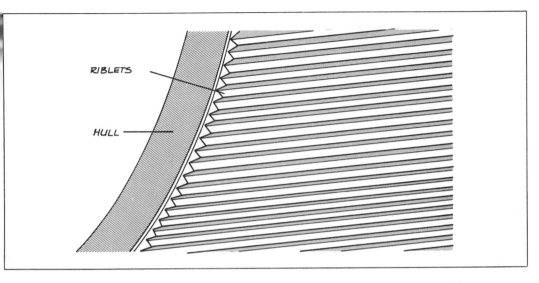

RIBLETS

HULL

Riblets are .007-inch-thick V-shaped grooves on plastic film manufactured by the 3M corporation. We applied the plastic shells to *Stars & Stripes'* hull. By loosening up the flow of water next to the hull, the riblets reduce friction and so increase boatspeed.

drag. Viscous drag—the drag that results from water flowing over the surface of the hull, the keel, and the wings—can be 40 percent of the total drag. Conventional wisdom says that smooth is fast. But our research suggested some things might just be faster than smooth.

"One was long-chain polymers, that could be released into the boundary layer to stabilize it. A proven technology, its applications have been relatively obscure. In one, polymers injected into the water big-city fire departments use to extinguish fires in tall buildings help reduce drag as the high-pressure water is pumped up very long hoses. The polymers reduce the frictional loss of the flow up the hose, resulting in more pressure in the water delivered to the fire. Polymers were tried on sailboats but quickly outlawed by the IYRU back in 1967. Since then a variety of attempts have been made to invent a polymer paint that would skirt the rule. The rule states you can't eject or release polymer, so that eliminates devices such as a holding tank and tubes attached to orifices all over the boat by which the stuff could be squeezed out like spaghetti. But what about a polymer in some kind of paint that could leech out at the correct rate? We asked 3M to work on that.

"But the riblets were by far the most promising for the short term.

Riblet technology has appeared in the professional literature for over ten years now, and it is a proven fact that riblets can reduce surface viscous drag. The idea was to have many thousands of tiny little longitudinal grooves etched along the hull. Boeing had experimented with etching grooves along the skin of its airplanes, but that was obviously impractical for a boat like a 12-meter. 3M had been developing much the same technology using plastics, so they joined forces with Boeing to produce riblets now being tested at their Seattle labs and on a 757. Boeing had also helped the U.S. Olympic rowing team reduce the fluid drag on their racing shells. Tom Darling, one of our crew, had been an Olympic Silver Medal oarsman, and he was familiar with that project. He reported it had been tested on a single scull and had definitely made a difference. Rowing was one of the sports in which Americans were not expected to do well against the Europeans and yet they had won a Silver Medal. Though not conclusive, it was certainly very promising. All the evidence suggested it ought to work. The 3M company sent Frank Marentic, one of their top laboratory managers, to Fremantle to help us with it. The irony was that 3M handled this through their Decorative Products Division. The basic adhesive film technology is the same as that used in household and automotive vinyl trim—it's low-tech in many ways. Just the little scratches are important; they help reduce the amount of energy lost through drag. If we could look through a very powerful microscope at the water close to the hull, we would see a series of widely spaced but dramatic explosions or upbursts rather like the towering formation of thunderstorms sometimes seen over a prairie on a very hot day. The riblets help reduce this kind of energy loss. The effect is most noticeable in light air, where we were most vulnerable.

"At a distance of some few inches from the hull, water is flowing at what the scientists refer to as its 'free stream velocity.' This means its flow is pretty much unimpeded.

"However, at the absolute contact surface of the hull—at the molecular level—the water isn't moving at all. There is actually a very thin layer of water bound to the hull. The transition zone is known as the 'boundary layer.' Successive layers of water are flowing at successively higher speeds depending on their distance from the hull. Between these layers is shearing in the flow. What happens is that the tension in these forces builds up until there is an energy release (like stretching a rubber band until it breaks). In turn, an upburst penetrates up through the boundary layer adding to turbulence and frictional drag.

"The riblets—these microscopic, sharp-edged channels—cause

much smaller and more frequent releases of shear stress, thus preventing larger columns of disturbance to go towering up through the boundary layer. The small, contained bursts of energy never get too far off the hull's surface and as a result, there is very much less disturbance in the overall flow.

"The frictional drag reduction on the hull of *Stars & Stripes* probably amounted to about 4 percent, thanks to the riblets. In moderate air that translated into a net gain of something like fifteen seconds over the entire America's Cup course. But in light air, it probably meant a gain of more than one minute—a significant improvement in a boat that had not shown terrific speed when the wind wasn't blowing hard."

Once we had gained in efficiency, the design gurus next turned their attention to how to apply that gain strategically. We knew that the riblets enhanced our light-air performance much more than our heavy-weather performance because viscous frictional drag is a more important part of the total drag when a boat moves slowly than when it's hauling the mail. Once the designers saw they had bolstered our potential in light winds, they set about looking for ways to increase our performance in 16 to 20 knots—the range that had always been our prime target. Their conclusions led to the keel-design changes we made at the end of the December trials.

The press probably gave the riblets issue more play than it deserved. There was talk that the Kiwis might protest, that we were using some exotic material, that the riblets had some mysterious qualities that only trained chemists in arcane methodology could recognize. Nothing came of all this speculation—except perhaps higher newspaper sales —and as we prepared to meet New Zealand on the race course, our attention was occupied by other, more important issues.

There was a tremendous buzz of excitement around the Fremantle waterfront when we cast off and began our tow-out behind *Betsy*. The dock was crowded with hundreds of supporters, many outfitted in special *Stars & Stripes* rugby shirts. It was a great send-off, with all the women and kids cheering like crazy and the guys on board grinning like a bunch of Cheshire cats. The theme from the movie *Top Gun* was blaring over the stereo speakers on *Betsy*, and all along the harbor's jetties there were thousands of people with flags and bunting yelling and cheering for us.

I couldn't believe it. There we were aiming to take the America's Cup away from them, and they were out there shouting, "Go Dennis . . . Yeah, you Yanks . . . Good on yer, Dennis." There were a few Americans but mostly they were Aussies. I think that they identified strongly with our guys coming back from the defeat of '83, hauling our rear ends off the mat, and punching our way through to the big showdown with the Kiwis. There also seemed to be quite a bit of animosity toward the Kiwis. New Zealanders and Australians are always at each other's throats on the sporting fields, and yachting is certainly no exception.

Although the forecast for the first day of the finals called for 20 knots at the start, building to 25, it looked to us like it might be even windier. So the first major decision we had to make was which mainsail to use. We had one we felt comfortable with that was good up to 20 knots. But we weren't completely convinced it was right so we talked and talked and finally talked ourselves into putting on our medium-heavy WeBe main, one of the sails we had made ourselves.

Just sixty minutes before the start, we decided to put up our heavier sail, anticipating stronger winds. That was a tough choice, although our weather guys Lee Davis and Chris Bedford made it a little easier by advising us to count on heavier wind. So we prepared to use the sails with the higher numbers. They were spot on with that call.

The start of the race found us at the right-hand end and the Kiwis at the left. The plan aboard *Stars & Stripes* was not to play Chris Dickson's circling game. *New Zealand* was the more maneuverable and faster-accelerating boat, and so Dickson would find it easier to end up directly behind us. Due to the complex regulations that govern racing maneuvers this position offers a competitor the most control over how the two boats will cross the starting line. And as the results showed, the majority of the races that season were won or lost at the start. Instead, we planned to jibe around the committee boat and head off on port reach away from the Kiwis. After several minutes, we would come back with very little time left for Chris to maneuver against us before the starting gun.

In fact, that is exactly what transpired during the prestart. The two boats met with about four minutes to go. Dickson was coming at us on port tack. He jibed on our leeward bow as we approached him on starboard tack and led us back to the line as we followed in his wake. Naturally, he had a little advantage by being ahead and to leeward, but it was not very significant. We sailed up to the line on starboard with about the right amount of time to go, and I tacked to port. We crossed the line three seconds ahead but because the wind wasn't exactly perpendicular to the starting line his end of the line was favored, and so we were still a little behind. We continued on port tack as did *New*

Zealand for about three or four minutes after the start, and during that time, *Stars & Stripes* was gaining ever so slightly.

Our first interesting decision was whether to tack underneath *New Zealand* and save the starboard side, or to continue across and make him duck beneath us. Our forecast called for the wind to go left later in the day, so we chose the left side of the course. As it turned out, there wasn't much wind in the left side so when the boats came back together again, we had to tack underneath him because I was afraid of a possible foul even though we were maybe three-quarters of a boat-length ahead. He immediately tacked back to port when we tacked to starboard under his bow. We went for forty-five seconds and tacked again, and then both boats settled into a speed trial on the left-hand side of the course. *Stars & Stripes* gained another half-boat-length, so the next time *KZ-7* came across on starboard we were able to cross her bow, giving us the right side. From there, we pretty much controlled the last half-mile to the weather mark and rounded fifteen seconds in the lead.

Heading down the first run, we jibe-set our spinnaker and Dickson bore away. We jibed in front of them and went down the rest of the leg on starboard with both boats seemingly tied together by a string. Officially, we rounded the leeward mark two seconds further ahead, but couldn't see much difference.

We stretched the lead out a little as Chris rounded, but he soon had *KZ-7* back up to speed and was smart to drive away from the wake of the spectator boats. We both tacked at approximately the same time, and soon it was apparent we had gained another two lengths.

We held that lead up the second beat and then rounded the weather mark thirty seconds ahead. *New Zealand* came at us on the reaches and picked up twelve seconds, so our lead was now down to about three boat-lengths. They were right back in the race. The third beat found us trying to keep a loose cover on *New Zealand* and at the same time to stay in phase with the wind shifts. Near the end of the beat, they got a little fouled up in the wash of the spectator fleet, so we gained about twenty seconds. We went around the upwind mark this time with a fairly comfortable margin of forty seconds, with no chance for them to get on our breeze downwind.

The run was uneventful. *Stars & Stripes* picked up two more boat-lengths to go around the leeward mark fifty seconds in front. With just one more leg to go for our first victory in the finals, we were feeling pretty comfortable. We were about to even the score with the Kiwis at two all and I knew the guys felt we could take them now. The mood on board was completely calm. It was just another race, but drawing first blood was nice. I was glad to have that one under our belts.

There had been a lot of dockside speculation that Dickson might buckle under the pressure, but at the press conference that night the kid looked pretty calm to me. I was impressed. It didn't seem like the loss had bothered him at all. He wasn't quite as cocky as he'd been, but he still had a lot of fight left.

I had a lot of respect for the entire New Zealand team. After all, we had sailed the first beat just a boat-length and a half apart. It could have gone either way.

When the ten-minute gun sounded for the second race, *Stars & Stripes* was on the left end of the line and *Kiwi Magic* on the right. That morning in taped interviews, I had predicted exactly what would happen at the start. Later, when the action was shown live all across Australia, the United States, and many parts of the world, my interview was juxtaposed with what was actually happening. It appeared as if I was giving a blow-by-blow account, that I must be talking from the cockpit. A lot of people commented to me about this and I felt it helped establish who was really in charge out there.

Dickson jibed under our bow onto port and chased us over to the spectator fleet on the right-hand side. That was exactly where we wanted to be because we could waste a couple of minutes as we reached downwind on port tack. We had no intention of mixing it up. We came in toward our VIP boat *Carmac VI*, then hardened up while Dickson tacked inside. Now the roles were reversed, with *Stars & Stripes* chasing the Kiwis back toward the line on starboard.

We went for the line a little sooner than Dickson as we headed down toward the left-hand end—the end we wanted. We went through a few feints, tacks, and bear-offs, all of which didn't matter much until about forty-five seconds before the gun. *Stars & Stripes* then tacked onto port and got up to speed, while *Kiwi Magic* tacked onto port to cover. We jibed under their stern to clear our air and Dickson tacked into a position on our hip that I wouldn't have liked in the same situation because *Stars & Stripes* had enough wind to build speed.

Both boats crossed the line fairly even, but *Stars & Stripes* was going 9.3 knots and that became the deciding factor on that first leg. The line was definitely skewed. The race committee had originally set the course to the first mark at 215 degrees, but they must have felt the wind was going left because they then changed it to 205 degrees in an attempt to keep the starting line at a right angle to where they thought the wind would be coming from when the race began. That was a big mistake because the wind didn't go left. In fact, it went right. So now we had the wind at more like 220 degrees, but the heading the committee had changed to, 205 degrees, had left absolutely no chance for the Kiwis to pass us because we had the controlling position between the line and the Kiwis. With the line so screwed up, all we had to do was protect that position.

One thing that definitely helped us a lot was that we didn't come right up underneath Dickson and force him to tack. We let him live there to encourage him to think he might be gaining, while we were actually pulling ahead rapidly on VMG up the course. It was like having a fish hooked on a line. We didn't want to reel him in right away, so we played a game while we were gaining nicely. Tom Whidden was right next to me calling out the numbers while I concentrated on the water in front of us. Finally the kid woke up to what the old man was doing and he tacked to port. We tacked right after him and promptly realized a two-boat-length lead.

As we both headed for the first mark, I noticed we would go for a long distance without making any gain. We'd just keep going even, even, even. Now and then we'd get a little gain like we did against Blackaller, but there was nothing too dramatic.

We rounded the mark thirty-eight seconds in the lead, but on the run the kid really got his boat flying and he cut off twenty seconds. But we still had eighteen seconds at the leeward mark and with that kind of lead, we never felt the kind of pressure he had exerted on us the day before.

The mood on *Stars & Stripes* was controlled. There was no relaxation, but neither was there any tension. We had the Kiwi bird where we wanted him and we knew we could keep him there. We now had three great advantages over Dickson. First, we had the lead. Second, the course was so skewed he really didn't have a chance to pass us. And third, we would get through the spectator wash and into smoother water before him, which would mean another boat-length or two on the beats.

We could see that a much fuller jib than what we had up was required for the initial part of the final beat, but I wanted to keep that particular card up my sleeve until the actual Cup races. For the same reason, we also chose not to use our best sails against *New Zealand*.

We won the second race by 1:36, sixteen seconds better than Race One. Once again at the press conference the kid handled himself well. I thought he was a little more subdued, but he certainly was a good sport about the losses. That's more than we ever got out of Tommy Blackaller. But I think the losses did shake the kid up a bit. He mentioned we had two races to go before it was over, when he should have been thinking they had four races to go. The 4–0 prediction he considered a joke just two days before suddenly didn't seem quite so funny.

People wonder if I eyeball the other guy and whether there's any tension between us. I never feel it and I rarely looked at Dickson. I had Tom Whidden look at him and tell me what he was up to. Tom has a good eye for that sort of thing and I trust what he has to say.

Tom and I sail the boat a little differently than most of the other 12-meter afterguards. I call the shifts and Tom tells me to go either faster or slower. I call the shifts because I look at the wind constantly and have a good feel for the wind shifts. While he dictates our boatspeed, Jon Wright makes it possible to go exactly as fast as Tom wants by trimming the main. If we need to increase speed, J.W. eases the main a bit. If Tom wants to go higher into the wind, J.W. pulls in the main. J.W. is very attentive. He has a very acute power of concentration, which has made him the great tailer he's been in four different America's Cup events.

Concentration by the mainsheet man has to be at least as intense as the helmsman's. In fact, the mainsheet man should really have more concentration than anyone else. Back there in the cockpit the tactician and the navigator can look around, fool with the running rigging, bail the boat, and do all types of things. But the mainsheet man and the helmsman are locked into specific tasks.

During the final Challenger races, among the Australian Defenders no one was confident of winning the finals before they started. That's why there had been so many protests—approximately forty-five—against each other. Sometimes there were as many as four or five in a single race. If you are confident in your boat, why risk the jury room? Why involve yourself in any incident that might jeopardize all those millions of dollars and three years of your life? So often in a protest room it comes down to whoever can tell the best lie. That's why I couldn't believe it when the jury disqualified both *Australia IV* and *Kookaburra III* in their first race. Although they both completed the entire course and *Kookaburra* did win, it went for naught because the jury tossed them both out. It was incredible. I'd never heard of it happening before.

In the third race, we used the same stay-away tactics to frustrate Dickson at the start. He clearly wanted to mix it up, but we figured the best strategy was to run off into the spectator fleet to keep him at arm's length. We knew we could beat him and we didn't want to get into a foul-out situation before the gun.

We had a slightly better start than they did, and at the gun we were ahead on starboard at the leeward end. After two fairly quick tacks, *KZ-7* went off on a long port tack to leeward. It was touch-and-go, up and down, and by the time we reached the starboard layline and *KZ-7* finally tacked, *Stars & Stripes* was able to tack underneath, forcing the New Zealanders beyond the layline. We rounded twenty-one seconds ahead.

For the run, we hoisted a three-quarter-ounce spinnaker we had borrowed from *America II*, but somehow the snap shackle on the halyard wasn't closed properly. As its name implies, the snap shackle is supposed to snap shut with a very definite sound when it's shut properly. There was some kind of gunk in the mechanism that prevented it from closing adequately, but John Barnitt, the mastman, thought it was okay so up it went. It flew for about ten seconds before the shackle opened and the spinnaker came down in the water on our port bow. My heart sank down around my ankles as I watched it descend. It was like watching twenty-five years of America's Cup effort flutter into the sea, and there was nothing we could do about it.

I didn't say a damned word. I just stood there with my mouth open and thought, Oh, my God. No! But the crew pulled together immediately. Everyone but Tom Whidden and myself went forward to pull the big sail onboard. When the spinnaker went up the crew was pulling the jib down so that was in the water too. *Stars & Stripes* slowed considerably. The guys did a superb job to rehoist in just ninety-one seconds. There was no yelling, no accusations, no blame leveled. That's not our style.

It was a great recovery, but in the mad scramble on the foredeck, the port halyard was attached to the spinnaker underneath the headstay. That meant that we couldn't hoist a jib without preventing the new chute from coming down. So, one mistake led to another. At that point Scotty Vogel had to go up the mast and clear the mispositioned halyard. While Scotty was up there I steered a little high to protect ourselves in case the Kiwis tried to pass us to windward. That meant we had to give up a little VMG, and it also meant we had to jibe for the mark a little later down the course. When we did jibe, *New Zealand* continued on port even though we were on the layline. Dickson soon bore off and sailed by the lee, which slowed us down. Then he jibed onto starboard, tucking her bow under our stern so he could ride our wave while the boat got up to speed.

KIWI TRAGIC

By the time we reached the leeward mark, the Kiwis had established an overlap, but it was very close.

Sometimes they had the overlap and sometimes they didn't. We had Peter Isler in his bright-red foul weather gear standing right aft on our transom, sighting across the water at them. If I denied them room at the mark, then under the yacht-racing rules, the onus was on me to prove I had broken the overlap. I wasn't confident I had, and I certainly didn't want to blow the race in a protest, so I allowed them into the inside and they rounded six seconds ahead.

That was the boat race right there. We spent the next two hours trying to pass, but with 20 knots of wind and the boats so close in speed, there were no passing lanes. We threw everything we had at them but they hung on tenaciously. We were fifteen seconds behind at the next mark and after the two reaches, we lost another four seconds to round nineteen seconds astern at the leeward mark. On the third beat we hit them with thirty tacks, but each was met with a beautifully executed covering tack by the Kiwis. *New Zealand* was certainly a great tacking boat and her crew had plenty of heart. Our guys could have gone on tacking all day and all night too, if necessary. We did everything we could. We threw false tacks at them, we tried down-speed tacking (with our boatspeed as little as 3 knots), and yet we still couldn't wriggle off the hook. It was pretty frustrating choking on their gas like that.

We went around the top mark twenty-nine seconds astern and on the run were able to close the gap to just fourteen seconds. But that was still not enough to allow us to bust through. Coming around that leeward mark in the lead gave Dickson a tremendous advantage. On the last beat we went all-out to tack them down. I told the guys, "Get ready, we're going to kick their ass and grind them down." "All right, we're ready," they replied. It was a great challenge but it was tough. The breeze was really howling in, and there was a big, steep chop on top of three-foot swells. The guys themselves never really said much. They were too busy catching their breath in the fourteen seconds or so between tacks. We established an America's Cup record by throwing fifty-five tacks at them up that last 3.25-mile leg to the finish. It was a tremendous display of courage on the part of both crews. We knew at the leeward mark that being fourteen seconds behind a boat of similar speed meant there was no way we could get ahead in the fourteen or fifteen minutes to the layline. The only way to pass was to force a mechanical or human error on their part. We tried, but the Kiwis held their ground.

When you're part of a great struggle like that you come to know the

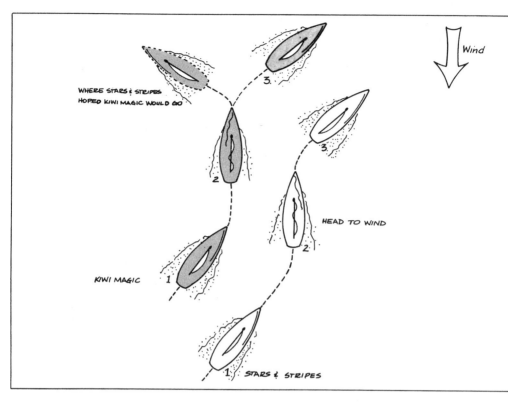

Finals, third race, January 1987. *Stars & Stripes* initiates a false tack going head to wind but *Kiwi Magic* is not fooled. (1–2). *Stars & Stripes* falls off onto her original tack (3) without managing to steer clear.

meaning of the word guts. True intestinal fortitude is a rare combination of raw courage, iron determination, and brute strength. My guys had all that and more. I was very proud of them. It would have been easy for them to slacken off, to take it easy, to say, "Look, we're behind. Can't you see there's no point to all this tack, tack, tacking?" But they were so fired up, if anyone had been dumb enough to say those things, they probably would have eaten him alive or at least tossed him overboard. Instead they stuck together, backing each other up, muttering words of encouragement to each other. It was like combat. When you're staring death in the face you either fight your way out or you go under. There was no way the *Stars & Stripes* crew were going to lie down and die. At the end they were all smiling in defeat. That's the mark of a great team. There they were, all grinning and backslapping as if they had actually won the damned thing. That's what sailboat racing is all about. We all knew that we couldn't win every race. The important thing isn't always losing, but knowing how to lose.

The day of the fourth race started out like it might be the windiest we had had all summer. In spite of our forecast, which called for weather similar to the first three days, we knew in our hearts it was going to blow so we picked our medium-heavy air WeBe mainsail—the same in-house sail we used in the first race. We tuned up against *Australia IV* before the start, and it was clear that we had pretty good speed. We were all very relaxed, though I felt as if I were at death's door. During the lay-day called by the Kiwis, we went out testing sails and I got hit on the head by the boom. It was a pretty solid whack. I felt sick to my stomach and was very dizzy. I was also terribly dehydrated. I don't think it had anything to do with the pressure of the races. In years past, I've sometimes felt a little sick to my stomach before the start, but usually I'm fine by the fifteen-minute gun, when the adrenalin really begins to flow and I'm concentrating 100 percent on racing. But this time I felt sick and I stayed sick throughout the entire race. In fact, I felt so uncomfortable at several points that I found myself crying. The tears just kept rolling down my cheeks. There was nothing I could do but stand there, hold the wheel, and keep driving. At the end of the race I got straight off and onto *Betsy*.

As we went out for the start, I was shocked to see that the course officials had marshaled all the spectator boats onto the left-hand side of the line. In previous races, I had always been able to count on having our VIP boat *Carmac*, or a boat of similar size, on the right-hand side of the course when I had to enter on the left. I certainly didn't ever want to be trapped on the right side of the course, because I felt if I was pinned in there by my opponent, I wouldn't be able to get back. If you want to have your opponent follow you in a match race, you want him following on port so that you can jibe onto starboard and come back. When you come into the starting area from the left side, he is going to drive just downwind of you and trail you closely into the spectator fleet. But if you start on the right, you can just jibe over there and have two minutes of rest. That makes it much harder for your opponent to attack. In this instance, there were no spectator boats on the right for me to use to brush him off. Through a series of maneuvers including tacks and fake tacks, I finally managed to get rid of him and come back to the line on starboard. We liked the left-hand side today and he seemed to favor the right. I couldn't figure out why.

He was smart enough to realize that the left was the favored end, but I guess he wanted the starboard tack advantage on the right side of the course, or he believed the wind was going to go to the right against the forecast. In any case, we were freely given our way.

Chris did try a clever tactic by attempting to get me up to the line early so that I would have to reduce our speed to prevent crossing early. But I realized quickly what he was doing and I was not about to fall for that. I didn't really go for the line. When he came charging over at me, I responded by speeding up just enough to protect our position.

At the moment I chose—not the one he wanted to force on me— I went for the line. When the gun sounded, we had a nice three-boat-length lead. That's the only thing that saved us, because when we tacked to port to cover we were going very slow. It was chicken-bone-in-the-throat slow. This occurred because between the time that we tuned up with *Australia IV* and the moment the gun went off, the wind had come up considerably, bringing with it steeper seas and increased spectator chop. The waves went from being quite smooth to rough, and yet we were still in our smooth-water trim with hard sheet, traveler down, and not much twist in the sails. We were slow to change gears. Dickson had *KZ-7* set up with her sails out nice and easy, which is a much better way to go through a chop. We needed to ease things out, open her up, and let *Stars & Stripes* find her legs, but in the five minutes it took us to do that, *New Zealand* came 7 degrees of bearing closer to us.

This amounted to three boat-lengths so they had now drawn even. We sailed into a slight hole in the wind, but Dickson failed to come across at us. That was his big mistake. If he had engaged us then, taken the aggressive role at that moment, he probably would have been able to snatch the lead. But when he drew even with us, he kept going. I really can't blame him because he was abiding by one of the great axioms of yacht racing—if you're winning, don't change what you're doing. Dickson had gained three boat-lengths and he must have felt he finally had *Kiwi Magic* on the move. We were going slow and he was hauling the mail, but the real turning point in the race came when he tacked onto the starboard layline as the wind shifted to the left, just as it had done at the start. Now the wind was coming from ahead of him and he could no longer sail directly toward the next mark. I saw an opportunity to move in while he was temporarily out of phase, so I tacked and went at him. We crossed underneath his bow and made the tack work. He backed off and after a few more tacks, we made the layline a little in the lead. Then we stretched it out, as he had to make several tacks to find clear air. The first mark was ours by thirty-one seconds because we seized the moment while young Mr. Dickson played by the book.

The Kiwis were forced to press hard in the strong wind and sea, and as so often happens in such a situation, things began going wrong for them. Their first gear breakage was a small link between their boom vang and its travel car. The vang holds the boom in a locked position and is used on windward legs. As it came off, the boom skyed up into the air. That caused a chain reaction that turned *Kiwi Magic* to *Kiwi Tragic.*

As the boom pointed upward, the mainsail went limp and the luff zipper caught on the spreader. This forced the Kiwi crew to send a man aloft while they also tried to repair the vang. Preoccupied with damage control, they didn't have time to set up for the leeward mark rounding, which was fast approaching. When they finally got things squared away, they were forced into a pressure preparation.

Dickson wheeled *KZ-7* into a flying jibe, perhaps his only hope of keeping her in the race. But since the boom hadn't been secured properly, it flew through an arc of close to 180 degrees at a tremendous speed. There was a terrifying noise as it smashed into the permanent backstay. The force of the impact buckled the masthead wand containing the boat's wind, speed, and direction sensors. It also bent the masthead crane off to starboard. That meant that at the beginning of the second beat, when they tacked from port to starboard in order to clear their air, their headboard was caught on the crane. That prevented the normal set of the sail so they had to tack back. They put in two quick tacks and found themselves up on our hip with nowhere to go while attempting to make repairs. That allowed us to straight-line out to the right side of the course in a commanding lead that was continually opening up. Yet even with all their problems, the Kiwis lost only forty seconds.

We went around the second windward mark and down the two reaches with the wind howling like hell. It was up to 28 true with big seas breaking all around us. As far as the eye could see there was nothing but white water. This is when all those months in the big winds of Hawaii paid off. There was a fantastic sensation of power in the boat. These were *her* conditions, and she really flew along on those reaches with the speedo numbers hovering close to 13 knots at times. We gained nine seconds on the reaches, although to be fair to the Kiwis, they were wounded and no doubt had to take it

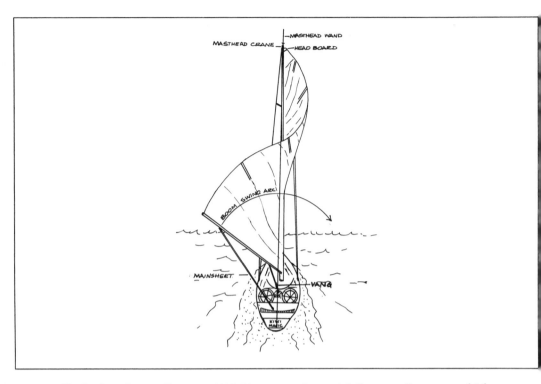

Finals, fourth race, January 1987. Due to equipment failure on the vang, which holds the boom down on leeward legs, *Kiwi Magic*'s boom flies high in the air during a jibe. The boom crashes into the permanent backstay, pulling the mast crane off to one side and damaging valuable instrument sensors aloft.

easy on the jibe since they now were without a permanent backstay.

We came around the leeward mark with *Stars & Stripes* really steaming along. We got off a few nice shifts up the beat and held them even on the run. Down that run, they had trouble with their luff zipper opening up again. We extended the lead by another two minutes to win by 3:38. Right at the moment they crossed the line, their main ripped right up the luff. It just wasn't their day.

Perhaps the most dramatic moment came when they sent their bowman, Earl Williams, aloft to cut the main down. He was hauled up on a bosun's chair as far as the hounds because the crane was broken off right there, and there was no gantline to haul him all the way up to the top of the mast. That meant that the kid had to climb hand over hand another twenty-two feet. It was like shinnying up a greasy flag pole, except in this case the flag pole was moving violently through an arc of 60 degrees. In those big seas and 28 knots of wind, young Mr. Williams risked his life. The guy was either very brave or very foolish.

That race made the score: Good Guys 3, Black Hats 1. It put the Kiwis in a pretty tough spot because it meant they had to win three races in a row. Of course, there was some talk about *Australia II* being in the same position back in '83, but I don't think anyone really believed the situations were similar. Here, the two boats were pretty close in speed and both had exhibited fine teamwork. But *Stars & Stripes* was just a little better and our crew a little more experienced.

And yet to listen to young Dicko, as his friends call him, it was no big deal. After all, he liked to remind everyone, *New Zealand* had won forty-one of forty-two races going into the finals. But what he didn't mention was that the one boat to beat him was *Stars & Stripes*, and that boat had just taken three out of four off him. I wasn't counting my chickens, but I felt pretty strongly we'd be on the line come January 31.

It was about that time that a local newspaper ran a story about our good luck charm being a clove of garlic hidden in the bow. It's an old seadog's trick—supposedly to ward off evil. Though it made good copy, I didn't think it was true. I guess a guy with an Irish name like Conner is expected to be superstitious, but I don't go in for all that blarney. As I've said, I believe luck is 99 percent skill and preparation. You make your own luck by making sure everything and everybody functions optimally. My credo is that there's no excuse to lose.

But the story turned out to be true. Apparently, we'd been sailing with that clove of garlic for some time. The guys could have stashed all kinds of good luck charms on board and I would never have known. They figured it had been there the whole time and we'd been winning, so why change? That sounded good to me.

On the eight-mile tow out to the line in what we hoped would be the last race against *New Zealand*, it was obviously going to blow hard again so we debated which mainsail to use. *Betsy* was loaded up with dozens of sails so we had quite an inventory to choose from. Jon Wright and Tom Whidden were all for using the same WeBe main we had up in the first and fourth race. It was slightly smaller than our full-size number-three main, and though it looked good, I talked them into using an even smaller sail since our boat just didn't seem to go when she was heeled over. While we won the fourth race in a real blow, I had felt that *Stars & Stripes* just wasn't going the way she should. We ended up going with our smallest sail—a brand-new America II main made by Larry Leonard. It had never been flown in a race before.

Just before the start, it was blowing 25 knots true from the southwest and I felt we might have been better under a number-six jib. But *KZ-7* had a bigger main and a bigger jib than ours so I figured we should match their sail selection.

When we went into the prestart, the Kiwis tried something different. Instead of chasing us from afar as they had before, they didn't engage us at all. Because they wanted the left-hand side, their plan was to come at us with a minute to go, and tack underneath us up near that side of the line. We tacked and jibed around so we could come back at the pin with good speed at the line.

The Kiwis were over the line before us and yet within three or four minutes, we were clearly going better than they were. They tacked and couldn't cross, and had to tack back under our bow. This was a wasted effort because Peter Isler had noticed that as we crossed the line, the race committee hoisted the general recall pennant, summoning both boats to return for another start. Their justification was that the buoy was drifting. If so, it hadn't moved very far because it was on the same approximate station for the forty-five minutes prior to the start. I've heard of both boats being over early and being brought back, but I cannot remember another general recall in any other 12-meter race I've been in. In fact, I can't recall there ever having been one in America's Cup history. At the time I felt the recall may have had more to do with the race committee's timing being off than with a drifting buoy. I was pretty unhappy because *Stars & Stripes* had won the start and we were going well, and now I had to perform the same trick all over again. I felt like a trained seal being brought on stage for an encore.

Then we had a forty-five-minute delay while the committee set up to start the race again. The recall was of course a godsend for *KZ-7* because they saw they were a little slower than *Stars & Stripes,* and were able to adjust to match our speed. They changed to smaller sails during the break, otherwise they would have faced a difficult situation.

The second starting sequence was identical to the first except that the Kiwis were going better because of their adjustment. Even so, within three or four minutes it was obvious that we were still faster. They tacked from underneath our stern onto port and we put a nice slam-dunk on them. That left *Stars & Stripes* clearly in the lead. After several tacks during which we gained, we straight-lined for the rest of the beat. *Stars & Stripes* went around forty-two seconds ahead. Although the pressure seemed to be off, they certainly weren't quitting and they had *Kiwi Magic* going extremely well downwind. They got on our wind and began closing the gap.

KIWI TRAGIC

We were sailing very conservatively and didn't open the luff zippers because now the breeze was definitely up and we didn't want to experience the problem that plagued them in the previous race. Although we were using one of our biggest spinnakers—one that was fifty feet on the midgirth—the Kiwis opened up their zippers, which gave them an extra eighty square feet of sail area. This allowed them to pick off almost twenty seconds. On the second beat we put on our number-six jib, enabling the boat to move through the sea almost perfectly straight up and down. We were going nicely and making gains, but with about one-third more of the second windward leg to go, we suffered a bit of a breakdown.

Apparently, the Maori wind god answered the prayers of the Kiwis in the spectator fleet. On race mornings, with thousands and thousands of people lining the harbor, Maoris would visit *New Zealand* in their war canoes, beseeching the great god of the winds to blow our sails to bits. Sure enough, our jib exploded like a lightning strike in a thunderstorm. The stitching came out of the vertical mitre on the foot and bam!, it was gone in an instant. We were left with a narrow ribbon of Kevlar fluttering from the forestay while the rest of it went straight into the water on the port side. The crew responded magnificently. Everyone except Tom Whidden and Jon Wright raced forward to clear the mess away and get a new jib bent on.

I didn't cry out or curse or sigh. I didn't slash my wrists or quote Shakespeare. I just told J.W. to ease the traveler down while I kept sailing the boat for maximum VMG. We didn't miss a wink. John got the traveler down and eased the main a bit, and I kept our speed on the right number. Unfortunately, we were within two minutes of the port layline when this occurred, so I had to tack while the guys were all on the foredeck. That put us on port with no rights, and *KZ-7* came right at us with a big white bone in her teeth. I felt like a sitting duck waiting for the Kiwis to take aim with a double-barreled shotgun. The big question was if we could cross them on port with only the mainsail powering us. If we could not, they would be able to force us off our course, since they had the right of way. Fortunately, I kept my cool, and sure enough, the guys got the new jib up just in time for us to come together. As we pointed higher they tacked underneath because they could see we were going to cross their bow. As fast as you can say Jack Robinson, the new sail was up hard and sheeted in. Our lead was cut from forty-eight seconds to just fourteen seconds, but at least we were still ahead. I doubt whether many other crews could have performed as well under so much pressure in so much wind. All their

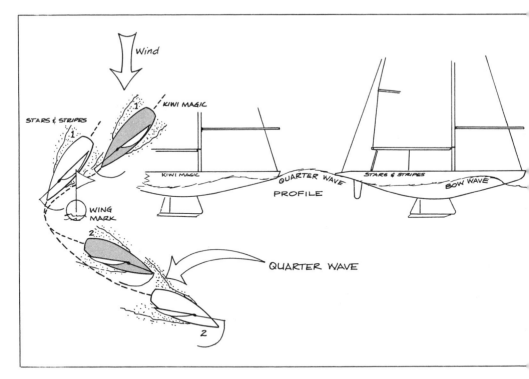

Finals, fourth race, January 1987. *Kiwi Magic* (1) rounds the wing mark with her bow ten feet away from *Stars & Stripes'* stern (1). *Stars & Stripes,* traveling at 13 knots, kicks up a large quarter wave (2), which *Kiwi Magic* is unable to drive over. *Stars & Stripes* maintains her lead.

experience, all their strength, all their skill and their seamanship came together in that moment. It was a great display of overcoming adversity.

Once we recovered, we got the spinnaker set up for the first reach and went around the weather mark onto the first reach with that slender lead. That's when the Kiwis put up their gennaker and started gaining, gaining, gaining. We tried everything we knew to counter them. We put the staysail up. We put the staysail down. The Kiwis just kept coming, coming, coming right down on top of us. It was touch-and-go as to who would get to the wing mark first. I feared they might roll right over our top. We barely beat them to it and with clear air, we jibed on the inside with them overlapped to windward. Their bow was only ten feet from our stern. But once we were around, we had them trapped in our wave. With *Stars & Stripes* doing almost 13 knots, we threw up a big quarter-wave that rose up like a wall of water right in front of them and effectively blocked them from climbing over us. We held them off by sailing high down the next reach and then running almost square to the mark. This tactic worked because *KZ-7* was still wearing the gennaker, and under the rules that sail has to be flown from the pole on the boat's centerline. Once we started squaring up for the mark, Chris had to try to match us by changing spinnakers. That's when *KZ-7* really came undone. The spinnaker and the gennaker got all fouled up and they had to take both chutes down just before the mark rounding. Basically, what had happened was that when the gennaker had been jibed, the halyard ended up inboard of the headstay. Until the halyard got squared away, they couldn't put anything else up. Meanwhile, we were able to move away from them. Although we had been through two very tight reaches, they were no closer to us at the bottom than they were at the top. They hadn't capitalized on their opportunity, and I wasn't going to give them another.

The third beat was by far the windiest of the race. There were gusts of 31 knots true. In the harder conditions we weren't gaining. We had a six-boat-length lead on the Kiwis and we went all the way up the leg at about that distance. On the run, they were all over us again but they never seriously threatened to get by. They were almost over-lapped on the outside at the leeward mark, but that inside position is so powerful that there was no way they were going to sneak by. We made a real nice early spinnaker drop and we rounded well ahead but *Kiwi Magic* was breathing down our neck and I anticipated a great battle. With so much pressure on him to round quickly and set out after us, Dickson came too close and hit the mark. That was the ballgame right there. Under the rules he had to reround, and once he did, there was no way he could catch us. Tommy Whidden simply said, "They're going back," and I replied, "Well, that takes a little pressure off." And it did. We were going to beat them anyway because our speed was at least as good as theirs, and we were three boat-lengths ahead. From then on, we just cruised up the last beat with a loose cover on them all the way to the line. About halfway up they quit their tacking, cruised out to the layline, and that was it. On the way up there, the guys had some fun taking pictures of me imitating the Boston Celtics' legendary coach, Red Auerbach, with a big cigar in my mouth. The party was over and the fat lady was singing. The song was "The Stars and Stripes Forever."

When we crossed the line, the crowd on the spectator boats went wild. It was just like Newport all over again. There were horns and whistles and people going crazy with flags and balloons and streamers. They were chanting "Dennis, Dennis, Dennis." There must have been three hundred big spectator boats behind the line, and as we passed there were shouts of encouragement and congratulations from each. We knew we had sailed well, and it was gratifying to know our efforts were appreciated. I also felt a tremendous sense of satisfaction at beating a boat that had set an historic record. She had defeated every boat out there that summer except ours. They had a record of forty-two wins and five losses.

The guys on *Stars & Stripes* were really excited although they didn't go overboard with emotion. They shook hands and did a little back-slapping, but no one leaped up and did a jig on the foredeck. We were all quietly pleased that we had been able to beat *KZ-7* and Dickson. However, the Kiwis did a magnificent job and the kid was good. But when it came right down to it, I guess we showed him who's boss. As we sailed back to Challenger Harbor with our enthusiastic escort, we got the word that the measurers wanted us to report to the pen over by the Kiwi dock. This allowed us to keep our sails up and we barreled right in through the narrow harbor entrance. There must have been ten thousand people, mostly Kiwi fans, standing on the big stone break-water, and they gave us a tremendous reception. All those people standing up applauding and waving flags for us was an incredible experience. No one had ever sailed right into the harbor with a main and jib up before so that was a special treat. We did a kind of victory roll and dropped our jib right outside the *New Zealand* dock on Kiwi Point.

Behind us came *New Zealand* under her main. After that great struggle, it was quite a sight having the two twelves together there in the little harbor. The Kiwi crew gave us three cheers and we returned them. It was as if we had suddenly come home with the Cup under our arm. The most extraordinary thing was that people actually seemed to be rooting for us. I couldn't believe it but there they were —Aussies and New Zealanders, everyone cheering for the Americans. All summer we worked hard at creating a good public image Down Under and at last it was paying off. I got the distinct impression that we were more popular than the Aussie Defenders, and ultimately we were.

During one of the earliest Challenger meetings at the Yacht Club Costa Smeralda at Porto Cervo, it was unanimously agreed that we would continue to uphold the long America's Cup's tradition of Challenger solidarity. The New Zealand syndicate was represented by Aussie Malcolm, who was in complete agreement that all Challengers should stick together with one goal in mind: to defeat the Australian Defender. Nothing was set down in writing—it wasn't the sort of understanding that needed to be spelled out.

So we were surprised and annoyed when the New Zealanders announced after the final race that they were scrapping the agreement and would help the Australians. We had expected them to help us. Instead, they switched sides and sided with the enemy. If we were at war that would be treason. We certainly felt betrayed. After all that close racing against us, they probably knew as much about the performance capability of our boat as we did. That intelligence would have been invaluable to the Aussies. Malin Burnham tried to talk some sense into Michael Fay, the New Zealand syndicate chairman, but all he got was lame excuses.

The Kiwis supposedly based their decision on the close cultural and sporting ties that have always bound New Zealand and Australia. But the truth was that the Kiwis wanted to cut the costs of their next challenge. It would be a lot less expensive to come to Fremantle in 1991 than to go after the Cup in the United States. I guess Michael Fay also felt pressured by the folks back home to atone for the way we had handled the fiberglass issue. To the Kiwi partisans, we were the Black Hats because they thought we had called them cheats. We had to be punished.

The Kiwis' decision to turn their backs on us really gave the Aussies a big leg-up. They would know how we tacked, how we straight-lined compared to their boat. But we would benefit too, when the Aussies realized that *Kiwi Magic* was a faster boat than *Kookaburra III*. They had been fairly confident of their boatspeed, but once *Kiwi Magic* bested *Kookaburra* and they realized they didn't have the edge in speed, they would lose the psychological edge as well. Suddenly their $28 million program would be teetering on the brink of disaster.

A lot of people were hoping *Australia IV* would be the Defender so the 1987 America's Cup would be a rematch of DC and the guys versus Bond, Lexcen, Jones, et al. But all summer I knew that Bondy was going to lose. We had trialed with *Australia IV* before the races, and the boat was so slow we just couldn't imagine it beating the *Kookaburra*. Although we never let the Aussies know, we sandbagged them a little during those trials. We used to overtrim the main, and have the trim tab down a few degrees and the rudder up to induce a little drag. We never really trimmed the gear the way we would in a real test to deliberately keep them in the dark. Every once in a while, we did floor it to try to measure it without their knowing what was going on. I think the Aussie skipper, Colin Beashel, picked up on our ploy, but I doubt he wanted to admit it. That's when we realized *Stars & Stripes* could be upward of fifteen seconds a mile faster. It gave us a lot of confidence because the Kookas didn't seem to have that kind of speed on *Australia IV*. We didn't want to show the *Australia IV* guys how fast we really were because we knew that they might help the Kookas like the Kiwis did.

In all fairness to the New Zealanders, their point of view made sense. I don't blame anyone for looking after his best interests. I would do the same. Even so, we certainly tried to pressure them to change their mind or at the very least to stay neutral. We even had a very high official in the U.S. government try to influence the Kiwis. Did they want continued good relations with the United States or not? We also had a couple of financial heavy-hitters call the Bank of New Zealand to tell them the score. Michael Fay is a merchant banker so he would have understood better than anyone. Soon after, Fay called a press conference to announce that although the trials against *Kookaburra III* would proceed as scheduled, there would be no transfer of technology and their dossier on us would remain under lock and key. It was at least a partial victory. At the press conference Fay was asked if he'd been put under any pressure by the New Zealand Prime Minister David Lange. Fay refused to comment, but we knew the answer.

It was too bad Bondy had to miss out. We were certainly looking forward to a rematch. We had a score to settle with those guys. It was unfortunate that Bond's design plan was flawed. He entrusted the entire design plan to Ben Lexcen. But as brilliant as Ben is, it was unreasonable of Bondy to expect him to carry their entire design program on his shoulders. John Marshall had a team of three great designers, Bruce Nelson, Brit Chance, and Dave Pedrick, and more guys backing them up. Poor Ben was left all alone.

In 1983, the Bond camp set the pace by having Benny head an excellent design team at the Dutch tank. But they didn't follow up this time. I'm not saying Ben Lexcen wasn't smart enough. The guy is a genius. But no one should have expected him to do everything on his own. Eventually we passed them, and so did the Kookaburras.

I also think Bondy made a mistake in choosing a young guy like Colin Beashel to take the helm. Beashel is very good but he's not in the same league as John Bertrand and Iain Murray. If they had been able to persuade Bertrand into returning, they might have stood a chance. He may not be the best sailor in Australia, but he's one of the best and he has good leadership qualities and experience. Hughie Treharne, the *Australia IV* tactician, told Tom Whidden that Beashel sailed the boat in a straight line better than Bertrand. This may be true, but you can't just ignore a guy like Bertrand and bring in a youngster and expect him to fill his shoes.

It's possible that Bertrand was afraid to come back and have a shoot-out with DC. He quit while he was ahead, and that was a smart decision. Otherwise he would have been defeated—not by Dennis but by Iain Murray. If that had happened he *really* would have looked foolish. Bertrand was too smart to put his newly acquired good life on the line. He had made a lot of money from his Cup victory and he wasn't hungry anymore. Even if Bondy had dragged Bertrand back, I doubt the outcome would have been different. There's no one in the world who could have sailed *Australia IV* fast enough to beat the Kookas.

The Bond camp hung in only because of the power, influence, and drive of Warren Jones, their executive director. Jones realized that *Australia III* was slow, and he made a good call in getting rid of her and concentrating all efforts on *Australia IV*. Jones also did an excellent job of putting pressure on Parry and Murray in the media, especially when the Kookas started their protest campaign. The Kookas protested anything and everything. That upset the Bond guys, who were forced to attend boring hearings often until the wee hours of the morning. But it was Jones who hit them where it really hurt. He publicly ridiculed them and demeaned their public image by accusing them of "howling like dingoes." The dingo is not just Australia's wild native dog—it is a term of the utmost contempt. Call an Aussie a dingo and you better be prepared to fight because it's the equivalent of calling him a coward. Jones did it deliberately. He used the media like a club to beat Parry, Murray, and the Kookas on the head. He used it precisely the way he did in Newport in 1983.

That is why I always maintain it was Warren Jones who beat me then. It certainly wasn't John Bertrand because we outperformed him on the water. I was beaten in '83 by the decision to use the Dutch test tanks. That was what I call a gutsy move. If someone had come to me with a proposition as wild as that I would have laughed in his face. In fact I did laugh. Whoever heard of an upside-down keel with wings on it? It sounded crazy. It *still* sounds crazy.

The lack of espionage did us in in 1983. This time, though, we were much better prepared. We sent our spies to the World Championships

in Fremantle in January-February 1986. Also our coach, Robert Hopkins, went there to talk with people and gather intelligence. John
Marshall had sources among the Challengers, and Tom Whidden
knew pretty well what the Australians were up to. He knew what
Bondy's guys were doing even before they did. Tom used to spend a
lot of time with Hugh Treharne because of their business association
and personal friendship. They shared information that helped both
camps. For instance, Tom gave them some good advice on how to
speed *Australia IV* up. He told them how they could get rid of their
weather helm problem by moving the mast. They did it, and the very
next day they were much faster. I had my own sources. I used to hang
out with the guys at Lombardos, a waterfront bar on Fishing Boat
Harbor. I got a lot of good guff there. I think the Aussies liked the idea
of hanging out with Big Bad Dennis. They were very open and always
willing to talk about their boat. If loose lips sink ships, those guys were
going down fast. We cast a very wide net. Mostly we would haul in
minnows, but once in a while, there'd be a pretty good-sized fish. We
tried harder on that score than anyone else.

People have asked me what brought the Kiwis down. It certainly
wasn't their boat alone. We could go seventeen minutes on a leg and
they would do the same speed. Their big asset was that they could tack
better. Dickson could never get ahead of me at the start to take advantage of that strength. If he had been able to get his nose in front he
could have won, as he did in Race 3. She was very, very fast and she
was around 800 pounds lighter in the hull than *Stars & Stripes* because
she didn't have to be faired off with all the filler we needed to use.
Fiberglass is definitely better in weight distribution even when it's
used legally. It has been suggested that not being able to change their
hull might have been a disadvantage. But we didn't change our hull
very much either. All we changed was our winglets, our spars, and our
sails. We added twenty inches or so to the transom, and we did move
the rudder post once. These changes could also have been made on a
glass boat.

I'm determined to do everything I can to make sure the 12-meter-
class association outlaws glass. It's too easy to bend the rules. And
glass offers a weight advantage that was never supposed to be allowed
in the 12-meter class. If they decide to go with fiberglass the costs
(which are already very high) are going to skyrocket. We will all have
to go out and build ovens to bake the hulls to keep pace with German
technology. That means that boats are likely to cost $2 million apiece.

13

Countdown

O it had all come down to this. America's Cup 1987. Forty months ago *Australia II* had beaten us on Rhode Island Sound and brought the Cup to Australia. Ever since the day I decided to attempt a comeback, I had looked forward to January 31.

My frame of mind was a little different from September 1983. Then we knew we had a slow boat. Now we knew we had a fast one. For me, '83 was agony. This was fun.

It all seemed worth it. From the first receipt in the shoe box in San Diego, through all the cigar smoke, the thousands of miles flying, the fund raisers, the speeches, the assembling of the design team, the selection of the crew, the building of a sail inventory, the move to Hawaii, the months of practice and testing on the water, our families' concerns about living in another country, the media hassles; it was all worth it. Getting to the starting line of the actual America's Cup match, having the opportunity to win the Cup back, made it all worthwhile.

I went into the first match believing we would win. We were faster, better prepared, and more experienced. Deep down I know I can beat anyone. That's not a boast—that's the record. Over the last fifteen years, I have won more major regattas than anyone else. No one has a record like mine.

In my previous book, *No Excuse to Lose,* I made the mistake of saying that I had no natural ability on the water, and that whatever talent I had was the product of relentless practice and preparation. I wish I had never uttered those words. The truth is, that was a damned lie. In those days I was trying to shed my image as a brash young guy full of braggadocio. I was the quintessential smartassed kid and I loved to hear people say how good I was. I loved the ego-stroking.

I guess the truth is that I had an inferiority complex and that's why I loved the compliments. I responded by working twice as hard. The few strokes I got felt so nice that I'd go crazy doing things to get more and more. Finally, when I realized I really was good, I also realized that I didn't need the stroking anymore. I decided to get out of being the smartassed kid and get into being a regular person. I thought the way to do that was to play myself down, to tell people I wasn't really all that good and that I had simply worked hard to overcome my lack of natural ability.

It's more honest to realize that a guy with no natural talent couldn't win five straight races in the Star Class World Championships against eighty-nine boats. That wasn't exactly an interclub dinghy meet. You don't do something like that unless you have some natural ability. I believe it was one of my greatest achievements and I regard it as highly as Charlie Barr's three America's Cups or all of Paul Elvstrom's Olympic Medals. What won me those races is what has helped me establish the record I have: a good crew, a good boat, good sails and hard practice. I even went to the factory and helped build the boat.

Part of the reason I have the record I do is that I don't like telling my rivals how I beat them. They're all nipping at my heels as it is. It's hard to stay ahead. Actually, that's the thing that saves me. They can't catch me if they don't know which way I'm moving next. As soon as I stop, though, they'll all be alongside. It's like I'm being pursued by a pack of wolves. I can hear them out there howling through the waves. It's a sound that haunts me.

If my fierce determination to reach my final goal helps me stomach all the unpleasant aspects of an America's Cup campaign, the equally fierce loyalty and support I have received from my family, friends, and colleagues make it all possible. I couldn't and wouldn't do it otherwise.

There have been enormous personal sacrifices. I've spent a lot of time away from my home and family. My wife Judy has been the mainstay of my life. Without her support, I would have crashed long ago. Judy knew what she was getting into from the outset, because even our wedding took second place to sailing. We had to postpone the ceremony while I went off to the Olympic Trials. Ten years ago if she had said, "Lookit, young man, if you practice on those 12-meters one more day, your clothes are going to be on the front porch when you get back," a lot of things might have been different. How could I go win the America's Cup under those circumstances? Our marriage hasn't always been easy but Judy has made the best of it over the years. She's been a real trouper and she deserves all the credit in the world.

She has raised two lovely daughters. Julie gets nothing but straight A's in all her classes. She's a soccer star and very attractive, and she has her father's drive and determination. Shanna has her father's outgoing personality. She has many friends, and is also very bright and talented. That my girls are so special is due to Judy. I was never home to raise the kids. While I was out on the race course, Judy did it all single-handedly.

So, as I prepared to take the helm of the *Stars & Stripes* for the first race of the 1987 America's Cup, I knew I was there because of the work and sacrifice of many other people. This was not just the DC show. That realization contributed in part to my decision to allow on-board cameras in *Stars & Stripes,* despite my initial reservations. I wanted to share 12-meter sailing with the world, to show the public what happens during a sailboat race.

I believe the addition of cameras and sound gear on board made the 1986/87 Cup campaign especially memorable. In America, ESPN broadcast live both our final races against *New Zealand* and the Cup races against *Kookaburra III.* In Australia, three different networks brought the races to Aussie living rooms.

I felt the production was spectacular and with the gang of commentators who participated, nonsailors got hooked on 12-meter match-racing. We kept hearing about viewers in the States staying up all night, glued to their sets. Before, watching yachting was believed to be as exciting as watching paint dry. The spectacular television pictures of the rough and windy Fremantle Cup course changed that perception completely. For the first time it became a contest the general public could understand and appreciate. Viewers got excited. No longer was it a bunch of rich men floating around in red pants and straw hats.

I allowed the camera on board *Stars & Stripes* because I could see it would be good for the sport. Tom Whidden didn't want it and neither did Jon Wright. They saw it as an invasion of our tactical privacy and felt that it could be used as a weapon against us. Although I agreed,

I also saw it as very much a positive thing. If we were confident, then why not let them on board? You have to be pretty damn confident, because it's like allowing people to come into your bedroom while you're making love.

The morning of the first race seemed to go pretty quickly. I didn't feel real nervous, but I was keyed up a bit. I attended to television and radio interviews and then took care of a swarm of important San Diego backers who had materialized. It seemed as though anyone who was anyone back home had hopped on a plane and ended up in Fremantle.

There was a great hubbub at the gate and extra security guards were brought in to help keep the crowds under control. Hundreds of fans had been waiting outside the compound since early morning, clutching American flags and wearing *Stars & Stripes* T-shirts and hats. Lots of pictures were taken, and there was a good deal of screamed encouragement to me and all the guys. We even opened up the big double gates that were usually kept shut to ensure our privacy. That day we just put a rope across the driveway so that the fans could watch us get ready to leave.

By and large the people were nice and friendly and very enthusiastic. What surprised me was that there were so many Aussies who were there rooting for the Americans. I don't think the *Kookaburra* guys had done much to endear themselves to the public. After all the protests during the finals between *Kookaburra III* and *Australia II*, and the obvious animosity between Alan Bond and Kevin Parry, the Australian people were a little fed up with their own guys. Aussies are an exuberant people and they like their sports heroes to be personable and visible. The Kookaburras maintained a business-as-usual approach with no fanfare, no theme songs blaring, and no battle flags. They did all they could to submerge their personalities.

But on this morning, they lightened up a little and gave out Australian flags to the crowd. Hundreds of people, all chanting and yelling, started an impromptu parade and carried all the flags past our compound. It was all in good fun, but I felt obliged to get out there with Old Glory. I marched right along with them, waving my flag, and they laughed and joked about Big Bad Dennis being in their midst.

Although I felt relaxed, I was concerned about one thing as I walked back to our dock. There was a strong, hot easterly wind blowing offshore. If it continued to midmorning, the southwesterly sea breeze would probably either be very late coming or it might not appear at all. A thick band of dull, gray, middle-level clouds covered the entire sky, effectively stopping the sun from heating the land mass (which would cause the sea breeze to be sucked right in.)

The atmosphere reminded me very much of a typical day in Newport, Rhode Island, during the Cup Races. That caused an alarm bell to go off inside me. I kept thinking that if it was going to be a real light day, our boat might have some problems. We had worked on improving her speed, but when you build a boat to perform best in heavy conditions, you are forced to accept certain trade-offs. Those trade-offs had caused four losses in November and I was concerned that they might hamper us today.

We cast off at about nine-forty A.M., earlier than usual. Jimmy Buffet's ballad "Take It Back" ("Call it pillage, call it plunder, we're takin' it back from the boys Down Under") blared from our stereo on *Betsy*. Buffet had been a fan and supporter of ours for a long time and we all loved his music. In fact, the day before, we had had a kind of "battle of the rock stars" as Jimmy sailed *Stars & Stripes '87* and Kenny Rogers sailed *'85*. Kenny and his manager had made a substantial donation to our campaign chest, and they brought a nice note to us from Dolly Parton, who was in Perth performing with Kenny.

We were towed out through the harbor and everywhere we looked we saw thousands of people waving banners and flags. The cheering was almost deafening. There were people dressed in kangaroo suits, kookaburra suits, Uncle Sam suits. I can't remember a warmer, friendlier send-off in all my years of racing. It was almost as if we were the Aussie Defender. I noticed a sign that said, "Iain Murray Walks on Water." I thought, "Oh yeah? We'll see about that."

Normally we were able to haul up our main as we left Fisherman's Harbor. But because the wind was out of the east, it was coming from astern, and we decided to continue our tow until we were well clear of the breakwater. While I was back in the cockpit worrying about the cloud cover and its likely effect on the breeze, the crew was in fine form, laughing and joking as if they were going on a Sunday cruise. I didn't mind. It showed they were pretty confident the wind wouldn't prevent us from performing well.

Stars & Stripes '85 was alongside as she prepared to help us tune up prior to the start. In the past, we had been able to rely on some friendly competition from one of the challengers or *Australia IV*. But on this day we were back in action against our great friend Jack Sutphen and the mushroom crew. The "mushroom crew" had named themselves—supposedly they had been kept in the dark and fed on bullshit. They

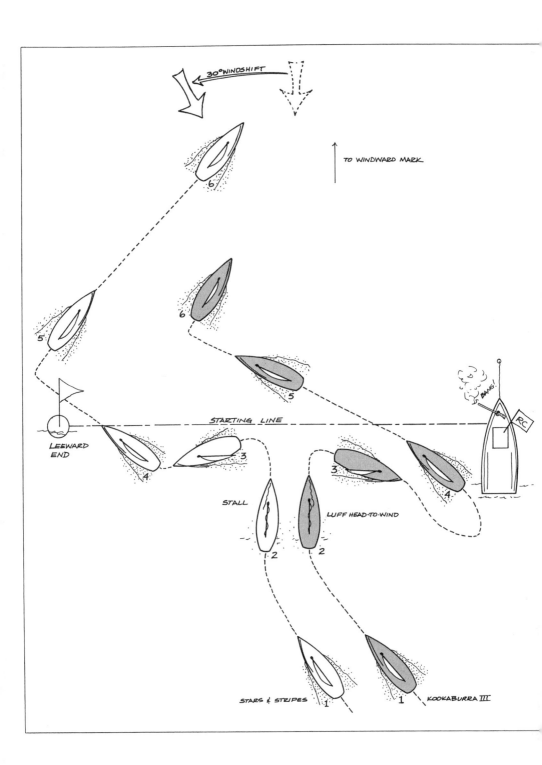

flew the mushroom battle flag (a large mushroom) and they joined their hands over their heads in the official "mushroom salute" (it looked like the cap on a mushroom). I wasn't particularly wild about it at first. But they persisted and before long we all had a lot of fun with it.

When we got to the course, the wind was very light and we changed from our medium main to our medium-light North main. That sail had been acquired from Tom Blackaller and we hadn't paid for it yet. When Tom Whidden was appointed president of North Sails International just a few days before, I asked him to arrange some kind of employee's discount from Blackaller, who runs the North loft in San Francisco. Whidden said he'd see what he could do!

As we tuned against '85, we readjusted our sail inventory to better prepare for the lighter winds. *Kookaburra III* also changed their main and jib in an attempt to match what we had on. That turned out to be a mistake because when the gun sounded, the wind was up to about 15 knots and the Kooks seemed a little underpowered, while our sails were just about right.

Stars & Stripes entered the line from the committee boat end, jibed around the boat, then headed off into the spectator fleet on port with *Kookaburra* trailing us by the length of the line. We sailed on port for several minutes before tacking back toward the Aussies. *Kookaburra* went beyond *Stars & Stripes* and followed us back toward the starting line.

When we neared the middle of the line, we hardened up with *Kookaburra* to windward. Peter Gilmour, who all summer long had been contending for the Defender's role in whichever *Kookaburra* boat Iain Murray wasn't helming, had now joined Murray in *Kookaburra III*. Known as "Crash" for his aggressive driving, Gilmour drove the boat during the starts and once on the first leg, he handed the wheel over to Murray. Today, Gilmour's strategy was apparently to run us up the line, hoping we'd run out of room and be over early. If that didn't

Opposite: America's Cup, first race, January 1987. As *Stars & Stripes* and *Kookaburra III* approach the starting line on starboard tack (1), they each luff head to wind (2). The Kooks are forced to tack away toward the race committee boat (3) to start at the windward end of the line, while *Stars & Stripes* bears off to a start at the leeward end (3–4). This is a favored end at that moment because of a 30-degree wind shift. When we tack (4–5) our position (5) allows us to point closer toward the mark than can *KA-15*, which began at the less-favored end. We catch a lift and soon gain almost a boat-length on *KA-15* as we cross their bow (5–6).

work, he hoped we wouldn't be up to full speed when the gun sounded. Attempting to execute his plan, Gilmour tacked and went to the right side of the line.

The starting line had definitely been set short by the Royal Perth race committee, and I suspected the committee was unfairly favoring the Kookaburras. My guess was that the Kooks probably told the race committee to have as short a line as was legal. I'm not saying they set out to cheat, but the race committee was dominated by Royal Perth people and *Kookaburra III* was sailing under the Royal Perth burgee. This is the big leagues and—like it or not—it's the way the game is played at this level. This was not just a boat race. This was big business.

I can't prove that the line was deliberately set short, but I do know that it was about half the length of the America's Cup starting line in 1983. There was a tacit agreement between the Challengers and the Defenders that the length of the line in 1987 would be the same. In the seventeen previous America's Cup races that I had participated in, I had never known a starting line to be so short.

When the matter was raised at the postrace press conference, Noel Robins, the executive director of Royal Perth's America's Cup Defense, said simply: "What you see is what you get." The truth was the Royal Perth Yacht Club could do just about anything it wanted out there. A shorter line made it harder for both boats to get an even start because there was less room to maneuver, and since *Kookaburra* was the better maneuvering boat, a shorter line should have favored them.

However, the strategy backfired on the Kookaburras because Gilmour was forced to tack just before the start and was unable to get his boat up to full speed at the gun. This maneuvering also placed him at the undesirable right-hand end of the line.

Almost immediately after crossing the starting line, we tacked because we were obviously ahead. As soon as we did, the bearing on *Kookaburra III* started going right, meaning we would definitely cross in front. At the same time, we caught a nice lift and when we did cross, we had almost a full boat-length lead. That really was the race right there because we soon caught another major shift. The wind went from 200 degrees to 170 degrees, and at the first mark we were well ahead by 1:15.

Although the second leg was supposed to have been a run directly downwind, the 30-degree shift changed it into a reach, where the wind came from our beam instead of our stern. The shift had been advantageous not only because we caught the lift, but also because we felt we might be vulnerable in light air going downwind. With the run changed, we found there was not much difference between the two boats on a reach.

Throughout the second leg and most of the third, the wind kept getting lighter and lighter. The start of the race had been in about 12 knots. It then dropped to 10, then 8. At the third mark, *Kookaburra* had climbed back into the race by knocking thirty-nine seconds off our lead. That illustrated just how vulnerable we were in light air. On that leg, the Kooks were gaining on us by about a boat-length per minute, and they would have caught us had the wind not piped up again toward the end of the leg.

On the first legitimate reach, the wind again played tricks that favored us. As we rounded the third mark, we set up for a reach (the point of sailing during which a sailboat will go fastest). But by the time Murray rounded the same mark, the wind had shifted back to the right, causing *Kookaburra* to set the spinnaker pole aft for a run. That advantage was seen most clearly by the wing mark when we rounded 1:41 ahead.

On the second reaching leg, both boats set gennakers. We had built ours shortly after *Australia IV* had revealed their "secret weapon" in the Finals of the Defender Trials with *Kookaburra III.* We knew *Kookaburra* would copy the design, so we decided we needed a gennaker of our own. However, near the end of the leg, we got hit by a squall that suddenly increased the wind from 8 to 22 knots true. I called for an immediate gennaker takedown and jib set, and though there was a scramble on the foredeck, the guys completed the maneuver quickly.

From there on, it was just a matter of sailing conservatively and applying a loose cover. Except for the third leg, when *Kookaburra* just kept gaining and gaining, there was not much pressure on us. What was unusual about the race was the number of sail changes we had made. I think we made more in that race than in all the races combined.

One thing that did seem strange was the silence at the end of the race. Normally, a winner gets a howling, hooting welcome home after the first race of the America's Cup. I think the Aussies were so confident that *Kookaburra* would win in the lighter air that they were a little in shock. There were some shouts of encouragement from Americans on the spectator boats, but for the most part there was just a very eerie silence. On board *Stars & Stripes* we shook hands and told each other, "Good race," but that was the extent of our celebration. One down, three to go.

★   ★   ★

COMEBACK

The second race was held on the first day of February, and it was sailed in wind conditions exactly opposite to those of the first race. It was a beautifully clear, cloudless day with brilliant sunshine; the kind of day we had come to expect in Fremantle. The southwesterly sea breeze started to come in early so we knew we were in for quite a blow.

First blood to *Stars & Stripes* had done nothing to dampen the enthusiasm of the Aussies. They were lining the roads around the waterfront, more than 150,000 strong, the newspapers said. That morning, a Sunday, it seemed like anyone anywhere near Fremantle had come by to watch the two "greyhounds of the sea" head out to do battle.

At the end of our dock, our huge American flag was snapping straight out in the strong onshore wind. Once again, a huge crowd had gathered outside our compound and there were many shouts and good-natured yells. The public support for this yachting event was unique in my memory. The folks in Newport only barely tolerated us and they certainly seemed glad to see us go. But in Australia, the people appreciated everything about the event. They loved the international competition, the sheer beauty of the sport, the life and sounds and images we brought to this little city by the ocean.

We received another spectacular send-off, and by the time we reached the harbor entrance, the wind was already blowing 23 knots true. While I was considering changing our mainsail to something a little heavier, the weather guys were confidently predicting that the wind would stay between 19 and 23 knots. There was a lot of discussion on board about what sails we should use. After listening to everyone's opinion, I called for a change to a Sobstad main, our heaviest heavy-weather sail. After the change, the weather team came back on the radio insisting that the wind would drop. They were stationed in a rubber boat near the weather mark, so I decided to go with their prediction. We changed sails again, but as it turned out, the wind held steady and even increased at one point to 31 knots.

Before the start of the regatta, Iain Murray and I flipped a coin to decide who selected from which side of the course to enter the starting area. The two yachts must keep away from the area and each other until ten minutes to the start. We then enter from opposite sides and begin employing whatever tactics we've chosen. Today, we entered from the port end, allowing *Kookaburra III* to pursue us from port tack. That meant that when she turned, she would be on starboard and have the right of way.

I quickly made for the spectator fleet with Murray in hot pursuit, trying to get the controlling position, on my stern. We headed over to the bow of *Bengal*, the big blue multimillion-dollar motor cruiser owned by Masakazu Kobayashi, who had paid almost $7 million for Alan Bond's boats *Australia III* and *IV*. When we got to his bow, we bore off and jibed around the *Bengal*. *Kookaburra* tried to bear off inside us, but there was no room, and as we jibed in front of her, their crew raised the red protest flag. We had been expecting them to do so because they were infamous for the number of protests they had lodged during the summer. This particular one seemed very cheap and the guys on *Stars & Stripes* just laughed. But I didn't take it lightly because protests can always surprise you.

The Kooka's superior maneuverability gave her an advantageous position on starboard tack to windward of us. They crossed the line three seconds before we did. Our telemetric readings (called "aheads and behinds") indicated they were about .9 of a boat-length ahead. But we had better speed, and I felt we could break away if we just continued on the same tack for about fifteen minutes. We did, and in that time we came from behind to take a one-length lead.

At that point, we landed the old sucker play. When the boats are that close and the opposing tactician is hanging down to leeward catching spray and wash in his face, he often can't know what the lead boat's doing until it's too late. By making no move, we let them think they were doing well. But actually we were slowly gaining. To zap them, we just came right up in front of them, eventually forcing Murray to tack onto port about two minutes short of the port layline. We tacked immediately, and the first ahead and behind Peter and Tom gave me indicated we were 2.1 boat-lengths ahead.

After rounding the first mark twelve seconds in front, we executed a nice jibe set of our spinnaker but theirs didn't do as well. They got trapped in our leeward quarter wave and we gained another boat-length. Halfway down the run, they decided to swap the leeward side for the windward side. They sailed above optimum velocity made good—the measure of how fast you're actually approaching the next mark. So that was another ten-second gift for us.

We went around the leeward mark twenty-nine seconds ahead, and on the second beat the wind was slightly lighter, down to about 23 or 24, but the seas were still large. These were just about the exact conditions the boat had been designed for, and she performed as we had hoped. By the end of the leg, we had extended the lead to 1:14.

From there the pressure was off, and I called for conservative sailing, which included a slow and safe spinnaker douse with about four minutes to go before the mark. I wanted to make sure we completed

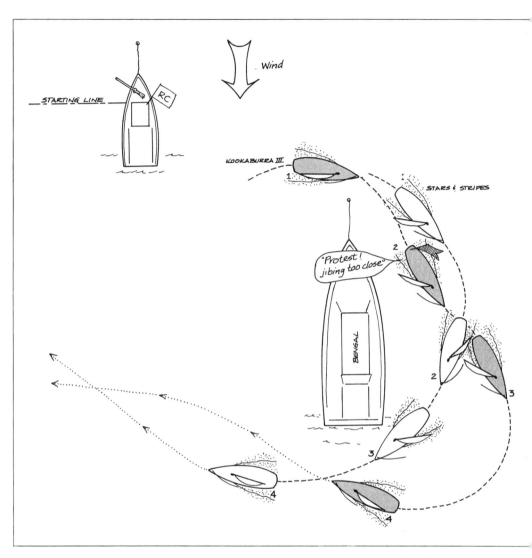

America's Cup, second race, February 1987. At the start of Race *Two*, *Kookaburra III* chases *Stars & Stripes* around the spectator boat, *Bengal*, to try to get inside (1). *Stars & Stripes* (2) jibes ahead of the Kooks (2), who can easily avoid her stern but attempt to protest for jibing too close. (Rule 41.2 states that a boat shall not jibe into a position that gives her right of way unless she does so far enough from a boat—here, *Kookaburra III*—to enable this yacht to keep clear without having to begin to alter course until after the jibe is completed.) *Stars & Stripes* completes her jibe (2–3) circling *Bengal*. *Kookaburra III* swings wide (3), jibes, and rounds *Bengal*, sailing higher (4) to get to windward of *Stars & Stripes* (4).

this maneuver, because at that point the only way to lose the race would be if something broke, or we were unable to get our spinnaker down and our jib up. Now all I had to worry about was the pending protest meeting, but after the race Murray and Kevin Parry decided to drop it.

The time at the finish was 1:10. Two down, two more to go.

I got down to the dock about seven-thirty on the morning of the third race, February 2. The atmosphere was electric even then. Again, the crowd outside the gate was raucous and enthusiastic. There were a lot of people wearing *Stars & Stripes* shirts and sweaters, and carrying placards urging us to "Throw another Kooka on the barbie." Almost overnight the Americans in Fremantle, as well as all those watching at home, had been caught up in our effort. There was a genuine excitement in the crowds and in the messages from the States.

Again, a good number in the crowd outside our dock were Aussies. Their sportsmanship was always gratifying to me, and their shout of "Good on yer, mate" was considered the highest accolade. They don't say that unless they genuinely mean it. It was very moving to me and the crew.

On the tow through the harbor, the crowd was again staked out on every rock and rooftop. The silence that greeted us after the first race had changed to deafening cheers. I actually felt the crowd was noisier in their support for *Stars & Stripes* than for *Kookaburra*, which had left just before us.

Once we got outside the harbor lights and turned north for the tow to the course, we were engulfed by a huge armada of spectator boats. Several of the large power cruisers were from the United States and they were all decked out in red, white, and blue bunting and balloons. It looked more like a water carnival than a boat race.

The Australian forecast had been for a fluky 14-to-18-knot easterly blowing hot and dry off the land, but already we felt the sea breeze kicking in a little as Lee and Chris had predicted. By the start, the Fremantle Doctor was blowing at about 14 knots.

With ten minutes to go, we employed our head-for-the-spectator-fleet ploy, and Gilmour came after us on port about 150 yards astern. We continued to sail away from him until about forty-five seconds before the gun, when *Kookaburra* forced us to the right-hand end of the starting line. Both boats crossed the line at about the same time. We were on starboard headed left and they were on port headed right.

Right after the start, we noticed that the luff zipper on *Kooka* was

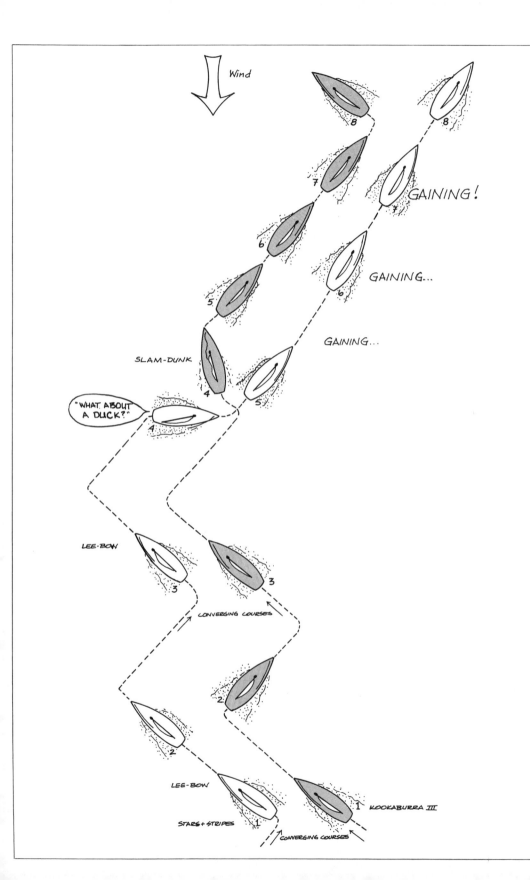

not functioning and Danny McKracken, their bowman, was sent up the mast in a bosun's chair to fix it. As the two boats headed at each other, we chose to bear off, and then when we came together once again about three minutes later, we did the same thing. When we had first converged, *Kookaburra* had a one-length lead, but now we'd gained just a little. Then on the fourth cross, the Kookas made their big mistake. They didn't make many in our series, but this was perhaps the most serious.

Up to that point, they had controlled the lead even though we were chipping away at it. After the third convergence, as soon as we got up to boatspeed, we tacked back at *Kookaburra*. When they tacked to cover us, they hadn't had enough time to build their speed for a proper slam-dunk. Right then Peter Isler asked, "What about a duck?" As soon as he said it, I agreed, so I put the helm hard over to starboard while Tom Whidden spun the trim tab at the same time. Between the two of us, we managed an incredibly sharp turn. At one stage, the boats were positioned at an angle of almost 180 degrees to each other. We had to bear away, to steer away from the wind, a long way to go underneath him and cross his stern. But when we did, we were suddenly on a reach and moving very fast. That extra speed enabled us to get *Stars & Stripes* back up on the wind and power right through his lee.

It was one of the most powerful moves of the entire Cup campaign. Later that night at the press conference, Murray said, "We've sailed upwind against *Stars & Stripes* in most conditions and the fact that they were able to sail around us on a weather leg . . . It's the first time a yacht has been able to do that to us all summer."

About a minute after we had busted loose, they realized the jig was up and tacked away because they were getting our backwind. When that happened, we reversed roles. *Stars & Stripes* now had the starboard tack advantage and *Kookaburra III* was on the left having to get by. From that moment on, we had control.

Opposite: America's Cup, third race, February 1987. On the first windward leg of Race Three, *Stars & Stripes* successfully completes two lee-bow maneuvers. *Kookaburra III* (3) converges for a third time just ahead of *Stars & Stripes* (3). This time Pedro Isler calls for an abrupt duck (4) behind the Kooks' stern. *Kookaburra III* quickly attempts a slam-dunk (4) but, with gradually superior boat speed (5–6–7), *Stars & Stripes* powers through to leeward. *Kookaburra III* is forced to turn away to starboard tack to avoid *Stars & Stripes'* bad air (8). The next time they converge *Stars & Stripes* will be on starboard tack and so have right of way.

A few tacks ensued, but there was no gain to either boat, so we decided to straight-line for the port layline. They were going every bit as fast as we were, but we were able to pull another fine maneuver that gave us twenty seconds. I sensed that we had already overstood the mark a little because I could see it out in front, and I decided to try a tactic I use only rarely. When a 12-meter is tacked, it should be sailed off the wind a few degrees while speed is building. Once boatspeed is reached, the yacht can be put back on the wind. But this time, instead of coming back on the wind, I held the boat substantially below the mark, which caused *Kookaburra* to duck our stern about twenty seconds later. After they went by, I just put the boat back up into the wind, and with the speed I had built, we rushed ahead by about three boat-lengths. We rounded the first mark with a fifteen-second lead.

I think right then Murray knew he wasn't going to beat us. After the first race, he could rightfully claim that we caught all the shifts, and after the second race, he could say there was too much wind. But now he saw that we could take them in anything, in any situation. His feeling of frustration and disappointment was almost tangible out on the water.

The next key gain came because the wind went left relative to the course. Normally going onto a run with a small lead we would have jibe-set the spinnaker, but Peter suggested we use a bear-away set to hoist the spinnaker. This technique allowed us to get the chute up a little quicker in light wind. As we bore away, *Kookaburra* went into a jibe set, which took her off our wind. As we set off in two different directions, the pressure was off. That allowed us to go for about three minutes, settle down, collect our thoughts, and prepare for the next move.

That move was to jibe and cover *Kookaburra*, and when we did, we discovered our lead had doubled to thirty seconds. At the end of the run, we had blown out to a fifty-seven-second advantage. From there, we sailed safely with me calling the shifts and Tom and Peter helping with boatspeed. We just kept pouring on the heat and finished 1:46 ahead.

Three down, one to go.

During that third race, there was a very unusual incident. On the last beat, we noticed that *Kookaburra*'s chase boat increased speed and came to the racing yacht's side very quickly. As this is strictly forbidden by the rules, we couldn't figure out what was happening. At the press conference, Iain Murray explained: "Dennis explained today's race pretty well, but he missed out the bit on the last leg when our rubber boat came alongside and told us we had a bomb on board. They asked us what we wanted to do. We checked our option list and our immediate response was: 'So what's the bad news?' "

Murray took his defeats well and with a sense of humor. But even though that power move through his lee probably made him realize his was a lost cause, I think now our victory in the first race was by far the most significant of the series. Light wind was supposed to favor him, but our sheer sailing ability took that race. They were vulnerable to the knockout punch and we delivered it in that third race. They had spent several years tacking, tacking, tacking every forty-five seconds in prescribed tacking duels, practicing for just such an eventuality. But when it came right down to it, they let DC and *Stars & Stripes* sidle right up and pick their pocket.

It also gave me great pleasure to sail into the harbor under our big blue Pepsi spinnaker. The "Today Show" was in Fremantle at the time and they showed that sail to millions of Americans back home. I had worked very hard to involve Coca-Cola in the early days, but their marketing guy turned us down. I'm sure it was coincidental, but he happened to be a director of the NYYC-dominated United States Yacht Racing Union and a member of the New York Yacht Club. In a wonderful twist of irony, he was on the water off Fremantle for the third race and saw his competitor's logo being cheered home.

Pepsi had made a generous donation, but even more importantly, they had offered us a substantial additional sum for our Defense fund should we win the Cup. Already, thoughts of 1990 or '91 were not far from our minds. Someone called me the "Michael Jackson of the sea," but I was very happy to tell Pepsi's president, Roger Enrique, that we were glad to be part of "the Pepsi generation."

I was also pleased for major backers, guys like Edsel Ford and Mike Dingman, who had come to our aid in the dark days. A lot of heavy-duty financial types had tried to keep DC out of the Cup Challenge, but fortunately, we found people who really believed in us. I was proud we were able to deliver on the promises we had made.

We called a lay-day for February 3 because the forecast was for very light and variable easterlies. So Cy Gillette just wrote down the request and it was granted. As it turned out, the meteorological team's forecast was spot on.

In the afternoon, we did have a chance to sail and Edsel Ford joined us. The guys enjoyed having the auto man on board, and all of a sudden they turned into hard-nosed businessmen. Adam Ostenfeld told Edsel he wanted to open a Ford dealership in New York City. Then J.W. mentioned he was thinking about doing the same thing in Philadelphia. Tom Whidden said he'd already picked the spot for a dealership in Essex, Connecticut. Edsel jollied them along, and in the end, said there was nothing he could do. "I'm in charge of Lincoln-Mercury, and you guys want Fords. Sorry."

On the day of the fourth—hopefully, final—race, I had mixed emotions. This was D day for the Kookaburras. To beat *Stars & Stripes* would have meant four straight victories against us—something that hadn't been done all summer. The Cup was at last truly within our grasp. I had pictured that moment so often in the past, and yet now I found myself unwilling to conjure it up in case it might somehow jinx us and turn the dream into a nightmare. I am definitely not superstitious, but I don't believe in counting my chickens before they're hatched. I didn't want to do anything that might jeopardize the job. That is why I agonized over taking eleven bottles of champagne—one for each guy—for what Moët et Chandon confidently predicted would be the final race. Moët had been a generous backer and eventually I was persuaded to bring them aboard.

Our home in Fremantle was perched high on a hill and faced west over the deep blue of the Indian Ocean. Our front porch commanded a fine view of the port with all its cranes and big commercial ships. At about seven-fifteen, the normally quiet waterfront was already buzzing with excitement. I sensed this would be a big day not only in the history of the America's Cup, but in the history of Fremantle as well as of Australia itself. The entire Australian nation had embraced the victory of *Australia II* in 1983. It had united Australians more than at any time since the end of World War II. I wondered how a fourth straight win for *Stars & Stripes* would affect the national psyche. As it turned out, I need not have worried. The Aussies are a great, sporting people, and though in their heart of hearts they were rooting for their countrymen, their warmth, hospitality, friendship, and support clearly showed that they had also embraced *Stars & Stripes.*

For all our success on the water that summer, perhaps our ultimate achievement was on land. Australian-American relations have always been strong—we've been allies and friends for two hundred years. But during the Cup summer I felt the two nations drew even closer. The Cup's original deed of gift specifies that it be held in perpetuity for "friendly competition between nations," and in this instance I think we were particularly successful.

But it seems there are always jerks who try to spoil things. The Western Australian police received a tip that some guy had made a death threat against me, and the cops suggested I wear a bullet-proof vest under my T-shirt. It was so uncomfortable (not to mention unsightly), that I decided to take it off and get on with winning the Cup. I had to settle for bodyguards onshore.

Thursday, February 5, 1987, was a typical Western Australian summer morning with clear, pale blue skies dominating the horizon. There was virtually no wind—a good sign because such conditions usually mean that after the vast dry easterly has died, the Doctor will come in strongly. Our forecast called for 14 to 18 knots, but the old DC nose could smell it. I knew there was going to be breeze enough for the sail I really liked—the main we had used so successfully in the third race. We put it up with the number-four jib, and after only five minutes the breeze was at 17 true, 18 true, 19 true.

Finally, we decided to go with the bigger number-three jib instead of the four while *Kookaburra* got rid of their three in favor of a number-four jib. As it turned out we were right. The Aussies' decision to go with a smaller jib meant that they were forced to change halfway up that first beat. At the ten-minute gun, *Stars & Stripes* had to enter from the port end, while the Kookas came in around the committee boat on the starboard side. As in Race Two, they got to come at us much faster. About a minute after the gun, I headed off into the spectator fleet, with them right on my tail. They harassed me the whole way into the fleet, where I went around their tender. They followed me, chased me down on starboard, and finally got their bow on my stern, forcing me to come up onto the wind. They established an overlap to leeward, and as I tacked to port, I thought: "Uh oh, here we go again."

With thirty seconds to go, we weren't far from the pin end. Young Mr. Gilmour was pushing me plenty hard. But one of my greatest strengths is gauging time and distance, so without knowing it, he was playing my game. He was down there trying to push me over and I wasn't about to be pushed over. I stalled and luffed and stalled some more. Tom was a great help here. He was underneath the boom checking the buoy telling me how long he thought I had to go. I can remember him saying, "Don't EVEN THINK about putting your bow down until you have ten seconds." When we were no more than a boat-length and three-quarters from the buoy, I had to stall and watch the clock. *Kookaburra III* had put her nose on the line too early and had to back down. When she did, we had her by the throat.

I went for the line with 10.5 seconds to go. I put the bow right down at the buoy, started accelerating, told J.W. to trim the main, and off we went at close to 8 knots. I looked down at my watch as the seconds ticked away. Five, four, three, two, one, bang! I put the bow up as we crossed the line—looking back, I saw Murray in our wake, six seconds behind. The race was virtually over. The Kookas were doing about the same speed but they had to tack off immediately. We just got up to 8.5 knots, tacked, and had our nose abeam of him. A short tacking duel was instigated by *Kookaburra* and when we crossed, it was only by thirteen feet.

This time, I decided to go all the way across and take the right because he was getting my attention. I didn't want him to keep gaining so I grabbed the starboard tack advantage and let him take the left. From then on up the first leg, it was basically a matter of trying to tack on the shifts. There weren't very many of them and the Kookas were going well. Just as our weather team had forecast, the wind went down two knots from 19 to 17. The Aussies did a real nice sail change to a bigger number-three jib, then tacked. They put pressure on us immediately. It was very similar to Race Three except that we were maybe three boat-lengths ahead while we were straight-lining out to the starboard layline on port.

We tacked right on the layline, and again I tried to sucker them by heading below the mark. But they didn't buy it. They went half a boat-length beyond us and tacked so that consequently they were just as close as they had been in Race Three at the weather mark. The margin there was twenty-six seconds. They did a bear-away spinnaker set just like we did, and while they tried coming across first to windward and then to leeward, they were gaining just a few yards at a time.

Then they tried something I would never have done. They tried to set up to leeward of us, but in doing so they chose to ignore the fact that it was an all-starboard tack. We were on port tack for only three minutes at the end of the run, so they never really did get on our wind. Though at the end of that run they had gained four seconds to round twenty-two seconds astern, they never threatened us.

They were very docile, very well behaved behind and to leeward. They could have come up on us and attacked by forcing us high to clear our wind, but they didn't. I don't think Chris Dickson would have played it that way. But Dickson was much more aggressive than Murray. I'm not saying that is right or wrong. It's just different. The downside of the attack mode is that you run a greater risk of losing more ground. If you have to sail higher, the VMG is not as good, so you actually fall back by attacking. I tend to be very aggressive when

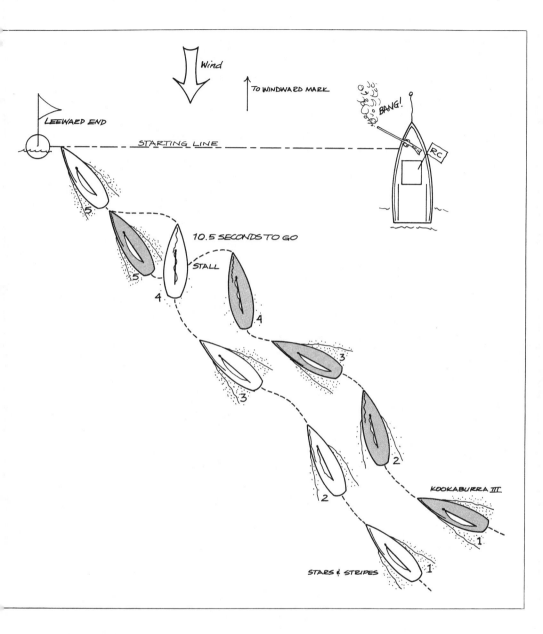

At the start of Race Four, *Stars & Stripes* and *Kookaburra III* are approaching the starting line with slow-and-go maneuvers on starboard tack with *Kookaburra III* to windward and *Stars & Stripes* in the controlling position (1–2–3). (The windward yacht must give way to the leeward yacht.) One and one-half boat-lengths from line both yachts luff and stall (4) for several seconds. With 10.5 seconds to go, I put the helm down and bear off for the pin end (5) and have a six-second lead at the gun.

I get behind, and attacking downwind has been one of my shortcomings. In Round Robin Race Two against the Kiwis, for example, I was fairly close at the end of the third beat, so during the run I went high, he sailed low and I sailed ourselves right out of the race. I was mad at myself later.

On the second beat we did use our number-four jib and we were really hauling the mail in 21 true. In those relatively stable conditions, I liked our situation. Unlike in Newport, there were no big oscillations to nail you if you didn't keep the other guy on a short leash. I tried to sail on the high ones, with Tom and Peter keeping me honest. I tend to be greedy when it comes to staying on the lifts, and Tom's job was to keep me on a short leash by giving me a few jerks on my choke chain whenever I got rambunctious. I feel I can sense where the wind's going to be, so if I'm on a lift, I don't necessarily want to tack. But even if you're right 80 percent of the time, you still pay a big price when you are wrong. It was good having Tom and Peter to keep me in line. They used to conspire to get me to tack back to cover. Peter would say, "Well, they're getting a little leverage over there now," and then Tommy would add, "So let's go!" I would usually tack, but sometimes I pretended not to hear them. Tommy humors me until he really gets nervous. Then he says, "DC, we'd better tack." That's when we go. The closer the race, the more likely I am to listen, but when we're a minute or more in front, I often get adventuresome.

It must have been extremely frustrating for the Aussies who, like John Kolius, had spent the past three years tacking every forty-five seconds only to come up against a guy who likes to sail on the windshifts. We truly fooled them completely, and right from the start I felt they had never raced a boat like ours. On the other hand, we had been racing boats like *theirs* all summer. From the outset, boatspeed was my whole strategy. We never really practiced racing in Hawaii or in Australia. Instead, we practiced going fast.

At the end of the second beat, we did have a little tacking duel because we wanted to herd Iain over to the right layline. When I got him over there, we tacked several times, guarding the left, and pretty soon were up on the starboard layline. He was forced to reach off, giving up a tremendous amount of VMG, which translated into time. We went up and layed the mark to round forty-two seconds ahead. That's when Iain Murray, Mr. Nice Guy, tried to foul us out. He kept going on starboard as I bore off to go round the mark. That meant I had to hold my spinnaker set and harden back up until he saw we were going to make it around him. It was a legitimate maneuver and one I

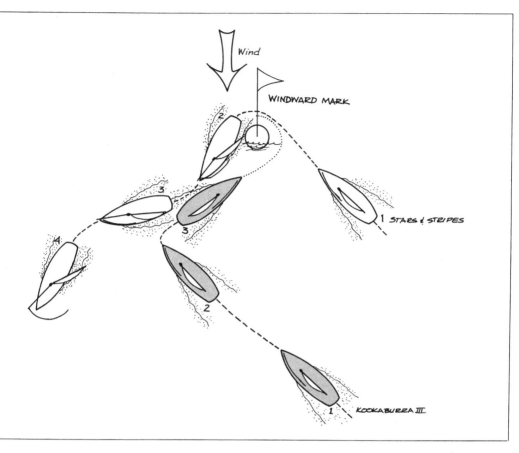

America's Cup, fourth race, February 1987. *Stars & Stripes* leads *Kookaburra III* to the right side of the windward leg and they both approach the mark on starboard tack (1). *Stars & Stripes* tacks around windward mark (2) on a course toward the wing mark. *Kookaburra III* legitimately tries to foul *Stars & Stripes* out by staying on starboard tack (2). Since the leeward yacht has right of way, *Stars & Stripes* must harden up and delay her spinnaker set (2-3). *Kookaburra III* then tacks to port (3) and rounds the windward mark 42 seconds behind.

would have tried in his shoes—in fact, I did try it once in the 1983 series against *Australia II*. Fortunately for *Stars & Stripes*, I was watching him under the boom. I told the guys, "Hold that spinnaker, trim the main," and I started back up. The rule says that a yacht on a free leg of the course shall keep clear of a yacht close-hauled. So the onus was on us to keep clear.

After that, we went down the first reach and gained 60 yards to round the wing mark forty-nine seconds ahead. That put the Kookas astern by about 205 yards. We held him on the second reach to round the leeward mark 260 yards ahead. The official margin was forty-eight seconds. On the third beat, we again applied our loose cover and steamed away to round the sixth mark one minute eleven seconds ahead.

We jibe-set our spinnaker and the Aussies bore away, and we jibed back to cover and layed the mark. We never really had any pressure applied all the way down. The spinnaker we really wanted was the one we used on the first beat, but it got ripped on the take-down and so we went with one of the chutes loaned by *America II.* It was a little smaller than the one we would have chosen, but it was a nice sail and we gained five seconds to round one minute sixteen seconds ahead. Once that jib was up and the spinnaker was down, the party was over. That was the last chance for the *Kookaburra* to capitalize on a possible *Stars & Stripes* mistake. We applied a very loose cover up the last beat and started savoring our victory, which turned into a margin of 1:59. When we got the gun, I couldn't help yelling, "God damn, we did it! We did it, guys!" I allowed myself a big smile, the kind that goes from ear to ear. I don't think of myself as a big shot but at that moment it was just as I had pictured it would be. It was a magic moment. To come back the way we did, with so many of the guys who were with me in '83, was the sweetest thing of all. Just seeing how excited they all were made me excited. We had pulled off the big one. The crew were ecstatic and yet I had mixed emotions. Naturally it put me over the moon to have won back the Cup that I had lost. I was aware that I had made sporting history, but at the same time I was kind of sad it was over. It had been a tremendous campaign with a lot of good, close friends.

I was very proud of the crew and I know they were proud to have been part of that campaign. They were the guys who really did have faith in me and we have stuck together through thick and thin. Their friendship and their camaraderie meant more to me at that moment than anything else in the world. The other Sail America crew guys came aboard and we finished up with thirty people sitting on the weather rail. We broke out a big American flag on our backstay and the eleven bottles of Moët that Bruno Troublé had stashed on board came bubbling to the surface. The French call Moët "le champagne des vainqueurs," the champagne of the winners, and at that moment it certainly seemed appropriate. It was a historic moment and, as I've always said, history is written by winners, not by losers. For myself there was a wonderful sense of relief and of accomplishment; I had come a long way from the shoe box to the cover of *Time* magazine. What gave me particular pleasure at that moment was the knowledge that I had been able to do it without all my friends at the New York Yacht Club who had tried so hard to stuff it to me. There was a lot of excitement aboard the spectator boats with horns blasting and people yelling at us. There were red, white, and blue balloons all over the place. After we crossed the line, Gary Jobson, the commentator for the American cable network ESPN, came aboard with a camera crew. Having them on board somehow spoiled one of the finest moments of my life. I wanted to savor the victory with my crew, just as I had imagined doing for the past three years. I wanted to cry but didn't dare in front of the TV guys. I wanted to wave to the crowd but the camera intervened. It made me a big-shot, something I'd tried hard not to be.

There were hundreds of boats all around as we turned and headed back toward Fremantle. They kept pace with us all the way in, even when we set our Merrill-Lynch spinnaker for the final triumphant run up the harbor. Tens of thousands of spectators turned out to cheer us in. They were waving their Aussie flags and yelling, "Good on yer, Dennis," "Good on yer, Yanks." I have seen homecomings before but nothing that resembled this. The Aussies were saying, "You beat us fair and square. Well done. No hard feelings." That spirit of Australian sportsmanship was something I'll always remember.

The Kookas had come in under spinnaker a little ahead of us, and there they were with their sails down and a big Aussie flag flying from their backstay, yelling three cheers at us. We returned the salute and headed into the dock, where an enormous American flag at least sixty by forty feet was flying from our big red crane. The sight of that flag will always remain one of my most vivid, moving memories. As the guys started tossing each other in the water, I skipped off to watch the homecoming on television aboard *Betsy*. That's where they found me. My crew dragged me out still clutching my bottle of Moët, and tossed me into the water, champagne and all. I hate to admit this, but I can't swim. I can dog-paddle, but not enough to save my life, so I made sure I went in alongside a rubber boat I could grab when I surfaced. One of my biggest secret fears is going overboard in an ocean race at night because I'd be a goner in seconds.

Having won the war on the water, the next great battle was getting out of the compound in our crew bus to go to the press conference. While we were celebrating on the dock, a crowd of thousands gathered. They were pressing on the gates and at one point, the gates threatened to cave in. There were mounted police and cops everywhere, but the crowd was so vast it threatened to go out of control. Eventually I had to climb out and address the mob. I clambered up on the wall by the main gate, raised my arms, and almost immediately you could have heard a pin drop. I thought, "My God, now I know how the Pope must feel." I thanked them for their support, said how much we appreciated it, and then explained that we had to get our bus out. None of the America's Cup team wanted anyone to get hurt. That did it. The waves parted, and we were on our way.

At the press conference, my heart went out to Iain Murray. He was up on the podium next to the Royal Perth Yacht Club Commodore, his friend Peter Gilmour, and his syndicate chairman, Kevin Parry. Their faces were like Easter Island statues. Seeing them so obviously drained made me flash back to the worst night of my own life, when I was the one up there facing the press alone and very close to tears. No one there to say, "Well sailed, DC." The Club had no further use for me, it was finished business. At least young Mr. Murray had a show of support at the end.

As my thoughts returned to Newport, I could suddenly see with absolute clarity the scene in our bedroom at Seacliffe the morning after the night before. I could see myself suddenly waking up and realizing the Cup was gone, and that I was the guy who lost it. I remembered trembling and yelling at the top of my lungs, "FFFAAARRK!" I could see myself getting out of bed, pacing up and down the room, and rubbing the back of my neck because I really had a terrible hangover. Every now and again, I'd feel compelled to shout again—"FFFAAARRK!" Having dragged myself out of that hole, I decided winning was a lot more fun. Yet the truth is that having endured so much for so long, I just couldn't savor the moment.

Just before we left for the press conference, we decided to haul the boat out of the water for the first time without the skirts around her keel. All summer long this had been our big secret—we would have risked our lives to protect it—and now the moment had come when the whole world would see our blue lady stark naked under all those floodlights. It wasn't quite the big deal that the revelation of *Australia II*'s winged keel was in '83. But I think those who saw the big blue beast for the first time were suitably impressed, especially by the sign that said, "Budweiser: The King of Beers." Budweiser had been very generous in their support of *Stars & Stripes*, and it seemed the least we could do to repay the debt of gratitude we owed them.

COUNTDOWN

As far as I know, the *Kookaburra* guys never did reveal their keel publicly, but we knew exactly what it looked like because Robert Hopkins was on hand during their prerace measurement check. His only really interesting observation about the Kooka keel was that some smart arse had drawn an American eagle being stuffed by a vicious-looking Kookaburra. It seemed a little childish to some of the guys, but to a lot of others it was like waving a red rag before a bull. They were fired up to knock the feathers right off that laughing little bird.

I had made a little wager with my good friend Bob Aron way back in 1984. I had taken a shine to Bob's magnificent full-length beaver coat when he wore it to a dinner in New York City. He let me wear it the next time we went out. There I was, the carpet salesman from San Diego, all dolled up in a magnificent beaver coat. I was so taken with it I didn't want to take it off, so to give me an extra incentive, he put the coat up as a special bonus for winning the Cup.

He and his wife Tracy had the thing air-freighted down to Fremantle in time for the final festivities, and he handed it over to me right there on the dock. There were plenty of wolf whistles and cat calls from the guys, but it looked and felt like a million. I didn't get to wear it very long because Julie and Shanna took it away from me. There wasn't much need for a beaver coat in Fremantle's hot, dry climate, but we weren't going to be there very much longer anyway. We had just been invited to the White House by President Reagan, and since Washington was knee-deep in snow, I figured the guys who'd laughed at the sight of me in a fur coat would probably want to borrow it once DC got to D.C.

14

✦

Coming Home

THE Cup was handed over on February 6, 1987, at the Royal Perth Yacht Club. It was a brilliant, sunny day, so it seemed entirely appropriate to hold the historic ceremony outdoors on the clubhouse lawns that roll down to the shores of Matilda Bay. It was a beautiful setting, and the thousands of guests who stood shoulder to shoulder in front of the podium all had a fine view of the Cup. It was sitting out in front, gleaming and sparkling in the sunshine.

There were a lot of speeches, but Bob Hawke, Australia's Prime Minister, seemed the most eloquent with his spontaneous comments. I think he expressed the sentiments of most of the people we had come to know in Australia. The Prime Minister had been clever enough in 1983 to time a cabinet meeting so that his presence in Perth coincided with *Australia II*'s great victory. In his opening remarks three and a half years later, he referred to the impact that event had had on the people of Australia.

It was, he said, one of the most memorable moments of his life. He had another memory of that day in 1983, one of "a very remarkable American, Dennis Conner," a man who had, to use the Australian jargon, just received "a fairly hefty kick in the guts."

"What we remember of that day," the PM said, "was the courage and the grace with which you took that blow. It's very difficult for any

208

of us to understand how you felt that day. I offer you and your crew our admiration and our respect and more than that, our deep affection. On behalf of all the people of Australia, I offer you our unqualified congratulations on a magnificent achievement.

"Over the years there has been a lot of nonsense spoken about the America's Cup being an elitist exercise, the plaything of the very wealthy. It's true that without those with wealth we couldn't have the America's Cup, but we shouldn't be jealous of them, we shouldn't write them off. We should say thank you for making this great event possible.

"We think these last few months have shown that the America's Cup, beyond almost all other sporting events, has the capacity to arouse the best in the spirit of the nation."

Bob Hawke was right. The America's Cup does have that special capacity and, like him, I can't think of any other trophy in any other sport that comes even close. We left Perth the very next day on a Continental DC-10, flown in especially for us and chartered jointly by Continental and Pepsi-Cola.

With the Cup strapped in a first-class seat right beside me, we took off for Washington via Hawaii and San Diego. The security guys at the airport had wanted to stash it in the hold, but I insisted it be brought into the cabin with us so that all those who had worked so hard to win it would at least have a chance to see it up close and maybe have their picture taken with it. Polaroid had supplied the entire crew with its latest automatic cameras, and during that initial 7,300-mile leg from Perth to Honolulu, the Cup must have been snapped a thousand times. For much of the trip it wore my beaver coat and the cowboy hat Prime Minister Hawke was sending to President Reagan.

Everyone knows the Cup has a personality all its own, but those little touches seemed to bring it alive. I could have sworn it was enjoying the fun along with everyone else. Although we were all pretty tired by the time we reached San Diego we were delighted by the Mayor's welcome. While the plane refueled, we were escorted to the B Street Pier for an incredible reception. Over 60,000 San Diegans turned out to welcome us home. It was all very emotional, especially for Malin Burnham and me, because we had grown up not so far away in Point Loma.

I don't think I've ever seen so many San Diegans in one spot before. They were ten deep on the sidewalk, yelling and cheering as we came by the waterfront drive, past the old clipper, *Star of India,* and turned into the reception area. This was just the kind of triumphant homecoming the Aussies had earned when they won the Cup in '83, but the hometown crowd made it even more special. The dream that had begun in a shoe box right there in San Diego had at last become a reality. I was very proud to have brought it home.

When we flew out of San Diego, the Continental pilot received permission to make a low-level pass over the waterfront, and as we whizzed by at what seemed like mast height, we could see there were still tens of thousands of people partying. The skipper wiggled the wings as if he were flying a Tiger Moth. That was Continental's way of saying, "Thanks, San Diego."

We pushed on directly to Washington, D.C. There, much to our astonishment, was another crowd that had turned out to welcome us despite the bitter cold of winter and the time—it was well after midnight. Right outside the hotel was a high-school marching band with drums and cornets, trumpets and bassoons all blaring away in a big, brassy welcome. It was a preview of what was to come the following day at the White House.

President Reagan and Vice-President George Bush were exceptionally generous in treating me and the entire crew to a private meeting in the Oval Office. Later, we trooped over to the East Wing where all the other team members and their families were assembled with what seemed like the world's media. With the crew on stage, the Marine Corps band struck up "Hail to the Chief," and then the President walked in.

Suddenly, all the effort of the past three years crystallized into a single moment. Being there, under the Stars and Stripes in that historic building, with the Big Chief himself paying tribute to us, made me feel more than a little overwhelmed. This was what we had all worked so hard for. This was our moment of greatest triumph.

I think it's appropriate to record here the full text of the President's remarks on that great day. After a formal welcome, he proclaimed his pride at being in front of the Stars and Stripes the day the boat of that name brought the Cup back up from Down Under. He reached down and plucked Prime Minister Hawke's gift off a chair. Saying how pleased he was to have won the bet, he put the hat on his head at a jaunty angle. The crowd loved it, and I couldn't help thinking that Australian-American relations must surely be at an all-time high.

The President then paid tribute to all the syndicates that had represented the United States in Australia:

There were six American syndicates altogether, and each had their own yachts and each involved literally hundreds of people bringing the best in American technology to bear on the complicated challenges of 12-meter racing. In designing *Stars & Stripes'* winged keel with its distinctive rounded nose, special computer techniques were employed, plastics experts gave the hull a coating that sheathed the yacht in thousands of tiny V-shaped grooves called riblets, sailmakers used a mixture of Kevlar, Mylar, and an entirely new fabric, Spectra, to produce hundreds of sails for every conceivable weather condition. *Stars & Stripes* was even fitted with an on-board computer that enabled her to communicate before the races with other computers ashore and on board her tender.

I believe it says something about the competitiveness of American technology that this time around the United States produced the best designed, most technologically advanced 12-meter yacht the world has ever seen. But no matter how slick the yacht, it still all comes down to what the skipper and his crew do with it. To the skipper, tactician, navigator, mainsail trimmer, tailers, grinders, pitman, sewerman, and bowman of *Stars & Stripes:* Congratulations! You performed to the highest standards in conditions that were exhausting and you made considerable sacrifices to do so.

Dennis, in 1983 you sailed against the Australian Challenger in what is universally acknowledged to have been a slower boat, but your skills were such that you forced the Challengers to go all seven races before *Australia II* finally took the America's Cup. In the races off Fremantle you showed your skill all over again. During the Challenger finals against New Zealand, *Stars & Stripes* blew her jib. To many skippers that would have been cause for panic, but you only said, "Hey, that's too bad." [It was at that point, while the crowd was laughing, that I leaned into the President's microphone and interrupted just long enough to confide that that was not all I said. That brought an even greater laugh and I think the President enjoyed it too because he answered, "Well, it was all you said that was printable." That remark brought the house down.]

Then, while your crew scrambled to replace the damaged sail, you calmly tacked to keep your opponent from gaining the wind. In just three minutes and two seconds, the new jib was up and *Stars & Stripes* went on to win the race.

Looking at the cup races themselves, there's no finer way to describe your victory than to quote the defeated Australian skipper, Iain Murray. To the suggestion that *Stars & Stripes* simply had better luck, skipper Murray said, "I'm not a great believer in luck in sailing. The wind Dennis left us with was pretty much zilch. He won because he was always in the right spot!"

Beyond your skill, Dennis, it was a matter of your commitment. One of your crewmen caught a glimpse of what it all meant to you. In his words, before the last tack, "Dennis said to the crew, 'Okay guys, this is the last tack in the 1987 America's Cup.' I turned around and looked back. He was crying. He had tears in his eyes." The crewman went on to explain that this had not been any gravy walk for Dennis. "He is a regular American guy, a smart guy who has worked his way up from the bottom and deserves credit for what he has done!" Dennis, today we congratulate you.

The President then paid tribute to the Australians who had so generously hosted us over those many months. "Of course," he said, "the outcome of these races must be a great disappointment to many millions of Australians just as many Americans felt the 1983 loss so keenly. I want everyone to know that I've heard again and again from Dennis and others that the Australian people could not have been more friendly nor more generous or sportsmanlike. On behalf of the thousands of Americans who visited Australia for these races, I want to thank Prime Minister Hawke, Royal Perth Yacht Club, and the Australian people. The America's Cup has brought our two nations, which were already close, still closer. In following these races, we have all been able to feel something ancient and deep within us, man's fascination with the water."

The President went on to quote Tony Chamberlain, the sports writer for the *Boston Globe*, who wrote: " 'In sailing there is a term called *lift,* which is both technical and poetic at once. It describes the moment of acceleration in a sailboat, the moment when the sails harden against the wind and the boat begins to slide forward faster and faster until you can suddenly feel what William Buckley meant by the title of his sailing book, *Airborne.* How something moving so slowly, about the pace of a moderate jogger, can impart something so exhilarating at this moment, is probably unanswerable.

"Hang gliding, dropping in a parachute, doing barrel-rolls in a light aeroplane—the thrills are easy to understand but the moment of lift is just as much a leap off the earth . . . airborne.' Gentlemen of the *Stars & Stripes,* for a few days you enabled all of us to become airborne."

After the President's eloquent remarks, there wasn't much more I could add. I agreed with the President that our win had indeed been a victory for American technology but more than that, I suggested it had also been a victory for the American will to compete anywhere in the world and for the American ability to be able to win. "It really was a victory for the American spirit. It means a great deal to me and to all the *Stars & Stripes* crew to have brought the Cup back home where it belongs."

I then read Prime Minister Hawke's message to the President and presented him with a beautiful half-model of *Stars & Stripes.* After the President and Vice-President left, the entire group moved to another of the historic rooms in the East Wing for tea and coffee before heading back to prepare for the journey to New York.

We flew in after midnight and there was still plenty of snow and ice on the ground. It was just as well I had my beaver coat because when it came time to assemble at Fifth Avenue and 43rd Street, it was way below freezing. Besides all the floats that Macy's had assembled for our ticker-tape parade, we had also managed to get *Victory*, the former British challenger, down from the Cove Haven Marina at Barrington, Rhode Island. There she was, with icicles hanging off her mast and hull.

The crew were all huddled together on a float that bore the enormous head of the Statue of Liberty, and as we headed up Fifth Avenue, with the Cup held high and all those people—100,000 of them—cheering and applauding, and the ticker-tape raining down, I couldn't help but wonder if they could hear the celebration at 37 West 44th Street, the address of the New York Yacht Club. The Cup that had remained there for one hundred thirty-two years was on its way up Fifth Avenue and on to a new home in San Diego.

We felt very special and very honored by the parade. Our good friend and backer Donald Trump was waiting on the reviewing stand outside Trump Tower. His belief in us had been one of the keys to our success, so it seemed only fitting that we should bring the Cup to his front door.

The Defense of the Cup is going to require many more gestures of the sort Donald Trump and others made for *Stars & Stripes.* With the prospect of Challengers coming from Japan, Germany, Sweden, Norway, Denmark, and Spain, as well as the traditional Challengers from Australia, Britain, France, Italy, Canada, and New Zealand, we are clearly going to need all the help we can get. In many ways, the Defense of the America's Cup now poses an even greater personal challenge for me.

I certainly intend to be there in the forefront of that effort. I will be steering what I hope will be one of three American Defenders. If we are to succeed again we will once more need to harness the national will and spirit that helped secure the victory in Fremantle. I think we can do it, but as I have said all along, Dennis Conner cannot do it all on his own. We are going to need commitment to the commitment. The three basic ingredients for winning remain the same: attitude, attitude, attitude.

GLOSSARY

●●●●●●●●●●●●●● ★ ●●●●●●●●●●●●●●

Aback: When the wind is on the incorrect side of the sails.

Abaft: Behind.

Abeam: Perpendicular to the boat's centerline.

Aft: Toward the stern or rear of the boat.

Aloft: Overhead in the rigging or on the mast.

Amidship: The middle of the boat.

Apparent wind: The apparent direction and strength of the wind as perceived from a moving boat. Movement alone creates the impression of wind coming from straight ahead, even if there is no wind. That plus the actual direction and velocity of the true wind combines to make what is called the apparent wind. *See also* **true wind.**

Astern: Behind the boat.

Back: When the wind fills the sail from what ought to be it's leeward side (given the way the sheet is trimmed) the sail is said to be *backed.*

Backstay: A stay running from the upper part of the mast to the stern. Keeps the mast from moving forward. Two types: permanent and running. The latter can be adjusted during a race to alter the shape of the mast, and therefore the shape or trim of the sails.

Ballast: Weight put in bottom of boat or keel for stability.

Batten: A strip of plastic or wood used to stiffen the rear edge of the mainsail.

Beam: The width of the boat at its widest point. See also **abeam.**

Bear away: To alter course away from the wind.

Bearing: The angle between the centerline of the boat or a point on the compass and another object, such as a mark or an opponent. To *gain bearing* is to point closer and closer to an object. For example, in a race a windshift might allow you to sail more directly toward (gain bearing on) a mark.

Beat: To sail to windward close-hauled, that is, pointing as close to the wind as is efficiently possible. To reach an upwind mark in a race one *beats to windward* by tacking back and forth.

Before the wind: Sailing in the same direction that the wind blows.

Beneath: To sail beneath is to sail to leeward of another boat.

Bilge: The lowest, rounded part of a boat's hull.

Blanket: To slow another boat down by coming between her and the wind. Your opponent's sails receive the weakened, turbulent air that spills downwind of your sails.

Block: Nautical word for pulley.

Boatspeed: A boat's speed through the water. Compare **Velocity Made Good.**

Boom: The horizontal spar that holds the foot or bottom of the mainsail.

Boom vang: A system using tackle or hydraulics to keep the boom from rising up, which would cause the mainsail to luff, and slow the boat.

Bosun's chair: The wooden or canvas seat used to hoist a man aloft. Alternately, a crew member can wear a web harness throughout a race that can easily be clipped to the line that will haul him aloft when the need arises.

Bowman: The crewman who works on the foredeck. Duties include attaching the jib to the forestay, bringing the jib onto the foredeck when it is lowered, managing the spinnaker pole, and calling distances to a mark or an opponent.

Broad reach: Sailing with the wind coming from astern over one quarter or the other.

Buoy room: See **racing rules.**

Centerline: an imaginary line from the tip of the bow to the middle of the stern.

Challenger of Record: the Challenger for the America's Cup that takes responsibility for establishing the bona fides of all challengers, scheduling the races that will determine the best boat, and establishing general procedures and rules that govern the Challenger series. For the 1987 America's Cup, the Royal Perth Yacht Club chose to name Italy's Yacht Club Costa Smeralda the Challenger of Record.

Chop: Seas with short, angular waves.

Chute: Another term for spinnaker.

Clew: The aft corner of a sail, and the lowest corners of a spinnaker.

Close-hauled: Sailing as close to the wind as one can.

Cockpit: The recessed area aft in which the helmsman, tactician, and navigator work during a race.

Coffee grinder: A big two-handled winch used for triming sheets.

Come about: to change directions from one tack (direction) to another while sailing to windward. To *tack* is to come about. Compare **jibe.** See also **port** (tack) and **starboard** (tack).

Cover: To maintain one's lead in a race by staying between one's opponent and the next mark, even if one must sail a longer or slower course to do so.

Displacement: The weight of the water that a floating boat displaces.

Downwind: To leeward, the direction in which the wind is going.

Draft: The vertical distance between the waterline and the lowest part of the keel. Also used to describe the fullness of a sail.

Drag: Resistance to boatspeed caused by the friction of water on the moving hull of the boat.

Duck: To pass behind the stern of a boat.

Feeder: The groove through which the luff or forward edge of a sail passes as it is raised or lowered.

Fetch: To be able to reach a windward objective, such as a mark, without additional tacks. See also layline.

Flying jibe: See **jibe.**

Fluky: Varying, weak wind.

Foot: a sail's lower edge. To foot is to steer slightly off of a close-hauled course, which, since a reach is the fastest point of sail, allows you to increase boatspeed.

Foredeck: The part of the deck between bow and mast.

Foreguy: A line attached to the outer end of the spinnaker pole. It keeps the force of the wind on the spinnaker from raising the pole.

Forestay: The stay running from bow to mast on which the jib is set.

Forward: Toward the bow.

Fremantle Doctor: See **sea breeze.**

Freeboard: The distance from the water to the deck.

Gantline: A line that runs through a block at the top of the mast. Used for hoisting.

Gennaker: A large headsail that is a cross between a genoa and a spinnaker.

Genoa: A large jib whose clew (aft corner) extends aft of the mast. Larger genoas are designated by lower numbers.

Grinders: Crewmen who operate the coffee grinder winches, which are used to trim the sails. A grinder must have great strength and endurance.

Guy: A line used to control a spinnaker pole. The *after guy* governs pole movement fore and aft, and the *fore guy* keeps the pole from rising upward.

Halyard: A line used to hoist a sail.

Harden: To *harden* a sheet is to pull it in. To *harden up* means to point upwind.

Headboard: A reinforced area at the top of a sail.

Header: A windshift whose direction moves further forward relative to the centerline of the boat. The usual response to a header is to tack or to bear off to leeward. The opposite of a lift.

Headsail: A jib or genoa, which are sails set forward of the mast.

Headstay: See **forestay.**

Head to wind: To point directly into the wind.

Heel: A boat heels or tilts over on one side due to the force of the wind on the sails.

Helm: The boat's steering wheel.

In irons: A term indicating the boat is stalled head to wind.

IOR: International Offshore Rule. A series of specifications that govern the design of a certain class of racing yachts.

IYRU: International Yacht Racing Union.

Jib: Alternate term for headsail or genoa.

Jibe: To jibe is to change course while sailing downwind. Requires that one move the mainsail and spinnaker from one side of the boat to the other. When, for example, the sails are trimmed on the port side of the boat with the wind coming over the starboard side, the boat is said to be *on starboard jibe.* In a *flying jibe,* the boom swings quickly from one side to the other, placing great stress on equipment and sails.

Jumper: A forward stay in the upper part of the mast.

Keel: A protruding section under the boat that provides stability and prevents sideways drift. After the 1983 America's Cup, keels with wings became the norm on 12-meter yachts. The wings enhance maneuverability and speed.

Kevlar: A material that ounce for ounce is stronger than steel. The gold-colored synthetic fiber is used in sailcloth, particularly in high-stress areas, and in ropes.

Kite: A word for *spinnaker.*

Knock: A header.

Lateral resistance: Resistance to sideways drift. Is provided by the keel.

Layline: An imaginary straight line tracing the course along which a boat can fetch a mark while sailing close-hauled. When racing to windward, competitors tack back and forth until they come to either the starboard or port laylines and then, unless the actions of the opponent dictate otherwise, each boat heads directly for the mark along the layline. If a boat sails upwind beyond the layline, it will have gone further than necessary (overstood) and, presumably, lost time. If a boat turns (i.e., tacks) toward the mark before reaching the layline, it will have to make a time-wasting tack *again* to round the mark. *Starboard layline:* the layline to the mark that is sailed on starboard tack. *Port layline:* layline to the mark along which one sails on port tack. The position of these imaginary lines is determined by wind direction. See also laylines drawn on diagrams throughout text.

Leeward: Downwind.

Leeward mark: The downwind mark. Approached on a *run.*

Leg: The passage sailed between two buoys on a race course is known as a leg. An America's Cup course consists of windward legs (also known as weather legs or beats), leeward legs and reaching legs.

Lee bow: To lee bow is to maneuver so as to direct the disturbed, weakened air spilling aft and to windward of one's sails toward the sails of one's opponent, thereby slowing him down. The correct position for using this tactic is just ahead and to leeward of one's rival.

Lee helm: When a boat tends to head downwind unless steered up, it is said to have a lee helm

Lift: When a windshift moves aft or away from the bow, it is called a lift. When sailing to windward it allows one to steer more directly toward the mark. The opposite of a header.

Luff: A sail's leading edge. To luff is to point up into the wind so that the boat slows—sometimes a useful maneuver before the start of a race.

Luff zipper: Main sails have a vertical zipper near the luff or leading edge, which, when opened, increases the area of the sail.

Louis Vuitton Cup: The trophy awarded the boat *(Stars & Stripes '87)* that compiled the best record against all other Challengers during the 1987 America's Cup and so won the right to challenge the defender chosen by Australia *(Kookaburra III)* for the America's Cup.

Mainsail: The sail hoisted *aft* of the *mast.* Its *foot* is attached to the *boom.*

Mainsheet: The line used to *trim* the *mainsail.*

Mark: In a race, a buoy that one must sail around.

Mast: The vertical spar that holds up the sails and that is itself held up by stays.

Masthead: The top of the mast.

Masthead wand: An antenna at the top of the mast.

Mastman: Crewman situated near the base of the mast whose responsibilities include control of halyards.

Match racing: Races involving two boats only as opposed to a fleet.

Mylar: A light, translucent material used in some sails and spinnakers.

Navigator: On a racing 12-meter, the navigator assesses the boat's position, speed, and bearing with respect to the opponent and to the marks that must be rounded to complete the course.

NYYC: New York Yacht Club.

Offwind: On a reach or a run you are sailing offwind.

On the wind: Sailing as close to the direction the wind is coming from as you can. Close-hauled.

Outhaul: A line or tackle that pulls outward, e.g., the mainsail outhaul pulls the mainsail toward the aft end of the boom.

Overstand: To overstand a mark is to sail past the mark's port or starboard laylines, that is, to sail farther than necessary to round the mark. When the wind shifts, the laylines leading to the mark change too, and so a skipper may find that he now overstands the mark through no fault of his own.

Phase: The match-racing textbook calls for the boat ahead to stay in phase with the boat astern, that is, to remain between her and the mark. If the boat astern is allowed to get out of phase, that is, go off on an opposite tack, then the boat ahead runs the risk of allowing the attacking boat to pick up a windshift, which could threaten his lead. In the '86–'87 Cup series *Stars & Stripes* was sailed for pure boatspeed. We didn't worry too much about close covering or staying in phase once we had established a clear lead. The term *phase* also applies to the wind and simply means the way in which the wind moves or oscillates about the course. The wind never blows from a constant direction.

Pin: A buoy.

Pinch: To sail too close to the wind.

Pitch: Fore and aft rocking of a boat in heavy seas.

Point: To sail close to the wind. The points of sail are the terms assigned to the directions you can sail with respect to the wind.

Port: The left-hand side of the boat as you look forward.

Port tack: Sailing with the wind coming over the port side of the boat The boom would, therefore, be the starboard side. Port tack does *not* mean tacking to the left.

Preventer: A line running from the foredeck to the end of the boom that keeps the boom from jibing accidentally as the boat sails downwind.

Proper course: The course a boat would sail in the absence of other boats to finish a course as quickly as possible.

Rail: The deck's outer edge.

Rake: To bend the mast forward or aft by adjusting the rigging.

Reach: To sail with the wind *abeam.* On a *close reach,* the wind is somewhat foreword of *abeam.* On a *beam reach,* the wind is directly abeam. On a *broad reach* the wind is somewhat aft of abeam. See endpapers.

Rhumb line: A direct line between one mark and the next.

Riblets: Microscopic grooves on plastic sheets applied to the boat. The grooves run lengthwise along the hull and are meant to increase boatspeed by reducing friction between water and the moving boat.

Rig: The way the spars, standing and running rigging, and sails are arranged. Spars and stays constitute *standing rigging.* Sheets and halyards are part of a boat's *running rigging.*

Rudder: An underwater flap operated by the wheels in the cockpit that changes the boat's course.

Run: To sail directly downwind, which occurs on the leeward leg.

Runner: Running backstay.

SAIC: Science Applications International Corporation.

SDYC: San Diego Yacht Club.

Sail plan: A boat's inventory of sails.

Sea breeze: Breeze blowing toward the shore as heated air over the sun-baked land rises and draws the cooler offshore air inland. The *Fremantle Doctor* is the nickname for Fremantle, Australia's prevailing sea breeze.

Set: To hoist and then trim a sail.

Sewer: The area under the foredeck where sails are stored. The sewerman organizes the sails down below and helps the bowman hoist and take them down.

Shackle: A fixture that fastens a line to a fitting, or one line to another.

Sheet: The line used for trimming sails.

Shift: See **header** and **lift.**

Shoot the mark: If you are sailing toward the windward mark on a course just below the layline you may avoid an extra tack by luffing up. This is *shooting the mark.* Ideally, you will be able to round the mark before the boat loses way.

Shrouds: Supporting wires on both sides of the mast. They give the mast lateral stability.

Slam-dunk: Maneuver used to deny a trailing opponent wind when maneuvering in close. Two boats approach each other on converging tacks. The leader (the boat that is likely to cross in front of the other) crosses in front of his opponent and then immediately tacks onto a course parallel to that of the trailing yacht. Downwind of the leader's sails the air is turbulent and weak; as the trailing yacht sails into this zone his boatspeed can be drastically reduced.

Spinnaker: A light sail with three corners used when sailing to leeward. When set it has a balloon shape. It is flown with the aid of a spinnaker pole.

Spreader: Struts on both sides of mast that spread the *shrouds* out from the mast as they travel down to where they're fastened to the edge of the deck admidships. Spreaders enhance the stabilizing effect of the shrouds.

Starboard: The right side of the boat as you face forward.

Starboard tack: Sailing with the wind coming over the port side of the boat. When you're on starboard tack the boom would therefore be trimmed to the port side. Starboard tack does *not* mean tacking to the right.

Starting line: An imaginary line between the mast of the boat of the committee that supervises the race, and a buoy. In the America's Cup the buoy or pin end of the line is always on the left and each mark is kept on one's port side while sailing the course. The ideal starting line is set at a right angle to the wind direction and is directly downwind of the first *windward mark.* This is meant to ensure that both boats have an equal distance to sail to the first mark regardless of where they cross the line. But, for example, if the wind shifts to the right after the line has been established, a boat starting on the right will have a shorter distance to sail on the *beat* to the first *windward mark.* In such a case the right side of the line is said to be favored. Until minutes before the starting gun sounds, the committee boat can adjust its position as the wind shifts to provide as fair a start as possible.

Stay: A wire that provides fore and aft support for the mast; part of the standing rigging.

Stay sail: Most often used during a run or a reach; it is a small jib flown between the spinnaker and the mainsail.

Stern: The part of the boat that is furthest aft.

Swell: The long, heaving waves of the ocean, caused by a combination of currents and wind.

Tack: To tack is to change directions while sailing to windward by steering the bow of the boat through the wind from port tack (wind coming over the boat's port side) to starboard tack (wind coming over the starboard side) or vice-versa. Tack also denotes the foremost corner of the foot or bottom of a sail.

Tacking duel: In a close race, a tacking duel occurs when the boat that is ahead tries to maintain its lead by tacking whenever its opponent does in order to stay between the losing boat and the next mark that they both must round.

Tackle: An arrangement of ropes and blocks (pulleys) that yields a mechanical advantage and so makes it easier to pull or hoist.

Tactician: The crewman who assesses actions of the opponent and offers tactical advice to the skipper, who concentrates on steering the boat.

Tailer: The port and starboard tailers are crewmen who trim the headsails. The port tailer, for example, is stationed on the port side of the boat and trims a jib or genoa when the boat is on starboard tack (in which case the wind blows over the starboard side and the sails are set on the port side of the boat).

Telemetry: Many of the vital moving parts and instruments of a modern 12-meter yacht are connected to sensors that detect movement or change and automatically send that information via telemetry, e.g., by radio to a computer on the tender or on land. A 12-meter's own onboard computer can also digest such information and automatically display such key data as boatspeed and Velocity Made Good.

Tender: A motorboat that holds spare equipment and sails for a yacht. *Stars & Stripes's* tender was a large catamaran named *Betsy*. She carried many sails to offer the widest possible choice before the start of a race, as well as spare parts from shackles to booms.

Time-on-distance: The act of precisely controlling one's boatspeed, course, the distance to the mark, and the time remaining before the starting gun so as to cross the line with the greatest speed exactly when the gun sounds. When maneuvering against another boat, the fight for the controlling position tends to prevent one from attempting a perfect time-on-distance start.

Transom: The back of the stern.

Travel car: The mainsheet leads from the boom to the travel car, a device whose position along a track (the traveler) astern can be adjusted according to how one wishes to trim the mainsail. From the travel car the mainsheet passes eventually around a drum and into the hands of the mainsheet trimmer.

Traveler: A track perpendicular to the centerline along which the travel car can slide.

Trim: One trims a sail by pulling in on a sheet.

Trim tab: At the aft end of the keel is a vertical, movable flap that acts as an additional rudder.

True wind: The actual velocity and direction of the wind. True wind combined with the wind one senses solely due to a boat's forward movement yields *apparent wind.*

Tuning: The act of adjusting a boat's sails, the shape of the hull and or keel, and the rigging to optimize performance.

Turtle: A bag that holds a folded spinnaker before that sail is set.

12-meter: A 12-meter yacht is not 12 meters long, rather, the term applies to a complex series of measurements and ratios having to do with various dimensions of the hull and mast, that when fed into a certain equation, must yield a sum of 12 meters.

Upwind: Toward the direction from which the wind is blowing, to windward or to weather.

USYRU: United States Yacht Racing Union.

Vang: See **boom vang.**

VPP: Velocity Prediction [computer] Program.

VMG: Velocity Made Good. The actual speed one is making toward a mark as one tacks or jibes back and forth. VMG is affected by such factors as ocean current, leeway (side slippage), boatspeed, and course sailed.

Wake: The turbulent waves a boat creates as it passes through the water.

Weather: In addition to the word's normal meaning, there is a nautical usage: to weather means to windward (upwind). The weather mark, therefore, is the windward mark.

Weather helm: When a boat tends to head upwind unless steered away, it is said to have a weather helm.

Winch: A drum around which one passes sheets or halyards; it enables one to trim or ease these lines even when they're under great strain from the pressure of the wind in the sails.

Wind shadow: The area of weakened, turbulent wind to leeward of a sail.

Windward: Upwind, to weather, the direction from which the wind is blowing.

Winglets: Roughly horizontal wings at the bottom of a keel that, when used on *Australia II* in the 1983 America's Cup, gave the boat increased speed and maneuverability. Winglets appeared on the keel of all 12-meters in the 1987 America's Cup except the yacht *USA*.

Wing mark: The mark one must round between the two reaches on an America's Cup race course.

Zipper: See **luff zipper**.

THE STARS & STRIPES
TEAM IN AUSTRALIA

224

THE TEAM

Stanley, Jon	Bowman
Steiner, Andy	Maintenance
Sullivan, Peggy	Physical Therapist
Sutphen, Jack	"Trial Horse" Skipper
Sutphen, Jean	
Trenkle, Bill	Tailer
Vogel, Dory	Navigator
Vogel, Scott	Bowman
Waite, Bill	Director of Hospitality
Ward, Charles	Marketing Director
Weinheimer, Mark	Sailmaker
Wenz, John	Tender Captain
Whidden, Betsy	
Whidden, Tom	Tactician
Wright, Jon	Mainsheet
Wuest, Donn	Shore Support
Weisman, Katie	Public Relations Assistant

RACE RESULTS

Round Robin 1   05/20-Oct-1986 Racing Day 13   1 point per win

	America II	Azzurra	Canada II	Challenge France	Courageous IV	White Crusader	Eagle	French Kiss	Heart of America	Italia	New Zealand	Stars & Stripes	U.S.A.		Provisional Points	Standing
America II		X	X	X	X	X	X	X	X	X	O	X	X		11	1
Azzurra	O		O	O	X	O	O	O	O	O	O	O	O		1	12
Canada II	O	X		X	X	O	X	X	X	O	O	O	O		6	7
Challenge France	O	X	O		O	O	O	X	O	O	O	O	O		2	11
Courageous IV	O	O	O	X		O	O	O	O	O	O	O	O		1	12
White Crusader	O	X	X	X	X		X	X	X	O	O	O	X		8	4
Eagle	O	X	O	X	X	O		O	X	O	O	O	O		4	9
French Kiss	O	X	O	O	X	O	X		X	X	O	O	O		5	8
Heart of America	O	X	O	X	X	O	O	O		O	O	O	O		3	10
Italia	O	X	X	X	X	X	X	O	X		O	O	O		7	6
New Zealand	X	X	X	X	X	X	X	X	X	X		O	X		11	1
Stars & Stripes	O	X	X	X	X	X	X	X	X	X	X		X		11	1
U.S.A.	O	X	X	X	X	O	X	X	X	X	O	O			8	4

Round Robin 2   02/19-Nov-1986 Racing Day 11   5 points per win

	America II	Azzurra	Canada II	Challenge France	Courageous IV	White Crusader	Eagle	French Kiss	Heart of America	Italia	New Zealand	Stars & Stripes	U.S.A.	Carried Forward	Provisional Points	Standing
America II		X	X	X		X	X	X	X	X	O	O	X	11	56	2
Azzurra	O		O	X		O	O	O	O	X	O	O	O	1	11	11
Canada II	O	X		X		O	X	O	X	O	O	X	O	6	31	7
Challenge France	O	O	O			O	O	O	O	O	O	O	O	2	2	12
Courageous IV														1	1	13
White Crusader	O	X	X	X			X	O	X	X	O	X	O	8	43	5
Eagle	O	X	O	X		O		O	X	O	O	O	X	4	24	9
French Kiss	O	X	X	X		X	X		X	X	O	X	O	5	45	4
Heart of America	O	X	O	X		O	O	O		O	O	O	O	3	13	10
Italia	O	O	X	X		O	X	O	X		O	O	O	7	27	8
New Zealand	X	X	X	X		X	X	X	X	X		X	X	11	66	1
Stars & Stripes	X	X	O	X		O	X	X	X	X	O		O	11	46	3
U.S.A.	O	X	X	X		X	O	O	X	X	O	X		8	43	5

Round Robin 3   02/19-Dec-1986 Racing Day 11   12 points per win

	America II	Azzurra	Canada II	Challenge France	Courageous IV	White Crusader	Eagle	French Kiss	Heart of America	Italia	New Zealand	Stars & Stripes	U.S.A.	Carried Forward	Provisional Points	Standing
America II		X	X	X		X	X	O	O	X	O	O	O	56	128	5
Azzurra	O		O	X		O	O	O	O	O	O	O	O	11	23	11
Canada II	O	X		X		O	X	O	O	X	O	O	O	31	79	9
Challenge France	O	O	O			O	O	O	O	O	O	O	O	2	2	12
Courageous IV														1	1	13
White Crusader	O	X	X	X			X	O	X	X	O	O	O	43	115	6
Eagle	O	X	O	X		O		O	O	O	O	O	O	24	48	10
French Kiss	X	X	X	X		X	X		X	O	O	O	O	45	129	4
Heart of America	X	X	X	X		O	X	O		O	O	O	X	13	85	8
Italia	O	X	O	X		O	X	X	X		O	O	X	27	99	7
New Zealand	X	X	X	X		X	X	X	X	X		X	X	66	198	1
Stars & Stripes	X	X	X	X		X	X	X	X	X	O		O	46	154	2
U.S.A.	X	X	X	X		X	X	X	O	O	O	X		43	139	3

RACE RESULTS

Round Robin 1 List of Yachts

	Yacht Name	Yacht Club	Country	Skipper
(F)	French Kiss	Societe des Regates Rochelaises	France	Marc Pajot
(A)	Challenge France	Societe Nautique de Marseille	France	Yves Pajot
(B)	Italia	Yacht Club Italiano	Italy	Aldo Migliaccio
(K)	Azzurra	Yacht Club Costa Smeralda	Italy	Mauro Pelaschier
(H)	White Crusader	Royal Thames Yacht Club	U.K.	Harold Cudmore
(I)	Canada II	Royal Nova Scotia Yacht Squadron	Canada	Terry Neilson
(D)	New Zealand	Royal New Zealand Yacht Squadron	New Zealand	Chris Dickson
(L)	Courageous IV	Yale Corinthian Yacht Club	U.S.A.	David Vietor
(M)	America II	New York Yacht Club	U.S.A.	John Kolius
(J)	Heart of America	Chicago Yacht Club	U.S.A.	Harry Melges
(E)	**Stars & Stripes**	San Diego Yacht Club	U.S.A.	**Dennis Connor**
(C)	Eagle	Newport Harbor Yacht Club	U.S.A.	Roderick Davis
(G)	U.S.A.	St. Francis Yacht Club	U.S.A.	Tom Blackaller

ROUND ROBIN 1—RACING DAY 1/ROUND ROBIN 3—RACING DAY 11

Stars & Stripes

Adversary	Round Robin 1 Result	T D	Round Robin 2 Result	T D	Round Robin 3 Result	T D	Averages Status	T D
America II	Loser	0:33	Winner	1:31	Winner	13:04	Ahead	4:41
Azzurra	Winner	3:19	Winner	0:37	Winner	4:11	Ahead	2:42
Canada II	Winner	2:19	Loser	0:29	Winner	3:46	Ahead	1:52
Challenge France	Winner	4:42	Winner	4:51	Winner	10:48	Ahead	6:47
Courageous IV	Winner	DNF		—:—		—:—	Ahead	6:47
Eagle	Winner	3:00	Winner	6:29	Winner	10:11	Ahead	6:33
French Kiss	Winner	3:40	Winner	2:34	Winner	2:07	Ahead	2:47
Heart of America	Winner	3:07	Winner	4:50	Winner	1:32	Ahead	3:10
Italia	Winner	5:49	Winner	5:15	Winner	3:37	Ahead	4:54
New Zealand	Winner	0:49	Loser	0:58	Loser	0:32	Behind	0:14
U.S.A.	Winner	0:06	Loser	0:39	Loser	0:42	Behind	0:25
White Crusader	Winner	1:16	Loser	2:18	Winner	4:12	Ahead	1:03
Averages	Ahead	2:30	Ahead	1:58	Ahead	4:44	Ahead	3:04

RACE RESULTS

Semifinals
List of Names by Yacht

YACHT NAME	YACHT CLUB	COUNTRY	SKIPPER
French Kiss	Societe des Regates Rochelaises	France	Marc Pajot
New Zealand	Royal New Zealand Yacht Squadron	New Zealand	Chris Dickson
Stars & Stripes	San Diego Yacht Club	U.S.A.	**Dennis Conner**
U.S.A.	St. Francis Yacht Club	U.S.A.	Tom Blackaller

Match Race Results

RACING DAY 1, DECEMBER 28, 1986 — TIME DIFFERENTIAL

New Zealand defeated French Kiss — 0:02:46
Stars & Stripes defeated U.S.A. — **0:00:10**

RACING DAY 2, DECEMBER 29, 1986

Stars & Stripes defeated U.S.A. — **0:03:02**
New Zealand defeated French Kiss — 0:02:40

RACING DAY 3, DECEMBER 30, 1986

New Zealand defeated French Kiss — French Kiss disqualified
Stars & Stripes defeated U.S.A. — **0:02:23**

RACING DAY 4, JANUARY 2, 1987

Stars & Stripes defeated U.S.A. — **0:00:43**
New Zealand defeated French Kiss — 0:02:44

Finals

RACING DAY 1, JANUARY 13, 1987

Stars & Stripes defeated New Zealand — 0:01:20

RACING DAY 2, JANUARY 14, 1987

Stars & Stripes defeated New Zealand — 0:01:36

RACING DAY 3, JANUARY 16, 1987

New Zealand defeated **Stars & Stripes** — 0:00:38

RACE RESULTS

RACING DAY 4, JANUARY 17, 1987

Stars & Stripes defeated New Zealand   0:03:38

RACING DAY 5, JANUARY 19, 1987

Stars & Stripes defeated New Zealand   0:01:29

Defender Elimination Races
Rounds A, B, and C and Semifinals
List of Names by Yacht

YACHT NAME	YACHT CLUB	COUNTRY	SKIPPER
Australia III	Royal Perth Yacht Club	Australia	Gordon Lucas
Australia IV	Royal Perth Yacht Club	Australia	Colin Beashel
Kookaburra II	Royal Perth Yacht Club	Australia	Peter Gilmour
Kookaburra III	Royal Perth Yacht Club	Australia	Iain Murray
South Australia	Royal South Australian Yacht Squadron	Australia	Phil Thompson
Steak n' Kidney	Royal Sidney Yacht Squadron	Australia	Fred Neill

OVERALL TOTALS	RACES SAILED	WON	LOST	POINTS
Australia III (withdrew after Round B)	20	8	12	12
Australia IV	38	27	11	83
Kookaburra II	38	22	16	70
Kookaburra III	38	29	9	77
South Australia (withdrew during Round C)	23	5	18	8
Steak n' Kidney (withdrew during Semifinals)	36	5	31	24

RACE RESULTS

Defender Races for the America's Cup Semifinals
List of Names by Yacht

YACHT NAME	YACHT CLUB	COUNTRY	SKIPPER
Australia IV	Royal Perth Yacht Club	Australia	Colin Beashel
Kookaburra II	Royal Perth Yacht Club	Australia	Peter Gilmour
Kookaburra III	Royal Perth Yacht Club	Australia	Iain Murray
Steak n' Kidney	Royal Perth Yacht Club	Australia	Fred Neill

Match Race Results

RACING DAY 1, DECEMBER 27, 1986	TIME DIFFERENTIAL
Australia IV defeated Steak n' Kidney	0:00:19
Kookaburra II defeated Kookaburra III	0:00:12

RACING DAY 2, DECEMBER 28, 1986	
Australia IV defeated Kookaburra III	0:00:12
Kookaburra II defeated Steak n' Kidney	0:00:41

RACING DAY 3, DECEMBER 29, 1986	
Kookaburra II defeated Australia IV	0:00:59
Kookaburra III defeated Steak n' Kidney	00:02:06

RACING DAY 4, DECEMBER 30, 1986	
Australia IV defeated Steak n' Kidney	00:00:14
Kookaburra II defeated Kookaburra III	00:00:50

Finals

RACING DAY 1, JANUARY 15, 1987	
Kookaburra III defeated Australia IV	00:01:32

RACING DAY 2, JANUARY 16, 1987	
Kookaburra III defeated Australia IV	00:00:46

RACING DAY 3, JANUARY 17, 1987	
Kookaburra III defeated Australia IV	00:02:06

RACE RESULTS

RACING DAY 4, JANUARY 19, 1987

Kookaburra III defeated Australia IV   00:01:13

RACING DAY 5, JANUARY 20, 1987

Kookaburra III defeated Australia IV   00:00:55

Defender vs. Challenger
Final Races for the America's Cup
Best of Seven Races

RACE 1, JANUARY 31, 1987   TIME DIFFERENTIAL

Stars & Stripes defeated Kookaburra III   00:01:41

RACE 2, FEBRUARY 1, 1987

Stars & Stripes defeated Kookaburra III   00:01:10

RACE 3, FEBRUARY 2, 1987

Stars & Stripes defeated Kookaburra III   00:01:46

RACE 4, FEBRUARY 4, 1987

Stars & Stripes defeated Kookaburra III   00:01:59

RACE RESULTS

Oct. 1 1986

The Yacht Club Costa Smeralda, Challenger of Record issued the following list of entries by each syndicate for the 1st Round Robin of the Louis Vuitton Cup Challenger Races for America's Cup.

Yacht	Sail #	Club of Record	Skipper
Canada II	KC 2	R.N.S.Y.S.	Terry Neilson
French Kiss	F 7	Ste Regates Rochelaises	Marc Pajot
Challenge France	F 8	Ste Nautique De Marseille	Yves Pajot
White Crusader	K 24	Royal Thames Y.C.	Harold Cudmore
Azzurra	I 10	Y.C. Costa Smeralda	Mauro Pelaschier
Italia	I 7	Y.C. Italiano	Aldo Migliaccio
New Zealand	KZ 7	Royal N.Z. Yacht Squadron	Chris Dickson
Heart of America	US 51	Chicago Y.C.	Buddy Melges
America II	US 46	New York Yacht Club	John Kolius
Eagle	US 60	Newport Harbor Y.C.	Rod Davis
Stars & Stripes	US 55	San Diego Y.C.	Dennis Conner
USA	US 61	St. Francis Y.C.	Tom Blackaller
Courageous IV	US 26	Yale Corinthian Y.C.	David Vietor

INDEX

INDEX

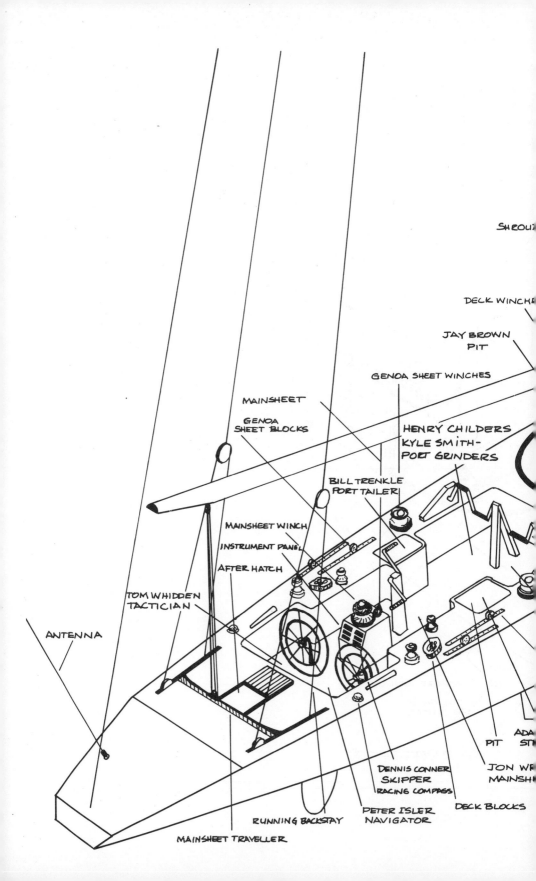

SHROU

DECK WINCHE

JAY BROWN
PIT

GENOA SHEET WINCHES

MAINSHEET

GENOA
SHEET BLOCKS

HENRY CHILDERS
KYLE SMITH-
PORT GRINDERS

BILL TRENKLE
PORT TAILER

MAINSHEET WINCH

INSTRUMENT PANEL

AFTER HATCH

TOM WHIDDEN
TACTICIAN

ANTENNA

ADA
PIT   ST

JON WR
MAINSH

DENNIS CONNER
SKIPPER

RACING COMPASS

DECK BLOCKS

PETER ISLER
NAVIGATOR

RUNNING BACKSTAY

MAINSHEET TRAVELLER